T0349363

AWAKENING ARTEMIS

life

AWAKENING ARTEMIS

Deepening Intimacy with
the Living Earth and
Reclaiming Our Wild Nature

VANESSA CHAKOUR

Penguin Life

VIKING
An imprint of Penguin Random House LLC
penguinrandomhouse.com

Copyright © 2021 by Vanessa Chakour
Penguin supports copyright. Copyright fuels creativity, encourages diverse voices,
promotes free speech, and creates a vibrant culture. Thank you for buying an authorized
edition of this book and for complying with copyright laws by not reproducing, scanning,
or distributing any part of it in any form without permission. You are supporting writers
and allowing Penguin to continue to publish books for every reader.

Illustrations by Vanessa Chakour

A Penguin Life Book

LIBRARY OF CONGRESS CATALOGING-IN-PUBLICATION DATA
Names: Chakour, Vanessa, author.
Title: Awakening Artemis : deepening intimacy with the living
earth and reclaiming our wild nature / Vanessa Chakour.
Description: New York : Penguin Life, [2021]
Identifiers: LCCN 2021025846 (print) | LCCN 2021025847 (ebook) |
ISBN 9781984882097 (hardcover) | ISBN 9781984882103 (ebook)
Subjects: LCSH: Self-actualization (Psychology) |
Plants—Social aspects. | Human ecology. | Consciousness.
Classification: LCC BF637.S4 C4928 2021 (print) |
LCC BF637.S4 (ebook) | DDC 158.1—dc23
LC record available at https://lccn.loc.gov/2021025846
LC ebook record available at https://lccn.loc.gov/2021025847

Printed in the United States of America
1st Printing

Book design by Daniel Lagin

To my loving mothers: Andrea and Mother Earth for nurturing, supporting, and guiding me. And to my wild green friends, especially the so-called weeds, who have led me back to myself and helped me heal. May the words in this book dissolve misunderstandings and awaken others to the depth and height of who you are.

CONTENTS

INTRODUCTION

The doors to the world of the wild Self are few but precious. If
you have a deep scar, that is a door, if you have an old, old
story, that is a door. If you love the sky and the water so much
you almost cannot bear it, that is a door. If you yearn for a
deeper life, a full life, a sane life, that is a door.

CLARISSA PINKOLA ESTÉS

Stories are alive. We breathe life into stories every time we tell them and
receive new insight every time we listen. Ancient myths speak to our
need for connection, share in our suffering, offer hope, and help to guide
our moral compass. As we retell them, generation after generation, they evolve—
told and retold in different forms. Revisiting traditional tales across cultures
reflects the fact that there are places—inside and outside of us—that are worthy of protecting, sanctifying, and remembering.

Artemis is the Greek moon goddess: a wild woman, eco-warrior, and activist who has lived for centuries through the power of story. She is a fiercely
independent woman who roams mountains, forests, and marshes with her
bow, arrows, and animal companions. She is a protector of women, animals,
wild nature, and the young and seeks vengeance on those who violate any of
the sacred life under her care. Those who believe in the goddess would not dare
harm the land under her watch. Thus in ancient Greece, her wild sanctuaries
were protected. Even as women and the Earth have been silenced, suppressed,
and abused, the story of Artemis has persisted, even intensified. She offers

women a protectress and a sacred warrior archetype. Artemis is a heroine who offers a new facet for each generation yearning for wisdom, and through which many cultures can express the value of the act of sanctity.

Science has given us clarity and invaluable information, but that critical lens has also silenced many of our Earth-based cosmologies. We have classified, objectified, and dissected nature into constituent parts, and with those parts under the microscope, we have forgotten how to step back, admire, and seek to connect to and understand the unified, animate whole. Luckily, science is evolving and realizing the incredible sentience of the natural world. As the methodologies and focus of science change, the truths we uncover actually align more and more with traditional stories and indigenous and ancestral wisdom—wisdom that has always known that nature is sentient and alive, and that we are inseparable from each other.

I have always gravitated toward wild places and, following Artemis, I have become a defender of nature, of women, and of our animal kin. My life's work has celebrated misunderstood species like wolves and other stewards of our ecosystem, and the essential wildflowers we call weeds. Stories like the Big Bad Wolf, the misconception that pegs the dandelion as an invasive weed, and the myth of human superiority over nature took hold in our collective imagination as people turned to agriculture, began domesticating land, and grew distant from wild landscapes. It is easier to "other" who and what we are destroying. But as we now know, stories that place humans above the wild perpetuate the illusion of separation and have caused great harm. They need to be peeled away.

Our bodies are living ecosystems, and like the cycles of nature, we also ebb and flow, go backward and forward, contract and expand, and move through necessary phases of growth, death, and restoration. Contrary to what we might want to believe, healing is not a linear process but an ongoing spiral into subterranean spaces of darkness where we confront the unknown. Where we rest, regenerate, and eventually expand outward into bloom. We might resist the dark spaces inside us but the truth is, most of our healing and growth happens underground and under our skin. We need dark, protected spaces to let the most tender parts of ourselves form. Rest and retreat are just as necessary as the warmth and illumination of light.

Through working with the plants and practices I share in this book, I've rewritten my own stories again and again, revealing blind spots and spiraling inward to shed old skins, confront shadows, and become more of who I always was. Plants entered my life as medicine but the real transformation occurred when I realized I was living among profound healers. All around me were green allies; strange and wondrous fungi; trees with rich history, life purpose, generations of family, and essential roles in our environment. As I began awakening to this complex, animate world, I understood, in a truly embodied way, the vast web of life that I was part of. I was in awe and compelled to share this wonder with others. I began to reintroduce plants, trees, and fungi to my friends and family, and eventually to the students I would teach; I pointed out healers like mugwort, dandelion, red clover, burdock, eyebright, and pine and asked my kin to look—*really* look—and listen to who these plants are. I apprenticed with herbalists, studied constantly, led plant walks and rewilding retreats. I began uncovering the ancestral roots of Earth-based healing that had been buried for generations in my family. I am still digging, exploring, learning, and awakening to more of nature's abundance.

Anthropocentric culture has been structured with a mindset to make us believe we are separate from, or different from, the rest of nature in order to justify the accumulation of supposed wealth, the injustices of colonization, a hierarchical power order, and patriarchal religious dogmas. But that foundational idea of hierarchy and separateness is not true. We are not separate from nature nor exempt from the natural world. Indeed we are inextricably connected to the plants, birds, fish, foxes, wolves, and fungi with whom we share ecosystems and exchange intellectual ideas, and on whom we depend for survival. I believe that humans were born to be ecological stewards, but many of us have forgotten this deeper purpose. We have been taught to tone down our instincts and have become desensitized and domesticated. We poison the land to get rid of weeds that could help us heal. We try to control and contain what will always seek to be free. We're wasting energy on a losing battle when we might instead awaken to the wonder and power that waits for us. When we remember our relatedness—as indigenous cultures throughout the world continue to do, despite the abuse, disruption, and corruption their populations have weathered in the throes of colonization—we *can* position ourselves to be guardians and caretakers of land, and feed the abundance that is already here and needs only to be seen and honored.

True abundance is not a wealth we can acquire but the infinite peace, wisdom, and stability that comes from knowing that the most valuable aspects of life are already sprouting under our feet, flowing through water, flying above us in air, and waiting patiently inside our bodies to be revealed. Intimacy with the inner and outer wild offers us a profound sense of belonging, something that no one—nor any life event, lost job, or missed mark—can ever take away. The faster we come to understand that we *are* nature and not separate from the web of life, the better off we'll be as individuals, and the better off our shared home, our planet, will be. The information we need to heal this world is not more statistics and stories of doom but stories about our interconnection, along with practices that slow us down and reinforce symbiosis. When we realize the incredible generosity of Mother Earth and our bodies, and truly see the awe-inspiring creatures we are related to, I believe we cannot help but fall in love. And when we fall in love, we become protectors and defenders like Artemis.

This book is a window into the way plants and practices like movement, meditation, and creative exploration led me home to a place of belonging. The first five chapters describe my initiation onto the path of holistic healing and bring context to the subsequent sections that move from my childhood into my present. Mirroring the seasons and ways in which a seed is propelled to burst forth from its shell and reach up through the dirt toward the surface, the five parts of the book chronicle the spiral inward to heal, restore, reckon with trauma, and acknowledge the gifts that presence has to give us. I offer these plants, discoveries, and my story in the hope that you might see something of yourself, something that inspires you to embrace the sacred relationship with your wise, beautiful body, and the incredible animate world. We don't have to cultivate a connection to the Earth, we only have to acknowledge and remember the connection that already is.

It is never too late to reclaim your wild nature.

AWAKENING ARTEMIS

The land knows you, even when you are lost.

ROBIN WALL KIMMERER

PART ONE

The Present

THE PRESENT IS ALWAYS UNFOLDING. IT IS REVISED MOMENT TO MO-ment, although sometimes we are not available to experience its potency. We might be living in the past, licking old wounds, projecting ourselves into the future, circling the perimeter of our lives, or simply be too busy. But sometimes we are startled awake. Love, tragedy, a breathtaking sunrise, or the scent of a flower can cause us to stop, breathe, drop into our bodies, and pay attention. In those pivotal moments, there is a gap where we can diverge from the traffic of paved paths and move in the direction of the unknown, where wonder and healing are waiting.

MUGWORT
Artemisia vulgaris

Family: Asteraceae

The botanical name for mugwort honors the Greek goddess Artemis, the huntress who sought vengeance on those unkind to animals or women and preferred the company of forest creatures and plants to humans. For many herbalists, the fierce protection and divine presence of Artemis is concentrated within the roots, leaves, and stems of this prolific plant.

Mugwort is a bitter, a nervine, an emmenagogue, and a potent oneirogen. As a bitter, mugwort moves the bile in our digestive system, helping us process food, emotions, and experiences to absorb their nourishment and release what doesn't serve us. As a nervine, mugwort repairs overstimulated nerves, frayed wiring within our bodies, to help us respond to stress with increased calm and presence. As an emmenagogue, mugwort eases the pain of childbirth and brings on delayed menstruation. And as a potent oneirogen, an herb that enhances dreaming, mugwort helps the subconscious emerge as we dream so we can see what it is we need to heal. One of my first plant allies on the road to becoming an herbalist, *Artemisia vulgaris* has helped me maintain boundaries and digest bitter experiences while I release deep wounds.

THE INNER WILD

Just as a snake sheds its skin, we must shed our past over and over again.

BUDDHA

I run my fingers along the silvery backs of mugwort leaves as the wolves howl. It's late September, harvest season, and the untamed land at the Wolf Conservation Center in South Salem, New York, is lush with tall perennials, blooming goldenrod, and carpets of diverse groundcover. Hours slip away as I study the unique shapes, textures, and colors of plants like chickweed, violet, mugwort, lobelia, burdock, and mullein, whose hair on their fuzzy leaves, like the cilia in our respiratory system, protect them from harsh and drying winds. The study and practice of herbalism has lifted a veil that stood between me and the natural world. Land that was once just a wash of green is now vivid, animate, and full of wonder for me. As I crouch among the plants, I put a mugwort leaf in my mouth to taste the familiar bitterness of her spear-like leaves. This fierce plant thrives among the wolves and, like Artemis, guards the boundary between the wild and the domesticated. I exchange breath with the plants, grateful for all they have helped me heal.

Breathing was a struggle for the first twenty years of my life. Diagnosed with severe asthma at age two, I learned that my lungs were weak and unpredictable. My inhaler, my lifeline, was with me at all times. If I couldn't find it, I panicked. When my bronchi seized up among friends, I snuck away into bathrooms or dark corners to inhale my lifesaving puffs like I was using an illicit drug. I was embarrassed to be so broken. I had a daily dose of pills, weekly shots, monthly visits to a specialist, and frequent home treatments from Mom when I woke up wheezing in the middle of the night. She would turn our bathroom into a steam room, pound my back to break up mucus, and sit with me, both of us exhausted, until I could breathe. Night after night, I fell asleep listening to the soothing sound of her voice saying, "It's okay, honey, you'll get through this."

Out of school for weeks, and sometimes months, at a time, I grew comfortable being alone. I even enjoyed it. With a piece of paper and pencil, I entered into imaginary worlds where mushroom gnomes and wise old trees melted pain away.

We lived in a green duplex in Western Massachusetts with two beloved dogs—one Newfoundland and one terrier—until I was twelve years old. The Mill River Conservation Area was just beyond our backyard. Wild raspberry bushes surrounded the perimeter of the forest, and at the far end, a narrow doorway between their dense thicket of thorns led to a world of woodland trails, brooks, and mysterious creatures. I wandered into those woods every day I could, listening to the brook and looking for evidence of a mystical world that seemed just beyond my reach.

At dusk, I called to the bats living nearby with high-pitched clicks and squeaks as they swooped down and circled above me. Who knows what made me think it would be a good idea to call bats but I've always had a special place in my heart for liminal realms and misunderstood creatures. In summer, I circled the perimeter of the forest, picking the ripe wild raspberries, and in autumn, I buried myself in the fiery colors of fallen leaves. In this early part of my childhood, I was never lonely because so much of nature was a friend to me.

What I didn't know then was that mugwort grew in and around the forest in Western Massachusetts. I wouldn't work with this wild, bitter medicine until I was living in Brooklyn, New York, fifteen years after a car accident I suffered in high school shattered me. When my spine and neck fractured in the accident, it was as though I was cracked open and trauma I'd been stuffing inside in my body subconsciously throughout my childhood was released all at once. Fifteen years on, in Brooklyn where I would discover mugwort for the first time, I still had much healing to do.

LATE OCTOBER, EARLY IN MY JUNIOR YEAR OF HIGH SCHOOL, I WAS ON MY WAY to a party in the backwoods of Belchertown with Ian, my high school sweetheart, and my best friend, Tonya. Ian was driving and I was leaning in close to him from the passenger's side as I turned around to talk to Tonya. We were following a friend whose lights we kept losing on the dark rural road, and then it started to rain. As Ian sped up to rejoin the caravan of our friends, the rain became a torrential downpour. Sheets of water made it impossible to see where we were going and suddenly Ian swerved the car to avoid an embankment. The car slid on layers of fallen leaves and flipped. I don't remember any of that. But Tonya told me that she remembers the moment it happened: "I looked up and all I saw was a tree speeding toward us."

She was knocked out by the impact and as she slowly woke, she heard the faint and then urgent sound of Ian yelling, "Get out! The car is going to blow!" She tried to revive me and couldn't. I had been thrown into the back seat and was upside down and unconscious in a car that now looked like a crushed tin can. It was smoking and she knew she had to get me out. Tonya later told me that as moved me, she thought, *I could have just paralyzed her.*

When I remember regaining consciousness, I was looking down as if from a great height at my body leaning against a police car. They were asking me questions and though I could speak, I didn't remember my name, who I was, where I lived, nothing. I was in and out of consciousness, and in and out of my body, until I finally found myself in the hospital, connected to machines, blinking into the glare of fluorescent lights and staring up while worried faces stared down at me. It was not an unfamiliar scene for me after all the asthma hospitalizations, but the difference was this time I had been thrown out of my body and when I returned, my body was broken. My spine fractured in three places. Ian walked out of the hospital that night and so did Tonya. They had glass in their heads, a number of bruises, but otherwise they were okay. I, meanwhile, was in for a longer journey.

The weeks in the hospital were a drug-induced haze. They strapped me into the bed before fitting me with a fiberglass back brace, afraid that if I moved at all, the fractures would get worse. So I lay there, frozen. Despite knowing that I came close to being paralyzed, the thing I feared most about my hospitalization and recovery was getting fat. According to Tonya, they tried to force-feed me with a feeding tube because I refused to eat. I don't remember that at all. But at the time, I was good at forgetting.

MY FLESHY FEMININE CURVES BEGAN TO APPEAR AS EARLY AS AGE ELEVEN and I immediately wanted to flatten them. My new body was a landscape that seemed beyond my control and brought the wrong kind of attention my way. I was hypersensitive to older men's stares that tripped unsettling emotional triggers. I hated those men and wanted to lash out, but instead I turned the anger inward. By age fourteen, I decided to tame my body by controlling the strongest impulse I could—hunger. I successfully arranged my days around avoiding food and obsessed about the carefully constructed "meals" I did eat. Lying awake at night, I made lists and counted calories: *the apple, 100 calories, the quarter of bran muffin, 75, the strawberry preserves on the muffin, 30, the salad with vinegar, around 175* . . . Denying hunger is very distracting, and moving beyond the intense desire for food each day gave me a twisted sense of strength. Somehow I felt more secure being close to the solid structure of my bones.

IN *WOMEN WHO RUN WITH THE WOLVES*, JUNGIAN PSYCHOANALYST CLARISSA Pinkola Estés begins with the tale of La Loba,[1] a story from the deserts and mountains of northern Mexico about an old woman who lives in the hidden place that "everyone knows, but few have seen." La Loba collects what she believes to be the indestructible force of all animals—the bones. Each day, she scours her landscape for skulls, limbs, ribs, vertebrae, and claws and brings them into her cave, which is crammed with the remains of all wild creatures. Her favorite, though, are the bones of wolves. On certain days, when she has found all the pieces she needs and the moon is full and the wind is just right,

La Loba sequesters herself deep in her cave and begins her work. She assembles skeletons but, most importantly, chooses a song to work with: an ancient, guttural howl that will sing flesh back onto bone. As she sings, the ribs, limbs, skull, and spine fill out and a wolf with lush fur and twitching tail begins to breathe. Suddenly, the ground trembles and the wolf opens her eyes and bolts out of the darkness of the cave, into the endless expanse of wilderness. As she runs toward the horizon, the wolf transforms into a laughing woman, feral and free with all of her animal instincts intact.

WHEN I WAS ABLE TO HEAD HOME IN MY FIBERGLASS BACK-AND-NECK BRACE, I moved slowly, tenderly, using the arms and support of others to sit and stand. I felt like a malfunctioning robot, rigid and covered in plastic. Worried friends and family got together and cooked meals to help out. I had to depend on others for my most basic needs, and so I had to eat. Feeling the food enter my body made me feel in ways I didn't want to and stirred intense underlying discomfort.

Unable to move or to distract myself, memories of sexual assault that I'd forgotten through denial of hunger and distraction of young love began to break free and invade my dreams. My nightmares were brutal. I was preyed upon night after night by men I thought I trusted, and began to remember. The power of those memories was excruciating. I turned to art, my instinctual form of release, and wrote and drew incessantly to liberate the tidal waves rushing through me; I couldn't get words and images out fast enough. My inner ecosystem had erupted. I was unloading, unpacking, releasing—with no idea where to put it all. The pain of my broken bones was nothing compared to the force of the memories, shame, and self-loathing rising up in their wake. Trying to bury what I'd been through had only made the wounds more insidious. Trauma therapist Dr. Peter Levine says, "Trauma is not what happens to us, but what we hold inside in the absence of an empathetic witness."[2] If I had been able to talk about the abuse instead of hiding it away, even from myself, perhaps the assault wouldn't have held such power. But I had done what my young mind told me was safe and right. If I didn't speak of it, I had told myself, it would disappear.

EVERY NIGHT FOR WEEKS, SOMEONE CAME OVER AND DROPPED OFF A DELI-cious home-cooked dinner, and my family and I ate together. It sounds amazing now, but then, it was absolute torture. So I discovered a new method of control. When I was able to shuffle from my bedroom to the bathroom, I began to purge. I figured if I threw up most of what I took in, I wouldn't get fat. I didn't want to feel fleshy. I wanted to waste away. I wanted self-control. After a while, though, after training my body to regurgitate like a mother wolf feeding her young, I could hardly keep food down. My digestive system was a mess. I had no idea what I was hungry for.

My boyfriend was the only thing keeping me afloat. He'd come to my house immediately after school every day, bring me schoolwork to catch up on, stay there as late as he could, and call once he was in bed, so we could fall asleep on the phone together. He was my lifeline. In the early months after the accident, I slept through most days, barely numbing my pain with the codeine I was prescribed while waiting for him to arrive. This went on for months until I was able to go back to school, wearing my brace and walking very tenderly. Some teachers got on my case for being late to class when simply walking there was a chore. I never liked playing the victim card, so I just sat and stewed. I couldn't keep up with papers or homework, was still in pain and barely holding it together, but, slowly, I was healing, and I had my love. Until the inevitable for teenage love: he broke up with me. The car accident consumed him with guilt and he wasn't living his own life. He had to "break free," he said. It was true. He was right. But losing our connection was the final rupture for me. I fully fell apart.

My previous distractions—my boyfriend, starving myself, or purging—were either gone or no longer working. As far as my food antics were concerned, everyone was onto me. Tonya confronted both me and my mom about my eating disorder, but I denied it. It took my mom a while to see that Tonya was right, that I was spending way too much time in the bathroom that was, unfortunately, in the hallway where everyone could hear me. I ran the water, the fan, everything I could to block the noise of throwing up. I did strange things like wash my face every time I entered and came out dripping. I shuffled food around on my plate. My incredible discomfort was obvious. I was still wearing the back brace and had to be extremely careful about how, when, and where I moved. I felt trapped. At night, images continued to surface through disturbing dreams, showing me things I didn't want to see. But somewhere in my psyche, something in me knew I needed to examine my inner world more closely. When I woke, I began the routine of purging my dreams through writing or visual art to get them out of my system. I did this night after night, day after day. I wrote and drew incessantly until I began to experience a little peace, and some clarity. My sweet and nurturing mom was always there too, in the background and steady. I entertained suicidal thoughts, but when I thought about her—how much we loved each other, and all that we'd been through together—any thought of suicide evaporated. With her help and Tonya's support, I scoured local bookstores and found writing to support me, including books on eating disorders. I was ready to admit I had one.

Crumbled in the cocoon of my fiberglass back brace, I had no choice but to eat, be in my body, and face the shadows I had desperately tried to avoid. I had admitted I was struggling, and now, lying in bed with a shattered spine, I felt overwhelmed, exposed, and panicked. Survival became my full-time job. I dropped out of high school and began to question everything.

And that is where my journey of healing really begins.

IN THE CHRYSALIS STAGE, A CATERPILLAR TURNS INSIDE OUT AND BECOMES liquid before transforming into a butterfly. That's exactly how I felt during my year of virtual stillness and intense inner transformation. Like goo. I woke up each morning and poured my insides out through stream-of-consciousness writing and drawing. I drew pictures of myself trapped in cages, cowered in corners of dark rooms while the walls around me wept. I studied wildlife photography in *National Geographic* and spent days drawing the details of fierce wolves, confident lionesses, and nervous rabbits, trying to master their body language, the textures of fur, and the fire in their eyes. Art and writing translated my pain, freed me, and brought me to a new level of awareness where I could, with regularity, empty out and enter a state of timelessness. I didn't know it at the time, but the creative release was beginning to reveal the root causes of my mental, physical, spiritual, and emotional challenges. With the eventual help of talk therapy and continued creative exploration, I created space within myself and began to tend to those intensely uncomfortable, wounded places. Somewhere within the abyss of my broken body, my inner wisewoman was at work collecting the scattered, yet indestructible, fragments of my spirit.

ARTEMISIA

My journey of healing has been an ongoing, spiraling journey of rewilding—peeling back layers of social conditioning, limiting personal narratives, and deep trauma. Just as plants grow in spirals—following Earth's rotation, reaching toward the light of the sun, resting in the dark of the night, ebbing and flowing with the pull of the moon—we heal that way too. When we go inward to uncover the root cause of a mental, physical, or emotional challenge and release it, we create space within us and expand outward. Eventually, we grow stronger and are ready to dive inward again . . . deeper this time, to expand further. This journey of depth and expansion goes on and on. Along the way, we might have to revisit pain we thought we'd overcome, only to find there's another layer of that same trauma yet to be lifted. Raw all over again, we must tend to our wounds and listen to what they have to teach us.

Bitter describes difficult experiences and also a taste that most despise. But like difficult experiences, bitter herbs like mugwort can increase our resilience and make us stronger. They can protect us from harmful microbes while creating a sympathetic nervous system response that increases blood flow to our abdominal organs; awakening our instinct. Ninety percent of our serotonin—a chemical that impacts our mood, memory, sleep, and stress—is created in our digestive system, so it is clear that psychosocial factors are impacted by the physiology of the gut.[3] Mugwort's unique bitterness also relaxes the nerves, calms fires of inflammation, and eases anxiety to bring us into states of presence and receptivity and as tension is reduced and blood flows, we enter into a relaxed state, and our innate wisdom, or what Jungians might call the unconscious, is more accessible.

In her book *Goddesses in Everywoman*, Jungian analyst Jean Shinoda Bolen explores a feminist revision of Jung's theory of archetypes by linking them to more goddesses from Greek mythology. According to Jung, archetypes are universal symbols that derive from the collective unconscious and seek actualization. Bolen criticizes Jung's theory for stereotypical and polarizing examples of the feminine: the maiden or the mother, and offers women instead the integrated and complex archetypes of the goddesses.[4] The Artemis archetype is the original "wild woman" who cannot be tamed. She is a moon goddess, a fierce defender of nature, and a virgin in the old definition of the word, meaning a woman unto herself who is complete with or without a partner. Women who are in abusive situations have called upon Artemis for centuries as a protector, and women giving birth can call upon her to ease their labor.

In Greek mythology, Artemis's mother was Leto, the beautiful Titan who in some versions of the myth represents motherhood for all she endured to protect Artemis and her twin brother, Apollo, from Hera's wrath. Hera, the goddess of childbirth and marriage, was married to Zeus, the philandering Olympian god and Artemis's father. Leto was condemned because of her relationship with Zeus and could not find a stable place on Earth to deliver her children, so Leto was on the run. At one point Leto shape-shifted into a she-wolf, finding refuge among a pack of wolves until she made it to Delos, a floating island, where she shed her wolf's clothing and gave birth to Artemis under a palm tree. Nine days later, Artemis acted as a midwife to bring her twin brother, the sun god Apollo, into the world.

Artemis would choose the wild as her domain, cultivate sisterhood, attend births of all kinds, provide refuge for women, the young, and nonhuman animals, and seek revenge on those who harmed her mother.

LIKE THE MOON THAT MOVES TIDES, MUGWORT HAS A RELATIONSHIP WITH THE water element, and when taken can dive into the subconscious, bringing forth buried experiences, patterns, and stories that we need to see in order to heal. As a potent oneirogen, mugwort delivers this important information to us through our dream life; when we are asleep, the subconscious stirs. As someone who has had vivid dreams my whole life, I was skeptical of this medicine at first, but while working with mugwort, I dreamt of things I thought I'd worked through, only to find more to confront and to heal.

While living in Brooklyn, I slept with mugwort by my bed, took drops of the tincture under my tongue, and burned dried mugwort before sleep, inviting the plant into my dreams. Each night I asked, "What do I need to see in order to heal?" In one experience, I dreamt of myself as a young child of seven or eight years old standing upon a tall tower, suspended in darkness, looking down at my life. In the dream realm, I was both the child and the dreaming self looking down on her, an experience much like the one I had after the car accident. As the child, I wasn't scared so much as bewildered and alone in response to confusing memories that separated me from myself. As the dreaming self, I felt deeply pained for her years of isolation. I woke up grieving for the bewildered and confused young part of me that had been stranded for so long. Though I'd done years of work to heal the secrets and shame of sexual abuse I experienced at that age, I realized there were parts of me that I hadn't accepted, nor fully integrated. It was time to uncover the remnants of that experience that were still embedded in my body and do the work necessary to bring the young me down from the isolating tower. I did this through talking to loved ones, journaling, and allowing the emotions to move through my body, with the help of mugwort as a dream-time ally and internal medicine. In doing so, pain and tension in my reproductive system, and menstrual irregularities that I assumed I had no control over and that had no medical explanation, began to shift.

Whether we like it or not, we must look honestly at every corner of both the dark and light within in order to heal. I see this dichotomy expressed in the leaves of mugwort, for one side is silvery and the other a dark green. The silvery, downy back of the mugwort leaf symbolizes the full moon—the tide-like ebb and flow of menstruation, the rise of subconscious emotions to the surface—while the opposite, dark green side symbolizes the new moon—a time to go inward, plant seeds, harvest roots, and conceive. This contrast becomes more pronounced as the plant ages. To me, the contrast symbolizes essential polarities—dark and light, masculine and feminine, dreaming and waking. The leaves change shape as they age and represent the three stages of womanhood: the maiden, the mother, and the crone. The look, feel, and taste of the young leaves contain the innocence of youth. They contain only a hint of her bitterness. The leaves of the crone stage are jagged and fierce, trident-like spears, the color darker and the bitter taste more intense. Mugwort at the crone phase in autumn is a medicine of self-confrontation. She must cut right to the chase, for time is precious.

Tinctures, teas, oils, steam, and other extracts of the plant are used to release tension that may have accumulated in an effort to protect us. Mugwort's power, that bitterness, is moving energy, and is thus essential for life and for healing. When things stagnate, they eventually disintegrate. As an emmenagogue, mugwort moves the waters of the body to ease the pain of childbirth and reinstate the flow of blood between our legs when menstruation is irregular or interrupted. I had phantom reproductive issues and intense menstrual pain for years after the sexual assault. Doctors assured me there was nothing wrong, but I experienced otherwise. Mugwort helped me release tension that had accumulated as my body made an effort to protect herself and process or at least bottle up my residual trauma. As Clarissa Pinkola Estés says, "where there is a scar, there is a door." I would add, where there is any imbalance, there is a door.

THE INNER WILD

We can describe how we feel in the most vivid detail, but in the end, we must traverse our inner landscapes alone. Our inner landscapes are forged by our unique experiences and the ways we handle them. They're formed by our ability to maintain boundaries, let them dissolve at the right moments, and rebuild them when they've been crossed without our permission. Our personal narratives and stories shape and influence our inner ecology, the way we see the world, and how we interact with everything in it. Our inner world is shaped by religion, media, culture, experiences, education, and family. From this infinite space within, we decide, consciously and unconsciously, how we relate to our body, and to others. Deep listening can be our greatest tool for healing. With consistent practice, we can separate the surface-level noise from our unwavering core of truth. As I heal, I spiral ever deeper toward my truth and my starring role in my own narrative: from victim to survivor to warrior.

One of the first assignments I give my herbalism students is to check in with themselves each day to become better acquainted with their inner terrain. I ask that they devote time, as little as five minutes a day, to tune into their body and journal about what they find. Physical symptoms are a message that something in the body, mind, soul, or spirit is out of balance. When we simply treat the symptoms of that imbalance we might mask them but we're not getting to the root of why they're happening in the first place. To move beyond this pattern, I always recommend meditation. Here, we can begin to witness our thoughts and can develop a practice of watching them with curiosity. We need this curiosity when it comes to rewiring our relationship with symptoms, and it is our curiosity that gives our body a chance to be embraced and heard. Some of my students use sensory reminders—Nathalie carries stones in her pockets, uses Post-it Notes, and creates mini altars at work and at home, reminding her to pause. Eventually, with practice, she learned to attune to the subtle nudges within and respond when her body is whispering to her instead of ignoring her body until symptoms and sensations scream out for attention.

Over the years, I've opened doors to all corners of my mind, spirit, and soul and created practices to help me cope, and eventually thrive, in the face of what I found. Disciplined meditation brought awareness to patterns of thought and calmed my mind; training as a professional boxer released anger and revealed innate strength I didn't know I had; visual art and writing helped me peel back layers through creative expression; and the study and practice of holistic herbalism transformed my relationship with my body in collaboration with the natural world. Throughout the years, I've integrated these practices to help me navigate empty, abandoned, or frightening places within me. I write from those places, I draw them, and tune in to find what's lurking there. When we push pain away, those wounds build in intensity and explosive power. There is really no "away" anyway until something is composted: transformed into a new state of being. From wood to charcoal to fertile ground. Still, the bones—the indestructible life force—always remain. Sometimes when I venture inward, I find empty rooms whose doors were closed years ago. The stale space needs airing out. It can be scary to create more room within, but on the ever-deepening and expanding spiral path of healing, I venture further—expanding, contracting, and learning—and broaden the scope of my inner horizon.

———

WHEN I SEE MUGWORT NOW, A PLANT THAT KNOWS MY BODY AND HAS HELPED me with profound healing, I feel love and a sense of belonging. This is the power of common wild plants. Each carries profound medicine, history, and connection to centuries of human and plant relations that many have forgotten. But we can remember. Conscious, direct encounters with nature are not only healing, but can help us develop a sense of the sacred and deeply affect our lifestyle choices. It's more difficult to care about something if we're detached. Experiencing interconnection and relationships create eco-defenders and sacred warriors—roles that are so necessary at this time.

Mugwort's rhizomes are relentless, continuously growing underground stems that allow this perennial to spread in dense, protective armies, creating a threshold. They thrive around forests and provide protective thickets for creatures like rabbits, who calm themselves on the bitter leaves. Mugwort, *Artemisia vulgaris*, has spread far and wide, at forest edges and seasides, in vacant lots and city parks, even through cracks in concrete, and in rural farmland, thriving along the boundary of wild and domesticated spaces.

Like the cycling seasons of nature and the waxing and waning moon, life is an ebb and flow of joy and pain. "The part that appears above ground," writes Carl Jung, "lasts only a single summer. Then it withers away—an ephemeral apparition."[5] Underneath the surface of it all, resilient rhizomes endure, ready and waiting to emerge. This is the power of mugwort. I've learned that true, everlasting life exists below the surface. And like the tenacity of our wild soul, it is difficult, if not impossible to destroy.

YEW TREE
Taxus spp.

Family: Taxaceae

Yew trees can live to be thousands of years old, rooting and forming new trunks where their branches touch the ground. In many Earth-centered traditions, this tree represents death, resurrection, and immortality. Native Americans of the Northwest coast used Pacific yew, *Taxus brevifolia*, as medicine and harvested branches and staves for bows and canoe paddles, whenever possible collecting sustainably from living trees. They made spirit poles, death masks, shaman's wands, and other ceremonial objects from the sacred wood. Some tribes call the yew the "Chief of the Forest."[1]

The English yew, *Taxus baccata*, was sacred to the Celts and is said to contain the experiences, knowledge, and understanding of the ancestors. In Ogham, the Celtic writing system, the yew tree is *iodhad*, the twentieth letter of the alphabet, and in the Gaelic spoken language, the yew is the ninth letter, *iogh*. Both systems of communication are embedded in the natural world and each alphabet is based upon trees.

BELONGING

Old Yew, which graspest at the stones
That name the under-lying dead,
Thy fibres net the dreamless head,
Thy roots are wrapt about the bones.

ALFRED, LORD TENNYSON

I arrive at my cabin, Eagle's Crag, and outside, a cavernous quiet echoes back where it should reverberate with wild noise. It's early March and I'm two hours north of Inverness at Alladale Wilderness Reserve among rugged, snow-capped mountains, rivers, and lochs. I'm the only human among 23,000 acres of wilderness, but I'm not alone.

Scattered Scots pine trees stand in the distance, a welcome sight amid the naked grassy expanse dotted by heather and gorse. The pines look like giant Moyogi bonsai trees, with curved trunks slithering toward the sky, and are the oldest living inhabitants of this land. These particular pines were "too twisted for felling," Innes MacNeill, native Highlander and head ranger at Alladale tells me. Their relatives that grew up straight and narrow like they were supposed to were cut down and used, among other things, as masts for English warships.

I walk along the pebbled road from my cottage and down a frost-covered hill to visit the Scots pines—descendants of the first pines to arrive in Scotland in about 7000 BCE. They once lived with a thriving multispecies family of aspen, juniper, oak, rowan, hawthorn, countless species of fungi, lichen, and medicinal herbs. Bear and lynx may have climbed their branches while wolves roamed the land. Roman naturalist and army commander Pliny the Elder—whose infamous book *Naturalis Historia*, written in 77–79 CE, includes myths and folklore, and information on trees and medicinal plants[2]—named the dense temperate rain forest the Caledonian Forest. The Roman army tried in vain to penetrate the wilderness whose surrounding land was inhabited by wild warrior people the Romans called the Caledonians. Historian James Hunter writes in *Last of the Free: A History of the Highlands and Islands of Scotland* that native Highlanders resisted the Roman Empire under warrior chieftain Calgacus, who called his people "the last of the free" and said of the Roman army, "They make a desert and call it peace."[3]

But the Caledonians couldn't defend the land for long, and over centuries people pushed their way through the dense woodland and the pines' family was destroyed. Wolves, bears, and lynx were hunted to extinction, trees were felled for building and cleared to make way for farmland, and indigenous Highlanders were forced from their homes and replaced with livestock. The Highlanders went from communal townships to planned single-tenancy crofting strips of land owned by absentee landlords based in England. These crofts are remnants of traditional townships or bailtean, which had common grazing, arable open fields, and sustainable subsistence farming. In the Isle of Harris, people were cleared from extremely fertile lands to the east side of the island, which has been compared to the surface of the moon.

Over centuries-long British colonization, and most dramatically during a period of time known as the Highland Clearances, native Highlanders were separated from the land that contained their stories, medicine, lore, and livelihood. Even the language that described their philosophical underpinnings and deep reverence for place was gradually silenced to the point of near extinction. People were shamed for speaking Gaelic, a language that embedded them in rhythms of the natural world. The language defined how they perceived themselves, their communities, and concepts of possession. There is no Gaelic word that can be easily equated with "ownership."

Colonization of Scotland has been subtle. Gaels are white Western Europeans and look no different to the casual observer from the Lowland Scots or English. Assimilation was thus achieved relatively smoothly when compared to the integration of marginalized people elsewhere in the world. The Gaelic language is one thing that made them different and potentially rebellious, so like other native languages during periods of colonization, its erasure was enforced as people were systemically "civilized." In schools, the teacher's armory included measuring sticks, belts, soap in mouths, and even human skulls, which were placed around children's necks. Using insidious methods of "self-policing," the last child caught speaking Gaelic by their peers had to wear what was referred to in Ireland—where the same treatment was meted out—as the "tally stick" and subsequently received the final beating of the day. As Irish poet and philosopher John O'Donohue said, "When you steal a people's language, you leave their soul bewildered."[4]

IN GAELIC, IT IS NOT THE USUAL PRACTICE TO ASK A PERSON "WHERE" THEY are from, but "who" they are from: Có ás a tha sibh? From whom are you? If I had been asked that question ten years ago, I wouldn't have known how to answer. Like many immigrants with mixed ethnic backgrounds, there were periods of time when I mistakenly thought that it didn't matter where my ancestors were from. My ancestors—Scottish and Russian Jewish immigrants with a mix of Irish, English, and Eastern European family thrown in too—had a desire to let go of hardship and assimilate when they set foot on so-called American soil. Some were peasant farmers who worked the land and wanted a perceived better life, some escaped persecution, and others, like the Gaels, were forced from their land. But as they reinvented themselves, the transmission of their stories and Earth-based cultures (which in most cases were lost long before they came) was ultimately lost in what became the homogenous melting pot of American culture.

My parents chose to raise me in the liberal college town of Amherst, Massachusetts. With a reputation for a good school system and its rich music scene in the early '70s, it aligned with their progressive sensibilities. With the help of my father's brother, they bought a large house that became a hippie, communal household after my parents divorced. In order to pay the mortgage, my mom rented rooms to musicians in the area and, when there was space, to those passing through to perform. We had a separate apartment in the basement, two extra rooms upstairs, and my mom and I slept on the ground floor. Music brought people from all walks of life through our door, people who sought to dismantle the status quo through self-expression. Music was a unifier and the closest thing we had to culture. She met my stepfather, Mitch Chakour, in that scene. He opened for James Brown at the Rusty Nail and played with people like Howlin' Wolf, B.B. King, and Joe Cocker. So I grew up with a soundtrack populated by Stevie Wonder, Donny Hathaway, the Beatles, Minnie Riperton, Joni Mitchell, and Jimi Hendrix. I was often excused from elementary school early because we had to drive to a concert and, on my little turntable in my bedroom, I listened to songs like "Mercy Mercy Me (The Ecology)," from Marvin Gaye's masterpiece *What's Going On*, on repeat as he sang about our abuse of the Earth and I grappled with the feelings of overwhelm the album stirred up in me. Artists told the truth, unlike many of the school teachings and textbooks I had to unlearn.

I remember reading Maya Angelou's *I Know Why the Caged Bird Sings* when I was ten years old. I found it in our house and I carried it everywhere until I finished. Though I caught glimpses of the things she was sharing with me—racism, rape, a woman coming of age in a male-dominated world—no one spoke openly about them. But even as a child, I could recognize the embodied resonance of seeing and hearing the truth, even if I couldn't articulate the lessons or takeaways clearly at the time.

Even though I was immersed in what seemed like a multicultural upbringing (as much as it could be in a mostly white liberal college town) and felt deeply connected to nature, for too long I was sorely ignorant of the land's festering wounds and the trauma of her indigenous people. Like many kids growing up in the '70s and '80s, I learned harmful myths like "Columbus discovered America" and "Thanksgiving was a happy gathering between Europeans and the Native People where they shared turkey and pumpkin pie." In my early education, even in a supposedly progressive town like Amherst, Native Americans were usually spoken of in the past tense. I recently spoke to my childhood friend Tonya about this to make sure I remembered correctly and she said, "Yeah, I didn't learn anything about Native American culture until I went to college." Like most school curricula in the United States back then (and probably now), our history books were populated by white men discovering things that already existed. The voices of women and people of color were faint and sanitized, if they were heard at all.

Amherst is located in the Connecticut River Valley, in an area known as "The Happy Valley," and has a reputation as a rural, left-leaning utopia that sits in the shadow of the beautiful Seven Sisters mountain range. Amherst boasts the home of poet Emily Dickinson, who wrote, "Pardon my sanity in a world insane" among other immortalized words, and there has been a decades-long debate whether to change the town's name to Emily because Amherst was named for Lord Jeffery Amherst, a sociopath and the commander of the British Army in North America, who oversaw biological warfare against Native Americans in the Siege of Fort Pitt using blankets contaminated with smallpox.

In my late teenage years, I finally learned that Amherst is Nonotuck land, with the Nipmuc and the Wampanoag to the east, the Mohegan and Pequot to the south, the Mohican to the west, and the Abenaki to the north. Having access to the Connecticut and Mill Rivers and the abundant vegetation of the area, those native populations thrived before colonization, and in many places are still stewards of the land I love so much. As I unearthed more sickness during my teenage years, and especially after the car accident and into my early twenties when I steered my own education, I thought there must be something empirically wrong with white people. I didn't identify with whiteness. I became much more interested in who and what I saw then as my spirit family, and I began to see my body as just a temporary apartment. By the time I was in my late teens, "white" had solidified as a derogatory term.

CHAKOUR MEANS "GRATEFUL." I STARTED USING THIS SYRIAN SURNAME AFTER my mom remarried when I was eight years old, because it seemed only right to carry the same name as my brother, sister, and mother, especially since I was estranged from my biological father. I hyphenated my name when I had to and changed it legally when I moved to New York City in my early twenties. Chakour gave me a sense of identity that resonated. An identity I also found through the ongoing exploration of consciousness and my "inner wild"—the arts, nature, boxing, passionate partnerships, and the study of spirituality. But there was an incessant seeking inside me that I couldn't seem to ground.

I thought I might find what I was looking for through a spiritual practice or philosophy that honored the Earth the same way that I did. I felt a profound and often painful emotional connection to the land and other species, and wanted a space where I could honor that with others. While it felt right to learn about the Earth-based cultures of the place where I was growing up, I knew I had to keep a respectful distance. I was humbled to learn from, exchange medicinal plant knowledge with, and engage in ceremony with First Nations friends and teachers, but I had no connection to any Earth-based culture that was part of my own ancestry. With the absence of my own heritage, the line between cultural appreciation and appropriation felt like a slippery slope. When I encountered blind spots, friends and partners had no problem keeping me in check, because no matter who I aligned with, or what I felt on the inside or in the realm of spirit, I was white on the outside. I knew that my skin afforded me privileges that some of my partners, friends, and colleagues didn't have. While the discomfort and glaring injustice of that reality initiated my work as an activist, it also made me feel displaced. My skin often felt like a barrier between me and the people and places I loved most. While soul connections and my growing inner landscape forged deep relationships, my surface kept some part of me at bay. I felt profound intimacy with the land I grew up on, but I came to understand that, from an ancestral standpoint, it wasn't my own.

The study of Western herbalism was a turning point for me. The practice addressed my longings to heal myself in relationship with nature, but also, unexpectedly, taught me about my culture. My teachers—Robin Rose Bennett and Matthew Wood, among others—validated my longings and understood the Earth as sentient and alive. I learned that the plants I felt most drawn to in North America—hawthorn, elder, mugwort, red clover, yarrow, nettles, burdock, wild rose, St. John's wort, dandelion, linden, eyebright, yew, many of them transplants like me—are found throughout Scotland and other ancestral lands of mine. As I learned about their traditional uses, I was unearthing my herbal heritage and, as I deepened my practice, I felt called to learn more about land I belonged to in my bones whose roots and Earth-based spirituality I could explore in all its depth. With Scottish blood on both my mother's and father's side, the pull toward that land and my Gaelic roots was strong.

While I learned about Scottish lore and traditional medicine from my teachers in the Northeast, the first person to really initiate me was Ancel Mitchell, a brilliant herbalist and folklorist, and now a dear friend, who grew up outside of Glasgow. Ancel runs a permaculture farm in Puerto Viejo de Limón, on the Caribbean coast of Costa Rica, and that is where we met eight years ago. I was staying nearby at my friend's ethnobotany center and studying plant medicine, learning from incredible curanderas and Afro-Caribbean healers, many of whom had been in Puerto Viejo for generations. One day, while discussing plants of the African diaspora, a teacher quoting Jamaican civil rights activist and proponent of the Pan-Africanism movement Marcus Garvey said, "A people without the knowledge of their past history, origin, and culture is like a tree without roots." I'd heard that quote before, but it really struck me in that moment, standing outside and studying *literal roots* with no real connection to my own. It was embarrassing, pretty pathetic, really. I suppose I was ready to hear that I was denying my visible, bodily truth. So when Ancel appeared to teach European herbalism a few days later, it was clearly a sign I needed to heed. We clicked immediately, and though I had been drawn to Costa Rica by the biodiverse landscape and teachings of other cultures, I knew I had to explore my own roots so that I could engage in traditional circles from a place of groundedness and integrity.

After we met, I rode my rickety rental bike along the beaches of the Caribbean coast to her farm and magical chocolate-making hut. Over the course of those few months, we spoke of the history, lore, and rich herbal heritage of Scotland. In the Costa Rican jungle that had pulled me in so deeply when I first visited in 2008, I began to unearth my ancestral stories and wove them into the holistic plant history I knew. And though surrounded by lush plant life, Ancel missed the yarrow, elder, and hawthorn of Scotland and yearned for home, so we designed a retreat together that would take place in Argyll—the part of the West Highlands where many of my family are from.

We went back and forth for a couple of years, mapping the route of the retreat and our intentions for the experience, and sought the right location that aligned with our ecological principles. We wanted to stay near Kilmartin Glen, a historic area filled with Neolithic and Bronze Age monuments: the stone circle at Temple Wood, the standing stones at Ballymeanoch and 350 other ancient monuments; a ritual landscape dating back five thousand years. Eventually we found a gorgeous off-the-grid space to host the retreat that was a short drive away. When I arrived, I felt plugged into source energy, and as we explored the land where my family had lived for thousands of years, my body, at least in part, felt like she was home.

The unearthing continued, and two years after the first retreat in Argyll, I was introduced to Àdhamh Ó Broin, a Gael of mixed Scottish and Irish ancestry who had singlehandedly revived from a state of virtual extinction the very Gaelic dialect that would have been spoken by my ancestors from the area, raising his family as first-language speakers. Àdhamh describes his work as "cultural rewilding," a term that both of us use. Just like I had with Ancel, we felt an immediate kinship. Since we met, we have found missing strands of our own stories in each other's work and have been weaving them together through the Gaelic language, Scotland's pre-Christian cultural legacy, and herbal lore. Gaelic offers a deepened interface with the Scottish landscape as I come to understand why geographical features received the names they did, revealing the worldview of our ancestors. Even though Àdhamh grew up in Scotland, he understood my feeling of displacement and, because of colonization, had felt severed from Gaelic culture and land. While we offer educational experiences for others, our collaborative work is synonymous with our own healing.

IN GAELIC, THERE IS THE CONCEPT OF DÙTHCHAS, NATIVITY, BELONGING TO place, and of dualchas, an inherited, intangible culture. Many of those who have come to my Sacred Warrior retreats with Àdhamh and Ancel grew up feeling displaced and looking to belong, like I did. Though root systems are unseen, their connectedness and well-being determine how we experience the surface of our lives. Likewise, traditional song and story that carry our culture within them reinforce our sense of shared identity with others, including our plant and animal family.

———————

IT HAS ALWAYS BEWILDERED AND INFURIATED ME THAT THE PREDOMINATE anthropocentric perspective sees our extended family of trees, fungi, pollinators, and keystone predators like wolves as something unrelated to us. Like us, they also have families of their own and experience trauma, and we depend on them to survive. Forester Peter Wohlleben writes in *The Hidden Life of Trees*, that "we have learned that mother trees recognize and talk with their kin, shaping future generations. In addition, injured trees pass their legacies on to their neighbors, affecting gene regulation, defense chemistry, and resilience in the forest community."[5] A healthy woodland is a multigenerational, multispecies family that, together, tends to the health and well-being of the whole.

THE RANGERS AT ALLADALE, LED BY INNES MACNEILL, HAVE NOW PLANTED nearly one million native trees and, like other rewilding projects around the world, may one day bring wolves back to their rightful place in the wild. A pack of wolves would restore ecological order and help heal the wounded land. They would keep the overpopulated red deer on the run and give saplings otherwise ravaged and uprooted by those deer time and space to assert themselves. While there are pockets of established forest in Scotland, where chaga and other fungi grow in relationship with birch, rowan, and Scots pine and support and sustain the health of the trees, in the areas of restoration at Alladale the soil is too depleted to nourish those organisms. The root systems lack elders or mycelial networks to help them communicate, share nutrients, and work as a unified ecosystem. This "woodwide web," as it's called by ecologists, is built by mycelial networks, protects trees from the poisonous effects of pollutants, and is particularly relevant for the full restoration of degraded land.

With no ancestral root systems to guide them, the young trees at Alladale are learning to survive on their own as they establish new ground. And though the plants may reappear, where are their stories? No one at Alladale seems to remember them.

WITH ALL OF ITS COMPLEXITIES, THE REWILDING PROJECT AND POTENTIAL reintroduction of wolves led me to Alladale three years ago. I've always had an affinity for those misrepresented stewards of the ecosystem, members of our extended family. And like the young trees, I have begun to reach into my own soil to restore broken roots and rewild my ancestral landscape.

NOTICING

"Won't you get lonely?" my father asked as we walked to breakfast. It was a bright January morning in Cambridge, Massachusetts, after my aunt's memorial service. "Not in the wild," I said. "I miss the people I love, but I'm surrounded by so much life. I don't feel lonely." It was the second time I'd seen him in two months, and also the second time I'd seen him in two years. My aunt's illness and subsequent death brought us back together. As we walked, we created a new path over freshly fallen snow.

"I've felt lonely throughout my life," he says.

My parents divorced when I was two years old, at the onset of the asthma I inherited from him. "One of the few things he gave me" was a crude joke I told for a while—a defense mechanism since he was rarely around, and when he was, our interactions didn't go very well.

As my father and I walk now, I point out rows of yew trees that line the sidewalks around Harvard Square and tell him about my visit to the Fortingall Yew in Glen Lyon, Scotland, earlier this year, the oldest living being in Europe, estimated to be anywhere from three to five thousand years old.

Àdhamh insisted I meet this ancient being, who may have known our family that lived nearby. I couldn't wait. I had high expectations for this tree and expected to get some sort of transmission, but when we arrived, something felt wrong. Church walls surround this elder that was sacred to the pre-Christian people of the land, and another protective wall surrounds this ancient tree inside of that. No longer free among the groves where people can gather, the ancient being seemed caged.

I sat with the Fortingall Yew tree and felt that sadness and constraint, and yet the tree is still thriving, growing over and beyond the protective barriers. I saw the cones and the ripe berries of this grandmother and grandfather tree. Yews are typically dioecious, meaning they are either male or female, but this tree is transforming—luscious red berries are appearing where cones once were. The balance of opposites—the stillness and steadiness alongside the intense, ongoing growth and life-force energy—that has persisted for thousands of years. A yew grows in almost every church and graveyard in Scotland. Though some of those yew trees were planted, most of the grandmother and grandfather trees were there first.

As my father and I walk, I imagine what these hedges would look like if their vast root systems were given room to grow, their branches liberated from constant clipping, and their wisdom remembered. In their natural state, these evergreens whose power is pruned into long, rectangular hedgerows might live to be thousands of years old, rooting and forming new trunks where their branches touch the ground. This supernatural power was harnessed in magician's wands, and the slow-growing, tightly grained wood was made into the infamous longbows of the Middle Ages. Native Americans of the Northwest also prized yew for archery: *haida*, their name for yew, means "bow tree."[6] In both cultures, arrows were tipped with poison made from the tree. The entire tree is poisonous—wood, bark, needles, and seed. The only edible part is the red berry (but the seed in the center must not be consumed), and the poisonous part of the yew, carefully extracted, is most frequently used in hunting and medicine.

My Celtic ancestors might have marked my aunt's grave with a branch of yew to help guide her to the Otherworld. My aunt had cancer. It's likely that Taxol, an extract from the poisonous tree's bark that inhibits cell growth and division, was used in her chemotherapy treatments.

MY FATHER AND I LOOK AT THE YEWS ALONGSIDE US IN HARVARD SQUARE, neatly tucked into their tight quarters, surrounded by concrete, and reflect on how much has been forgotten. "I wouldn't even have noticed them," he says. Invisible to most and robbed of their potential, I imagine these trees are lonely.

IF WE DON'T NOTICE THAT OUR EXTENDED FAMILY OF TREES, WOLVES, INSECTS, birds, or fungi exist, how will we know when they're missing? Corporations and consumerism will never fill the void that destroying nature leaves. Recent studies have shown that young children in the United States can recognize over one thousand corporate logos, but few can identify more than a handful of local plant or animal species.[7] What an isolating illiteracy.

When I walk down Brooklyn blocks, I marvel at the powerful oak trees that line streets; the cedar trees, also known as the tree of life, sacred to the First Nations people of the land; the mystical hawthorns protecting the school-yard with their boundary-keeping thorns; the dreamy, honey-scented linden trees, sanctuaries buzzing with bees throughout Prospect Park; and the syca-more trees in Grand Army Plaza that look like an army of spotted leopards in their speckled, smooth bark.

I often give my students the exercise of looking at the trees and plants around them as though for the first time and to notice which ones call to them. I tell them not to worry about their names and, if they're so moved, to give them their own based on what they feel, sense, and observe. When we name, we notice. As we name the countless trees around us—sycamore, juniper, yew, red oak, white pine, linden, hawthorn, elder, birch, beech, elm, maple—they come alive.

But it isn't enough to know the names or gifts of trees if our relationship with land is one of taking or penetrating without permission. Not long after Taxol was first isolated from the bark of the Pacific yew in 1962 as part of a National Cancer Institute study, these ancient trees were on the brink of ex-tinction.[8] Roughly six trees are sacrificed to treat one patient. This caused an uproar and ethical debate in the 1990s, not to mention the fact that Western science likely received information about the Pacific yew from First Nations people, who've used the tree to treat cancer and other healthy issues sustain-ably, long before Europeans arrived, and yet it is only Western science now reaping the monetary reward and credit for the discovery. Fortunately for the Pacific yew, methods have been developed to produce the drug without the need to further endanger wild populations. But the damage to these ancient, slow-growing trees, their forest families, and Indigenous people of the North-west has been done. It will take much collective work to begin repairing those wounds.

FAMILY RESEMBLANCE

That evening in Cambridge, my father and I walk ahead of the family, rushing after dinner back to the hotel, where he'd left his inhaler. It's freezing cold and my father has asthma. He speed walks. A man of seventy, he is in incredibly good shape. His nervous energy reminds me of my younger self—my panic at the onset of wheezing. He takes his two puffs and feels immediate relief. "Embarrassing," he says.

Once he settles down and catches his breath, we talk about our relationship with nature. He tells me about the cedar tree—arborvitae, the tree of life—in the woods of Norfolk, Connecticut: "The tree spoke to me, I can't explain it, but I'll never forget it." We listen to each other, mending strands of disconnection. I've done a lot of work to soften my anger toward him, and he's worked his entire life to heal his addiction to alcohol and the hurt he has caused because of it. "I drank to numb my incessant, gnawing feeling of loneliness," he says.

My father came from a broken family system. He and his siblings were sent off to different boarding schools in New England while my grandparents lived separate lives in Japan, and then Italy. My mom said that he referred to himself as the black sheep, the unwitting rebel of the family who resisted his elitist upbringing and stumbled through descendant ranks of Ivy League prep schools while his perfect brother (in my father's mind, at least) followed the set path and excelled. His sister had health issues so was often closer to their parents, living in Europe. When the family did see each other in summertime, gatherings were a show of accomplishments. Forced to act and desperate for authentic connection, my father felt like a failure inside.

My grandfather Robertson was named for family members of Clann Donnachaidh, otherwise known as Clan Robertson from the Perthshire area of the Scottish Highlands. Grandpa Robertson was intimidating. He had a photographic memory and could quote passages from every book he read (which seemed to be *all* books, especially obscure but "important" ones) and had a talent for making anyone, no matter how smart, feel like an idiot. And if there was a subject you loved? Forget it. He knew more. He must have been tapped into some otherworldly information portal. Listening to his monologues, I would drift away into my own peaceful worlds, and each time I came back into my body I felt increasingly blank and stupid. I can only imagine how my father felt in his formative years.

Robertson was the first to tell me the story of Romulus and Remus, the fabled founders of Rome who were fed by a she-wolf. I was twelve years old, visiting my grandparents in Italy and bored out of my mind listening to art history monologues, and after touring all of the Renaissance museums in Rome, I could not bear to look at another painting of Mary and baby Jesus. So when we came upon the statue of the two young boys suckling from the body of a female wolf in the Palazzo dei Conservatori, my senses were revived. I have always loved wolves, so I remember listening intently to that story and wondering, *If a wolf was the nurturing mother of Rome, why weren't her wild kin treated with respect?*

At home, I lived with a struggling single mom and my father didn't pay child support. But he was broke too, living in Cambridge and then New York trying to carve out a living as an actor, musician, and waiter. Meanwhile, I was whisked away to Italy on occasion by my grandparents, and spent some weekends at their summer home in the New England woods. I developed a real schism around money. On rare occasions, I visited my father as he moved from apartment to apartment, and from city to city.

Apparently, when I visited him in New York and my mom spent a day with us, he stood me on the crown of the Statue of Liberty to see the view, and when I was visiting him in Cambridge, he stood me up above the shark tank at the Boston Aquarium so I could look down at the predators swimming and stalking in circles. I remember seeing them and being mesmerized. They were beautiful. But my mom thought he was reckless. "He could've killed you!" she told me. I wasn't afraid in the moment, but I was afraid afterward. Like when I raced down a cement hill in flip-flops, scraped the skin off my knees, and tore my big toenail off. It makes me cringe even now, but at the time, when I fell, I merely walked to get help. I only cried when I looked down and realized the severity of my wounds and that the wet I was feeling was the rush of my blood. I never ran down a hill in flip-flops again—and soon, I felt like I should hold my father at arm's length too.

The wound between my father and me was a deep one. I'm the only child from the union between my mother and father and, for a time, she wanted to forget that he existed because of the pain he caused her. Aligned in their progressive, hippie sensibilities, they had some good years together, but because of his drinking, unreliability, and recklessness, my father transformed from a visionary to a villain in her story. She admitted to me, in one of the rare moments we spoke of him, "I was so relieved you didn't grow to look like him. And I was so glad you weren't a boy." My mother, my source of unconditional love, my best friend, didn't want to see that part of me. And for most my life, I avoided my connection to my father too. I was angry at him for hurting her, for his unpredictable behavior, and for his absence. I understood that something in me needed to be ignored and washed away. An impossible feat since his blood runs through my veins.

As we all grew older, his parents lost most of their money to bad investments, and so they had to live more simply. In his old age, my grandfather softened and started to listen a little more. My grandmother and I became close. Passion was the ruling force in her life, and she was proud of the way I created my own path. When I started boxing, she seemed to really get me. Like my grandfather, she was brilliant, though didn't wield knowledge as a weapon the way he did. But as intellectually driven as they were, they were wilder than other members of my family. They chose to live in beautiful but rustic settings— in an old converted stone barn amid overgrown olive orchards in Tuscany or on Doolittle Lake in Norfolk, Connecticut, deep in the woods. My grandmother was never ashamed of her body, and on summer visits she ran through the woods naked and barefoot to jump in the lake and go skinny-dipping. Little prudish me thought she was scandalous. But she was unabashed. She wanted to live passionately, that was her motto. And she did. She sucked the marrow out of life to the very end. Well into her eighties, she read voraciously, took philosophy courses, and gambled on backgammon games (she loved gambling), and when her car keys and alcohol were taken away by Tara, a neighbor and caretaker, she was seen walking to the liquor store with her oxygen tank rattling alongside her.

When Granny and I had moments alone over the years, she spoke highly of my father. She was one of the few who did. She told me, "Though he might appear to be a mess, he lives with passion and that's something to admire. And if you give him a chance, you might find you're very similar." She was his champion and they were close. As close as they could be across years of physical and emotional continents.

BACK AT THE HOTEL IN CAMBRIDGE, MY FATHER AND I SHARE WHERE WE ARE now. We're done blaming, carrying guilt and anger, and have exhausted the rehashing of old wounds. They are healing over now; it's time to stop picking at them and move on. We're at peace with ourselves. He has become a therapist, a drug and alcohol counselor, and has devoted his life to healing. Daily meditation and exercise have been his balm as they have been mine. After years of being on the edge of each other's lives, like the unseen yew trees, we are finally taking the time to notice each other. And as he speaks, I see myself in his stories too. Granny was right; wheezing and all, we are similar.

I've never called him Dad. I've never called him anything, honestly. Through the years, I've greeted him with "hello" and avoided naming him altogether. I still don't know what to call him, Van or Dad, neither feels quite right. But I know it's time I name him so he can come alive.

RESTORATION

Innes just sent me a list of native trees they are reintroducing to the land— hawthorn, crabapple, juniper, Scots pine, aspen, rowan, and dwarf birch and dwarf willow in the higher altitudes. As part of their herbal apprenticeship, some of my students in Scotland and in the northeastern United States are researching the ecological relationships of those trees and asking, What does hawthorn need in order to thrive? What wild relationships are vital to the tree's health and wellbeing, and vice versa? It isn't enough to simply stick a tree in the ground. Like our own familial networks, the tree is one part of a larger ecosystem and we want to understand how to nurture the soil and revive as many of the tree's relationships as possible so every individual in that community, including humans, can flourish. Like us, trees need diversity to thrive. Species diversity, racial diversity, a diversity of ideas, stories, roles, and paths—all nurture life while sameness stifles. Yet our instinct at times is to contort into linear shapes instead of embracing our beautifully twisted ones. For some, standing out can be dangerous and fitting in is a matter of survival. On a national level, one's appearance or ethnicity has no place in the ways that people of any region are regarded by law or discriminated against, nor what opportunities are afforded them, and it's tragic how many lose connection to their roots when forced to fit in.

Over and over again, I witness the ways in which the study and practice of herbalism guides us back to the land and the stories of our ancestors. My herbal apprentice Jessica shares: "While I am not living currently on the Land of my ancestors, connecting to the Land I love and honoring it by becoming friends with the plants outside my door has stirred me to seek the practices of the people of the Philippines in pre-colonial times. The plants have supported me by calling to me in visions and dreams. Decolonizing my mind, my education, my practice is a painful process, but a necessary one that is bonded to my relationship to plants. Building relationships with the Land is decolonization work: we are remembering the old ways, strengthening an ancient relationship with our Lands."

When I spent time on the Akwesasne reservation whose territory is in upstate New York and Canada, we spoke about the ways that they, like the Gaels, were sent to schools to be "civilized" and brutally stripped of their traditional language and culture. My friend Kim, a Mohawk who grew up on the reservation, has been working to reclaim her language and traditions and, along with others, revive the ancestral ways. But the trauma of colonization has had a devastating impact: many of those who experienced the boarding-school era that only ended in the 1970s suffer from PTSD, depression, and alcoholism, and there is glaring environmental injustice as the United States government continues to break treaties and exploit Native land. The St. Lawrence River that surrounds the Akwesasne reservation that was once teeming with fish is now toxic from being used as a waste site. The impact of those wounds make superficial appropriation of their culture all the more insidious. During my time at Akwesasne, we took a boat to the island where keepers of their traditional knowledge care for the community's plant medicine. We shared and compared notes about plants like goldenrod and elder that offer indiscriminate healing to all people. Robin Wall Kimmerer, member of the Potawatami nation and author of *Braiding Sweetgrass* writes that in some Native cultures the word *plant* translates to "those who take care of us."

WHERE OLD, DRY, COMPACTED SOIL HAS BEEN OVERTURNED AT ALLADALE, hundreds of medicinal plants appear—yarrow, red clover, eyebright, self-heal, St. John's wort, and sundew. The rare twinflower that hadn't been seen in hundreds of years reappeared in the area where new trees have been planted. "Disturbed soil" is where many of these plants like to grow. Like us, even the earth benefits from occasional disturbance and digging instead of being left alone.

Reconnecting to our roots can lead us home, to a place of belonging. It doesn't mean we'll change who we are on the outside, or even set foot on ancestral soil, but on the inside, finding a grounded sense of belonging can ease our grasping. Even if we've been torn from countries of origin or birth families, we are still part of a larger community and can listen to the land where we are. Like mycorrhizal mycelium, we can restore the web of communication with our multispecies family. I was much more prone to loneliness before I restored my relationship with land. Relationship with the Earth has given me the strongest sense of belonging I've ever known. For many years, like the young trees, I was seeking something, some level of understanding or connection that could only be found by reaching below the surface.

And there is still much to unearth.

There are many layers of healing, and for healing to be truly whole, we must do the uncomfortable, imperfect work of confronting our cultural and communal wounds as much as we tend to our own. Time, in Celtic cosmology, is seen as circular not linear, an ongoing spiral that never circles back to the same place. So as I unearth the stories of the plants, animals, and people that surround me, my inner narrative and external experience changes too.

After mending spaces of disconnection at my aunt's memorial service, my father and I went our separate ways and left each other feeling more grounded. As we said goodbye, we encountered the yew trees once again—those ever-present elders whose lives span all other trees and much of human history to date. The yew contains the cumulative lessons of their ancient forests, just as we contain the hopes, fears, dreams, and knowledge of our ancestors. Like our human family—chosen, biological, or spirit—the plants, trees, wolves, and wild ones deserve to be remembered, honored, heard, and seen for who they are too. As I learn about indigenous cultures and my own ancestral roots around the world, I find that at the core of many of them, there are principles that reveal our interconnectedness with nature; we are nature, and nature is alive.

In the process of rewilding my ancestral landscape, I strengthen my roots, extend my limbs, and rewrite history.

APPLE TREE
Malus domestica

Family: Rosaceae

In Celtic cosmology, the Otherworld exists along-side our own with an entryway signaled by sudden mists, change of season, and the appearance of unusual beings. Women guard the boundary to this Otherworld, an elusive place of beauty where gods and ancestors dwell. A seeker may be invited in by one of these powerful guardians through the offering of an apple or a silver apple branch. In Welsh, one of these mystical lands is known as Ynys Afallach, the Isle of Apples, otherwise known as the Isle of Avalon.

Symbolism of the apple is vast—ranging from the Sacred Feminine; the five elements, represented by the pentagram that is revealed when an apple is cut in half; the five wounds of Christ; the limbs of the human body; and even witchcraft. The apple has long been depicted as the infamous forbidden fruit, but centuries before Eve took her fateful bite, Gaia, who was Mother Earth in Greek mythology, gifted a sacred apple tree to Hera on her wedding day to Zeus, the sky god. The tree's glowing, golden apples were guarded by the three maidens of Hesperides, or "daughters of the evening," and a serpentlike dragon named Ladon. The serpent, an ancient symbol of awakening, coiled around the tree to guard the highly coveted golden fruit.

ORIGIN STORIES

A seed hidden in the heart of an apple is an orchard invisible.

WELSH PROVERB

It's February in Western Massachusetts, and as I write, Mother Earth rests under a heavy blanket of snow. With the exception of evergreens like pine, hemlock, and spruce, the trees around me are bare. White birch stand out like skeletons in the forest. Wild rose thorns grab me as I walk, making sure I pay attention to where I'm going. Burdock burrs attach to my pant legs, and as I pull them off, I scatter new seeds. And there are apple trees. Like wild rose, apple trees are in the rose or Rosaceae family of plants. As I walk among their gnarly, crooked branches, they remind me of old, wise crones. Moss and lichen cover their scaly, weathered bark.

I stand in front of what feels like the grandmother tree. Her trunk twists, turns, and expands to make way for new growth like snake shedding skin. Smooth layers appear underneath old, gray bark and young shoots spring up toward the sky from her limbs. And there is a bird's nest. Sanctuary.

A few withered and frozen fruits hang on. Soon, they'll descend with seeds in their bellies, ready to create new life. If these seeds germinate, these trees will be nothing like their parents, a characteristic known in botany as extreme heterozygosity. This ability to shape-shift and adapt has enabled apples to spread from the mountains of Kazakhstan—where *Malus sieversii*, wild ancestors of *Malus domestica*, still flourish—to the rest of the world.

These small, twisted trees look older than their years—maybe it's the weight of their stories.

IN GAELIC TRADITION, WINTER IS RULED BY THE CAILLEACH BHÉARA, THE Grandmother of the Clanns and Wisewoman of the Otherworld.[1] She controls the weather, builds mountains, guards sacred wells, and created Scotland's rivers and notorious deep, dark lochs—she is a fierce guardian of the wild. She also governs the invisible realms of our dreams and influences our internal inner wild. She has two famous haunts in Argyll, where my grandmother's people are from: Ben Cruachan, the largest mountain in the area, and the powerful whirlpool of the Gulf of Corryvreckan. In Argyleshire lore, the old people used to say "Tha a' chailleach aig glanamh nam breacan" (The crone is at the cleaning of the plaids) whenever the roar of swirling water was heard. The Gulf of Corryvreckan, creates a fine spray that mists over the inhabitants of Knapdale. Some refer to the force of the intense, ever-spiraling whirlpool as "the breath of the goddess beneath the waves."

THOUGH WE WEREN'T RELIGIOUS, MY FAMILY HAD OUR RITUALS. MY FAVORITE one took place in autumn. My mom, her parents, and I gathered at Atkins Farms in South Amherst to eat Mcintosh, Macoun, and Cortland apples straight from the trees in their orchards. We shared cider donuts and hot apple cider, and when my grandparents couldn't make the drive, we brought bags of apples to them.

When my parents divorced, my maternal grandparents' house, forty minutes away in Springfield, Massachusetts, was my sanctuary. My grandparents often said that I was their fourth child. "An apple a day keeps the doctor away" was one of my grandfather's favorite sayings. A physician and caring patriarch of the family, he was indeed like a father to me. A steady, stoic, and calming presence, he reminded me that "food is medicine," though he always laughed at how much salad I could eat in one sitting: "Somehow, you inherited the digestive system of a cow." (I love those sweet herbivores, so I didn't take it as an insult.)

There were stacks and shelves full of the very important-looking *Journal of the American Medical Association* magazines in the room where I slept at their house. I gazed at those periodicals, wondering about the American Medical Association logo that I now know is the serpent-entwined rod of Asclepius, the Greco-Roman god of medicine, who used nonvenomous snakes in healing rituals. Asclepius was trained in the healing arts by the centaur Chiron, but it was an encounter with a wise snake that imbued Asclepius with supernatural healing abilities. In the years that followed—right around 300 BCE—Asclepius became so renowned that pilgrims flocked to his healing temples where snakes slithered on the floor as they slept. Dreams were reported and healers would prescribe the appropriate therapy by a process of interpretation. I always felt my dreams held important messages for healing, but my grandfather and other doctors around me didn't seem very interested in their interpretation.

Where my grandfather was calm and steady, my grandmother, Dorothy Graham, was a fiery force of nature. She was fastidiously clean, the consummate fashionista (even on days she only puttered around the house), and had unwavering opinions about what everyone in the family should be doing with their lives. She was sure that Mitch, my stepfather and an incredibly talented musician, should take on a more consistent and reliable job as a postman. While we laughed about it, she drove us all a little crazy. But she was fun, full of life, and I adored her.

Dorothy was the daughter of churchgoing Presbyterians, and my grandfather had been raised by Yiddish-speaking Russian Jewish immigrants. There was a lot of tension around their religious differences. They met at Mount Sinai Hospital in New York City, where my grandfather interned and my grandmother was a young, freckle-faced, and strikingly beautiful nurse. Shortly after, my grandfather went off to be a naval doctor in World War II. They wrote letters back and forth over those years; we still have their correspondence, and what they shared was clearly true love. They married on August 14, 1945, at New York's city hall, on the famous V-J Day.

They then returned to my grandfather's hometown of Springfield, Massachusetts, where he opened a private practice; his relatives were not at all thrilled that he had married a shiksa and my grandmother refused to take the sacrificial bath in front of the rabbi that was an essential part of becoming a Jewish wife and mother. Over time, their different belief systems neutralized any sort of religious practice, though my mom tells me that my grandmother read Bible stories aloud on Sunday afternoons when my grandfather was at work. The book was abruptly put back on the shelf when he pulled into the driveway before dinner and it was never discussed. I doubt he would have cared, though he might have thought it was "ridiculous" (one of his favorite words). Ever rational and with a scientific mind, he felt that religions were filled with misinterpreted stories that divided people when what we most needed was to get along.

Though most of my immediate family are agnostic, when I was young, my stepfather and his father, a Baptist minister, warned me that "Oh, my god," which I often said, was terrible blasphemy. They told me that God was always listening and, in fact, "He" was watching my every move and ticking "good girl" or "bad girl" boxes according to my behavior. Punishment or reward would be dealt when I was dead, so I'd better be good. I couldn't stand the idea of this judgmental male hovering above me. Why an omnipotent, all-powerful, and supposedly loving figure had such a delicate ego made no sense to me.

My stepfather's parents ran a Baptist church and Sunday school out of their home, one hour away in Auburn. Adults sang hymns and had service in the living room, while their children attended Sunday school with Grammy, my stepfather's incredibly sweet mother, in one of the bedrooms. I loved her, but dreaded Sunday school. I felt a palpable dissonance in the violent stories that spoke of guilt, sin, and obedience. Where were the powerful women? Why did Christians, who supposedly taught love and acceptance, constantly try to convert and impose their beliefs on everyone else? And wasn't Jesus Jewish? I was confused. We went to their church once every couple of months, and I attended other services sporadically throughout my life. Every time I did, I felt more and more resistant to this God that was depicted as an angry, judgmental white man. Though I felt there was an animating force that coursed through life, I didn't believe he was it. But it took me a long time to shake the feeling that he was watching me.

———

I'VE BEEN LOOKING FOR THE QUINTESSENTIAL CELTIC OR GAELIC ORIGIN STORY and the closest I've come is the beautiful tale of Eiocha, the white mare of the sea. Scott Leonard retells the myth beautifully in his book *Myth and Knowing*. He writes, "Once upon a time, there was no time . . . But there was the sea, and where the sea met the land, a mare was born, white and made of sea-foam. And her name was Eiocha."[2] From there, creation continued and never stopped. An oak tree grew where the sea touched the land. Eiocha ate the white sea-foam seeds (mistletoe) and from those seeds gave birth to Cernunnos, the horned god, and together they created more gods. But over time, the gods felt lonely, so from the wood of the oak tree they formed the first woman, man, and all other animals. The oak, the tree of life, was sacred to the Celts, and many rituals took place in oak groves, their outdoor temples. The divine was free on the wind and among the trees.

In similar stories, Uranus, the husband and son of Gaia, Mother Earth, mixed sea foam with blood from his genitals to create Aphrodite, the goddess of love. In Peru, Viracocha, the great creator deity in pre-Incan and Incan mythology from the Andes, emerged from the foam of the sea. He was represented as wearing the sun for a crown, with thunderbolts in his hands and tears descending from his eyes as rain. And though the sky is often associated with masculine energy, in Native American tradition, there is Skywoman.

It is hard not to think of Robin Wall Kimmerer's stunning book *Braiding Sweetgrass* when reflecting on the story of Skywoman, a beautiful tale of reciprocity. Falling from a faraway planet with handfuls of seeds, Kimmerer writes that Skywoman "fell like a maple seed, pirouetting on an autumn breeze."[3] As she plummeted through the cosmos toward Earth, the animals on Earth conspired to ease her fall before she dove into the deep blue water that at that time completely covered the planet. A flock of geese caught her in midair and gently brought her to rest on the back of a turtle. Surrounding her, the animals convened. They understood that she needed solid ground. And after many unsuccessful attempts, a brave muskrat gave his life by diving deep to the bottom of the water to bring Skywoman a handful of mud to create land. His gift was placed on the back of the turtle and slowly, in collaboration with all the animals, land—Turtle Island—began to form. With her handful of seeds, Skywoman ushered the plants and sentient green life onto land to nourish the animals and the people to come.

The core of these many stories isn't that so different from the story that science tells us about the origin of life on Earth: Recent studies speculate that several billion years ago, enormous waterlogged asteroids began developing into planets while the solar nebula swirled around the Sun. These asteroids, known as planetary embryos, collided and began expanding rapidly until an intense collision introduced enough energy to melt the surface of the largest embryo into an ocean of magma.[4] The result of that collision is our beloved planet, Earth. And from there, we emerged over time from the sea. Since the microcosm is so often a reflection of the macrocosm, we emerge from the ocean of our mother's womb. From sea onto land, like Eiocha. In most stories, once the Creator has manifested, this entity creates male and female energy that join to manifest offspring. This union of opposites to create life gave rise to the concept of the holy trinity—mother, father, and child—that is found in pre-Christian imagery throughout the world. One of the earliest appearances of this holy trinity is the Egyptian father, Osiris; mother, Isis; and son, Horus.[5] Later, Christianity stripped the feminine from its versions of the creation trinity that became father, son, and the holy spirit, replacing the feminine icon with a dove.

FROM SEPTEMBER 2005 TO OCTOBER 2006 I WORKED ON BEHALF OF HIS HOLIness the Dalai Lama. I cocreated and coordinated an event called HOPE to raise funds and awareness for the Norbulingka Institute, a sanctuary for Tibetan refugees in Dharamshala, India, whose mission is the preservation of Tibetan art and culture.[6] For the previous several years, my world had revolved around boxing, day in, day out, and that narrow focus was beginning to feel like more of an obstacle than a gift. Tibetan Buddhism resonated deeply with me, so when I phased out of full-time training as a competitive fighter, I looked for work that felt less selfish. While it was a vital aspect of my own healing, I also thought that professional boxing would become a platform from which I could launch other initiatives, but it hadn't turned out that way. I felt like I had little to show for the years and countless hours I spent training in the boxing gym, and though I was engaged in activism—working on behalf of environmental causes, organizing events on behalf of Mumia Abu Jamal and other political prisoners, and going to protests—I felt like it wasn't enough. The HOPE event was an answer to my prayers. It was a cause I wholeheartedly believed in, plus friends and family were impressed by its status: Donna Karan generously donated her event space for the fundraiser, and as the overall event coordinator, I had celebrities like David Bowie and Susan Sarandon calling me, and I went to fancy "important" meetings. But I was wearing too many hats—fundraising, event coordination, communications, and constant problem solving. Despite rubbing elbows with the rich and famous, I was scrambling to get the money for the nonprofit so that there would be enough to pay me. I was stressed out and struggling. Apart from meditation, I barely had time for my practices or people I loved. The study and practice of Buddhism was one thing, but organizing an event in New York City for and alongside high-maintenance people was a different beast. I convinced myself that it was "sacrifice" for a good cause, but I was on edge, always on my phone, and I didn't like it.

The event was to take place in 2006, three days before my grandmother's eighty-eighth birthday. During the run-up to the event (and her big birthday), she got sick, really sick, and I wasn't as attuned to her as I wanted to be.

MY GRANDMOTHER'S BIRTHDAY IS SEPTEMBER 29, AND EVERY YEAR WE GOT A cake from Lederer's bakery in Springfield to celebrate—another family ritual. I can still picture sitting around the dining room table with our growing family: first my mom, aunt, and me, then my stepfather and uncle, and eleven years later my sister, brother, and cousins joined us as she blew out her candles. She always giggled as she took "just another little sliver" after her big piece with the pink rose made of sugary frosting. She loved her sweets. When I moved to New York, any time the city or my mom's house felt too chaotic for me, I went to my grandparents' spotless, organized, and predictable home on Pondview Drive for peace and stability. When my grandmother passed away in August 2006 at my aunt's house in Cape Cod just before her eighty-eighth birthday, I felt a void I'd never experienced before.

The night she died, I held my grandfather in the twin bed he occupied at my aunt's, next to my grandmother's. The brilliant family caretaker had been too ill to stand beside his wife and could do nothing but watch her struggle. It was absolutely heartbreaking. As my grandmother moaned and took her last breaths, one of my cousins whispered in her ear, "Accept Jesus Christ as your savior." I felt this was an unbelievable insult to my Jewish grandfather, my sweet and loving grandmother, and to many of us in that room. But my cousin truly believed my grandmother would be on her way to hell if she didn't. I thought, *What kind of God would send a loving, generous, and kind woman to hell?*

The day after she passed, I lay on my cousin's bed with all the shades drawn, in darkness next to my mom. We were silent. I sensed that we felt the same endless abyss. I was away from the city where the HOPE event was about to take place, and it was mere days before a treasured holiday in our family's calendar—my grandmother's birthday. I called my colleague to let her know of my family's loss and that I needed to stay longer but she pushed back, saying, "Don't be so heavy about it. We need you here. There's a lot to do." So much for Buddhist compassion.

Later that day, I walked to the beach where my grandmother and I spent summers burying ourselves and sculpting our own mythic creatures in the sand. As I walked along the shore, I imagined I saw their shadows rising and falling around me and I noticed a butterfly following me. She danced around me, even along the windy shore as the water smoothed the edges of sand. After a while, I lost her, but as I made my way back to the house, there she was again.

A few days later, I went back to New York. It was the first birthday I didn't celebrate with my grandmother. My mom, sister, brother, and stepfather all came to the HOPE event, which, for me, went by in a blur. All that work for something that looked good on the outside but left me feeling empty. The consolation was that the moment before the event started, the Dalai Lama walked over to my mom, looked into her eyes, and held her hand.

The bardo stage in Tibetan Buddhism is the state of intermediary existence after death and before one's next birth, when one's consciousness is not connected with a physical body. In the wake of the HOPE event and my grandmother's passing, that's how I felt. I was depleted. On my grandmother's birthday, all that work was over and she was gone. But she seemed to be visiting me. No matter where I was, I saw a butterfly. They landed on my windowsill in Brooklyn, fluttered around my head on the city streets, and when I sat down on park benches, they often landed on me. My aunt and mother saw butterflies in the most unusual places too. I can't explain it rationally. In Russia and Ireland, butterflies are seen as the souls of departed loved ones waiting to pass through purgatory, so perhaps the butterflies were her spirit in between births. If she did indeed reincarnate in another form, as many cultures believe, how can I call upon her spirit now? Isn't that spirit in another form? Why would the spirit of Dorothy Graham as we knew her continue to hang around?

I'M IN SCOTLAND AS I WRITE THIS. MY GRANDMOTHER'S ANCESTRAL LAND. OUR ancestral land. This afternoon I was talking with my friend Anna, a Tibetan Buddhist practitioner and teacher, about death and the pull that families can have on those who are trying to let go. Perhaps that's what happened to my grandmother. I didn't want her to go. None of us did. She got sick so suddenly and she wasn't ready either. And worse, no one asked her where *she* believed she was going and how we could make her transition more peaceful, even beautiful. She didn't know the story of Eiocha, the white mare. If she did, perhaps she would have galloped toward the Otherworld of our ancestors on Eiocha's back. But she wasn't given the choice of what to believe in. And even though our Scottish ancestors worked with horses and lived in harmony with the land, they had been indoctrinated with patriarchal Christian belief systems, and so my grandmother was too.

My grandfather died one year later. I often see them in my dreams, and feel their presence. Every time fall rolls around, and especially when I see a bag of freshly picked apples, and certainly butterflies, I think of my beloved grandparents.

THE GIVING TREE

When the reign of the Cailleach, the winter crone, wanes in spring, the time of rebirth, the Celtic goddess Brigid begins to rule. On Imbolc, her festival day, people watch to see if serpents come from their winter dens. A Scottish Gaelic proverb about the weather divination is this:

Thig an nathair as an toll
Là donn Brìde
Ged robh trì troighean dhen t-sneachd
Air leac an làir.

The serpent will come from the hole
On the brown Day of Bríde,
Though there should be three feet of snow
On the flat surface of the ground.[7]

As a symbol of the fecund earth, like an earthworm, the serpent stirred the soil awake, uncoiling and rising up toward new growth. A similar concept exists in India: Kundalini energy is symbolized by a serpent coiled at the base of the spine that remains dormant in an unawakened person. Like the serpent in spring, this energy can be called to rise as our inner soil is stirred through conscious movement, meditation, and in tantric traditions, sacred sexuality. As the energy awakens, our inner serpent moves through each energy center or chakra to eventually open the third eye.

When I came upon the notion of Kundalini energy during a period dedicated to meditation and yoga practice in my twenties, I theorized that my inner serpent had been startled awake when I fractured my lower vertebrae in the car accident, rising up my spine quickly and erratically, creating massive shifts and overwhelming, life-altering initiations. I assumed that "higher" states of consciousness were better than "lower" ones and that the goal of spiritual practice was to move beyond the cramped, painful apartment of the body. I was intent on awakening my third eye so I could truly *see*. I wrote words like *transcend* over and over again and even painted them on my apartment walls. I vacillated between animal embodiment with martial arts and meditations to transcend it. When I studied the samurai tradition (that I was inspired to learn about after watching the movie *Ghost Dog: The Way of the Samurai*), I came upon a meditation to imagine my body dying a gruesome death. The samurai did this to be fearless in battle and that made sense to me. After a while the idea gnawed at me, so I pictured myself dying in the most horrible ways, which was disturbing. But then one day, while doing the visualization in an empty basement gym before boxing, this meditation of my death didn't bother me. No attachment, no fear. The more I meditated, the easier it was to travel out of my body. And while this had been my goal, I think I went a little too far. Luckily, plants and herbalism practices brought me back down to Earth.

WHEN A SNAKE IS READY TO MOLT, THEIR OLD SKIN BECOMES DULL AND THEIR eyes cloudy, as though they have entered a trance. But unlike many of us humans, they know exactly when it is time to let go of that state. They stop eating, move to a safe space, and after a few days of molting, their eyes clear and they emerge from their old skin completely renewed. Because of this, the snake has been worshipped throughout the world as a symbol of rebirth. And in some traditions, the serpent symbolizes the umbilical cord between earth and sky, joining all humans to Mother Earth.

In ancient Mesopotamia and the early schools of mysticism, the snake was sacred to the Great Mother, symbolizing knowledge, healing, and awakening one's potential.[8] She often had snakes as her familiars, sometimes twining around her wrists or sacred staff, as in ancient Crete. The spiraling snake—like the moon, women's menstrual cycles, the spiraling Milky Way, and the cycle of the seasons—was a symbol of the never-ending cycle of life, death, and rebirth. The first known image of the famous caduceus, circa 2100 BCE, was a symbol of the god Ningishzida of Sumeria, who ruled the vegetation and the underworld. Ancient goddess temples used snake venom to enter a trance and see into the past, present, and future like the shamans of today might do with psilocybin mushrooms, peyote, or other entheogens. In Scotland, there is the earthen serpent at Glen Feochan, Loch Nell in Argyll.[9] Pictish standing stones, like the stones at Aberlemno, are often engraved with serpents and symbols thought to be connected to healing pools and springs.[10] Corra was the serpent goddess of Ireland.[11]

But in Genesis, the snake (in concert with Eve) is reimagined—a symbol of the goddess and her counterpart are cruelly rewritten to serve the story of a male god. Eve's sinful bite of the apple goes down with no problem but Adam's got stuck in his throat. Eve, sinful as she was, was able to digest this forbidden fruit and we women are still made to feel guilty for our hunger.

With the onset of Judaism in the sixth century BCE, Christianity in the first century CE, and Islam in the seventh century CE,[12] many cultures began to turn to something outside themselves to make sense of the world, and as people began to look up to the sky and worship a spirit perhaps beyond our realm, the feminine mystery of the earth became "heathen" and dirty. The bodies of both men and women became something to transcend. Prayers were sent to *Him* and away from the soul of wild, life-sustaining ecosystems. As Christianity took hold and in many cases was imposed, there arose an interpreter between people and spirit—the priest. These holy men were to deny sexual cravings and advise women to deny hunger for knowledge and for freedom.

When St. Patrick drove the "snakes" from Ireland, some saw that the story illustrated the violent imposition of Christianity over the Old Religion, the Druids, and the mystery of serpent goddesses like Corra.

FEW BOOKS BROKE MY HEART AS A CHILD MORE THAN SHEL SILVERSTEIN'S *The Giving Tree*. Rereading the book to write this passage brought tears to my eyes. Silverstein's story chronicles the unconditional love a tree has for a boy—a selfless, sacrificial love. Though the short trunk and gnarly branches of an apple tree wouldn't have been able to provide the wood for a house, the basis for a boat, or even a straight, solid branch to swing on, there is rich symbolism in Silverstein's choice. With curvaceous forms, intoxicating flowers, and sweet fruit, apple trees are often associated with the Sacred Feminine. The generous tree gives him her apples to eat, her branches to climb and swing upon, her canopy for shade, her leaves to build forts with. But as the boy grows older, he becomes restless. He wants money, a house, a boat to float away in. The tree gives him her apples to sell, her branches for building, and eventually her body for a boat. When the boy comes back as a sad old man, the tree tells him, lovingly as always, "I wish that I could give you something . . . but I have nothing left." He is unhappy, his belongings have faded, and his loving friend that he took and took from is reduced to a stump. He sits on her stump, and with a problematic ending, Silverstein writes "and the tree is happy." Really? To be taken for granted, pillaged, and reduced to a stump?

Growing up, I felt that *The Giving Tree* was about the unconditional love of Mother Earth and the lack of human reciprocity. And as I grew older, whether it was meant to or not, the story illuminated abuse of the Sacred Feminine and celebrated the notion that the role of a nurturing, loving mother is to give or sacrifice herself to the point of utter depletion. Others felt that way too. *The Giving Tree* was banned at a Colorado public library for being sexist, and on the flip side, was challenged by several schools, along with *The Lorax*, because it disparaged forestry.

Like the lessons in *The Lorax* and *The Giving Tree*, our current climate crisis is letting us know that we've been on the taking end for too long. If humans believe they have "dominion" over nature as Christian traditions led many to believe, how does our perceived power affect our relationship with the wild? Are we an integral part of the ecosystem or simply passing through on our way to paradise? These beliefs and their interpretations have done much damage to the Sacred Feminine in our bodies—male, female, and all animals— and the body of the Earth. We need to listen to, and create more stories about, acts of reverence and mutually beneficial reciprocity. As Bron Taylor writes in *Dark Green Religion: Nature Spirituality and the Planetary Future*, "Conservation is getting nowhere because it is incompatible with our Abrahamic concept of land. We abuse land because we regard it as a commodity belonging to us. When we see land as a community to which we belong, we may begin to use it with love and respect."[13]

ALCHEMY

I take a bite of an apple grown in the orchards here in Ashfield, Massachusetts. In it, I taste the land around me. The apple is sweet, sour, and bitter all at once— like life, the inevitable pain and sadness that courses through each of us when we become aware that one day will be the last day we see our mother or our grandmother, or walk in a beloved forest. Acceptance of this reality can help us cherish those we love and savor each drop of sweetness. By eating the fruit and exposing the seeds of these trees that keep growing, fruiting, changing, and expanding, I uncover deep resilience that guides me home to myself and unearths the practices of my people.

I reflect on the ways our ritual trips to the apple trees at Atkins Farms planted the seeds of my spiritual practice. I have been able to explore and accumulate wisdom through the sensual nature of experience in ways that were forbidden to women who came before me. Mother Earth is amply generous, and when we taste her fruit and revel in her sweetness, we can awaken to infinite wisdom. There is a saying in the Tibetan scriptures: "Knowledge must be burned, hammered, and beaten like pure gold. Then one can wear it as an ornament." According to Tibetan Buddhist teacher and scholar Chögyam Trungpa, this means that when we receive spiritual instruction from another, we need to look at it critically, "burn it . . . hammer it . . . beat it, until the bright, dignified color of gold appears."[14] Then we can mold it into a design that resonates as truth, and put it on.

While human stories, myths, and beliefs may change, evolve, and divide us, nature is honest and consistent—the medicine of birch, apple, wild rose, burdock, and all other plants are the same as they would have been thousands of years ago. These divine beings offer medicine, nourishment, and, in some cases, shelter to anyone who crosses their path. For those who choose to seek, each plant contains knowledge, lore, and stories to be told.

I WROTE THIS WHEN I AWOKE FROM A VIVID DREAM THIS MORNING: "OUR souls are rooted in earth and live underground, deep in our inner wells of emotion. They are heavy, rich with our experiences, our currents of love, solid and broken relationships, and our deep yearnings. Our souls speak to the truth of who we are. Spirit is something timeless, intangible, beyond our bodies. Spirit lives above the earth, sometimes passes through form, and is changeless as we move between dimensions, between lifetimes, between life and death. But the soul is unique to now. It is the reverence for which we live our lives and the rich, embodied awareness that is heavy with love, heavy with the bittersweet reality of interconnection and impermanence, heavy with who we truly are. The soul can be seen in and through the eyes of all species, and spirit is just beyond them. Sometimes I see spirit out of the corner of my eyes, but I see soul in the depths of them. Soul is water and earth, endlessly deep, dark, and mysterious. Spirit is fire and air, moving all around us, unseen and sometimes too dangerous to touch."

Like a snake shedding skins, my experiences of deep knowing have been a result of peeling back layers to come home to my innate wisdom where my instinct and intuition are intact. This is ongoing work, of course. Layers can accumulate too easily. So while the Cailleach Bhéara reigns and Mother Earth rests and renews herself underground, let me embrace this season as my sacred time of depth, introspection, and hibernation too. In many ways, the mystical Otherworld is right here. The veils between us might just be layers of conditioning. If we believe the wild world around us is inanimate, we shut ourselves out, are unable to sense the subtle, and will not have access to her wonder. It is time for us to shed our old, divisive stories, peel back layers, and see. The health and well-being of this wild and wonderful world desperately needs us to awaken.

EYEBRIGHT
Euphrasia spp.

Family: Orobanchaceae

Eyebright is a stunning little flower that helps us see more clearly. The botanical name *Euphrasia* is taken from one of the three Greek Charities, Euphrosyne, meaning "gladness." According to legend, the linnet, a bird whose Greek name comes from the same root, first used this plant to clear the sight of their young and then passed the knowledge on to humans. Eyebright was used in this way by the Scottish Highlanders, who mixed the plant extract with milk and applied it to the eyes with a feather.[1] When used at night just before bed, the healing ointment is said to induce prophetic dreams, and when used during the day, it makes what is usually unseen visible.

PERCEPTION

You can't depend on your eyes when your imagination is out of focus.

MARK TWAIN

A raven swirls above my head, in and out of the mists, and as she disappears, my eyes rest on shades of green that cover the ground as far as I can see. There are no billboards here, no one is trying to sell or convince me of anything in this expansive wilderness, as long as I don't reach for my phone, my portable distraction from reality. But I have no signal here, so the connection my phone promises can't tempt me—nothing competes for my attention except, maybe, the flowers. The deep fuchsia foxglove blossoms hang from their tall stalk-like bells (or small fox slippers, hence the name) and are impossible to ignore. The flowers face the ground, so bees have to enter completely to drink their nectar, and as they crawl to the end of the tunnel they are coated with pollen. The clever flower has marked the route with dark pinkish-red spots outlined in white that look like blood platelets; each bloom hanging from the stalk bears a unique design called a "nectar guide."

I'm looking to see if one of my favorites, eyebright, whose small flowers like to grow amid gray, rocky, depleted areas and overgrown grasses, is blooming yet. The labiated white flowers of eyebright can be easily overlooked, but once I attune my senses, I see their fiery yellow centers, purple veins, and deeply toothed leaves everywhere. I examine the lower lip of the flower that acts as a landing pad for tiny insect visitors that are guided to their nectar by the purple veins (I just love that flowers include directions for the busy pollinators). Eyebright is generally semiparasitic, feeding off the nutrients from the roots of relentless grasses, helping to keep them at bay so more delicate wildflowers can thrive. Today, I find eyebright alongside self-heal, clover, speedwell, and potentilla, perhaps gnawing at the surrounding grass underground to make space for their wildflower friends.

There is an intensity to this little flower and, as the name suggests, eyebright can help all manner of eye ailments, from conjunctivitis, red-eye, styes, itchy eyes, and stinging eyes to weak vision and metaphorical cloudiness. The plant combines soothing, astringent, cleansing, and anti-inflammatory actions that relieve eye pain or fatigue while lifting veils of illusion. Good medicine for the age of copious screen time and fake news. When my eyes burn from too much of either, I take an eyebright eye bath. I use an eyecup that has been rinsed with boiling water, fill it with cool eyebright infusion, and blink into it. Some herbalists like to tilt their heads back and tip the cup over their eyes, opening and shutting them a few times while looking in every direction: up, down, and side to side.

I SET OUT TODAY WITH INTENTION, TO FIND BOTH EYEBRIGHT AND THE LINnet, the small bird in the finch family that, according to legend, taught us how to use eyebright as medicine. These beautiful songbirds build their nests in thorny, protective bushes like gorse and feed on the seeds of wildflowers such as thistle, chickweed, yellow dock, and dandelion. I've been listening for their calls as I look for the tiny flowers. Once I find a patch of eyebright that welcomes my company, I sit hidden and protected by surrounding gorse and quietly become part of the landscape. Eventually, the linnet's sweet song emerges. The less I move, the more everything around me begins to.

When we look at nature, we often perceive it as a one-way street, but it isn't. Nature is also observing us. Plants notice changes in light as we walk by, and if we enter nature recklessly, we create a zone of disturbance that scatters wildlife and the land goes silent. Naturalist Jon Young in *What the Robin Knows* writes, "It is never just the robins communicating with the other robins, the song sparrows with the other song sparrows, the juncos with the other juncos. In the yard and in the trees, it's everyone communicating with (because they are eavesdropping on) everyone else—spring, summer, fall, and winter: ripples within ripples, a vast web with many seams and confusions; concentric rings bouncing off concentric rings; subtle sounds, subtle scents, subtle movements."

For many, the magic of the visible animate reality has become invisible. And why look for otherworldly creatures when we know so little about the sentient world around us?

PLANT BLINDNESS

When our eyes dart all over the place, so does our mind. When I began Zen and later Tibetan Buddhist meditation, I was taught to practice with my eyes open using a soft gaze. It was surprisingly hard, harder than practicing with my eyes closed. Whenever I had distracting or difficult thoughts, I had an impulse to look away and avert my gaze even though all that was in front of me was a hardwood floor or white wall. It took a lot of discipline to maintain my focus and presence and also not stare.

We rarely think about exercising our eyes, but during warm-up at the Shaolin (Kung Fu) Temple in New York City, that was one of the first things we did. As we stretched, we stretched our eyes too, moving them deliberately in every direction. In martial arts, looking down or away at the wrong moment can have serious consequences. "Look far!" my Shifu would say. When I stood tall and looked far for the first time, like the raven, I had big-picture vision, seeing peripherally and at the center simultaneously and could zoom in at will with laser-like focus when I was ready to attack. In boxing I was told to look "through" my opponents, not at them. "Keep your eyes wide!" was daily instruction from my boxing trainer. He didn't want me to close my eyes, flinch, or even blink while I was in the ring. With a constant expression of intense surprise, I earned my forehead lines, proving just how wide my eyes really were.

With disciplined meditation I cleared a lot of my mental noise and had more space to notice and listen without inference. And with the practice of martial arts, I awakened my animal instinct. In Taoism, the term *zhi* refers to plants, fungi, stones, or any living being that radiates shining light, and that's often what I feel when plants call to me; it's as though there is a spotlight on them. With senses more alive, receptive, and intact, I've attuned to the outer landscape in a new way and continue to see more as I move through the wild world around me. Embodied awareness grounds me, calms me, and brings me closer to nature's medicine.

In *Becoming Animal*, ecologist David Abram writes that cultures that have healthy relationships with nature don't just talk *about* nature, but talk *to* the plants, flowers, earth, water, and trees, "opening discourse to the more-than-human world."[2] Every living being speaks, but not necessarily in words. With more space to listen and an openness to nature's guidance, like nectar guides on the flowers, I have found that to be true. As I observe and communicate with the unique shapes and patterns of roots, berries, barks, flowers, and seeds, I deepen intimacy with nature and practice mindfulness. Plants and trees move at a slower pace, and the practice of herbalism has become a never-ending meditation. Even in the noise and chaos of city streets, I can stay aware and notice the intricate textures of trees' bark along the sidewalk and the powerful but unassuming chickweed surrounding the trees' roots.

MY FORMAL HERBALISM TRAINING BEGAN IN NEW YORK CITY WHERE I WAS filled with purpose, but starved for nature. Though it seems like a strange place to dive in, it makes perfect sense in retrospect. There was a gift in needing to connect where there was less; I paid close attention. It hadn't occurred to me to learn about the plants that grew through the cracks in the sidewalk, but I reached out to them in desperation. Like many people, I thought the exciting flora and medicinal superfoods were in the tropical rain forests of the Amazon or Costa Rica, not in New York City. But when I began to notice, really notice, the beauty of the so-called weeds, to learn about their ecological roles and their incredible cultural and medicinal history, my narrow, conditioned perspective shifted.

In abandoned city lots, where nature can do her own thing, plants and their pollinators thrive. These forgotten lots were some of the most stunning spaces in the city, full of mugwort flowers in bloom atop seven-foot stalks and arrow-like leaves; red clover, the gentle but powerful nitrogen fixer that makes way for more fertile ground; lady's thumb; wild mustard; violet; evening primrose; mullein; wood sorrel; thistle, with their purple petals atop sharp, porcupine-like leaves; and the confident flowers of dandelion.

Sacred medicine to some and invasive species to others, these ubiquitous healers are the epitome of wild nature. They're strong, resilient, and adaptive. They live with us in rural and urban areas alike, bursting through cracks in concrete and bringing beauty, color, and character to an otherwise boring lawn. *Wild* is often defined as being out of control, but when nature is healthy and functioning as she should, wild spaces are rhythmic, peaceful, and sometimes necessarily violent, but with every sentient being serving a purpose. Every wild animal and plant is clear about the role they play in an interdependent ecosystem.

THE LINNET WAS ONCE A POPULAR CAGED BIRD, CAPTURED FOR THEIR BEAUTY and melodic song. How anyone could ever find suffering beautiful is beyond me, but our species has caused a great deal of harm in the name of beauty. The linnet is now struggling in many parts of the world due to disruption of habitat, pesticide use, and the cutting of "'unsightly" hedges and weeds that the bird depends upon to survive. Our ideas of "civilized" beauty, tamed nature, and pleasing aesthetic principles have resulted in the planting of manicured gardens instead of old growth forests and—the bane of my existence—the removal of vital wild species to create useless, poisonous, carpet-like lawns.

We do this to ourselves too. I was talking to a woman recently who said that every woman in her country who can afford it now goes to a plastic surgeon to get the same button-like nose. Not necessarily the best to breathe through. Sameness is celebrated and yet monoculture, in our society and in nature, weakens us. Women's bodies and the body of the Earth are carved, cut, and poisoned to be more "beautiful" and appealing to patriarchal, capitalist culture where all is for sale—manicured lawns, manicured faces, bigger breasts, wrinkle-free faces, flatter stomachs, and bigger, brighter flowers that are shipped across oceans, laden with formaldehyde to keep them "fresh."

More than two thirds of the flowers sold in the United States now come from South America, where over one hundred types of fungicides, herbicides, insecticides, and preservative chemicals are used and approved by the United States in Colombia's flower industry, including those known as probable carcinogens. Flower workers in Colombia and Ecuador, the majority of them women, report that they are forced to reenter greenhouses soon after spraying to harvest roughly 350 roses a day.[3] A stupid and cruel exploitation of women and the Earth when we have such beautiful wildflowers that surround us—so long as we don't poison our planet. But then, we put lives on the line all the time for the sake of what our societies call beautiful.

When we manipulate flowers to get colors that we like, we screw with the specific shades and patterns that have evolved over time in relationship with their pollinators. Shades of red, pink, blue, and purple come mainly from the pigments called anthocyanins, which are in the class of chemicals called flavonoids. Other pigments called carotenoids produce hues of yellow, red, and orange in fruits like tomatoes and peppers. If reproduction through pollination is done by way of wind and air—which is the case with plants like ragweed—the pigments of the flower will be inconspicuous.

Birds like the linnet are tetrachromatic, able to distinguish four basic wavelengths of light, sometimes ranging into ultraviolet wavelengths, enabling them to distinguish more subtlety and hues of green than we do. Scientists believe that because our eyes are at the peak of their perception to detect the wavelengths corresponding with the color green, the shade calms us. With less strain to perceive the colors, our nervous system can relax, and yet many of us are losing vital green spaces and the ability to distinguish between plants and their unique adaptations.

THE LANGUAGE OF NATURE

I always try to look at the plants and trees outside my door as though for the first time. I begin with mindful walks in nature—noticing the patterns of tree bark one day, and the small plants that grow close to the earth the next. Each day, I attune my awareness to something different and use all of my senses—sight, smell, touch, taste, hearing—intuition, and instinct, and I can fill in the blanks with my imagination. The doctrine of signatures is a theory that states plants are communicating their medicine in this way through their shapes, textures, colors, and every other choice they make in their evolutionary process.

I think it's safe to assume that people have been pondering this concept since they began working with plants, but like many things in history, it formally dates from the time white men wrote it down. Dioscorides, Greek physician of the first century CE and author of *De materia medica*, an early pharmacopeia, described medicinal plants according to a divine intention and believed that the Creator marked objects with signs of their purpose. Paracelsus, the early sixteenth-century Swiss physician, developed the concept when he wrote, "Nature marks each growth . . . according to its curative benefit."[4]

But it was the German mystic Jakob Böhme who coined the term "the doctrine of signatures." He believed plants that resembled human organs, body systems, animals, or other objects were thought to have useful relevance to those parts, animals, or objects when he wrote, "Everything has its mouth to manifestation; and this is the language of nature, whence everything speaks out of its property, and continually manifests, declares, and sets forth itself for what it is good or profitable; for each thing manifests its mother, which thus gives the essence and the will to the form."[5] Böhme's 1621 book, *De Signatura Rerum*, or *The Signature of All Things*, gave its name to the doctrine. At the core of Böhme's philosophy was a mystical Christianity, and because his beliefs were far from the Lutheran establishment, he was persecuted throughout this life.

WE CAN USE THIS THEORY TO NOTICE WHERE AND HOW PLANTS GROW: DO they prefer the sun or shade? We might conclude that a plant that prefers direct sunlight might be more warming or drying in nature, while plants that prefer the shade might be more cooling. If our chosen medicine is a tree, we can sit with that tree in all seasons and witness the transformation. What direction do a plant's leaves or branches grow? Do they reach up and out or are they tucked in close? Does the plant grow counterclockwise or clockwise? Are the leaves smooth or rigid? A plant that grows alone, scattered throughout a field or forest, might offer more concentrated energy, or they might be conveying a message to use their medicine (if they indeed have medicine for us) sparingly. A plant that is capable of thriving in the city has incredible resilience and is a "people" plant. We can also observe whether plants offer food or medicine to others in the wild. Do they have symbiotic relationships with fungi, birds, or other mammals or seem to grow alongside the same plants everywhere they're found?

Oak trees line the New York City sidewalks; oak is a tree connected to the masculine energy of fire that we can see in the upward thrust of their branches like arms in victory pose. Like fire, oak extracts are drying, in contrast to the watery, weepy, and sweet-smelling linden tree that offers slimy, moistening mucilage. Cleavers resemble the lymphatic system that they treat; dandelion, a premiere plant for digestion, bursts out in spring exuding the confident yellow of our solar plexus. Purple in plants often signifies the treatment of stagnant blood, and mycelium, the communication center of forests, looks like and is used to restore our own neural networks. Chaga is a collection of mycelium that resembles a tumor protruding from birch trees and is used to treat cancer.

MY REWILDING EXPERIENCES IN COSTA RICA TAKE PLACE AT AN ETHNOBOT-any center in the jungle where hundreds of medicinal plants grow, many of them planted for conservation and learning, and some wild. Most people who attend these intimate retreats are unfamiliar with these plants, which is perfect for our exploration. The first full day, we do what I call plant ally exploration as a way to get acquainted with the land and for each person to find their own special plant among the hundreds of trees, herbs, shrubs, and flowers. After a grounding meditation, we walk together and I point out the textures, shapes, colors, and we wonder at what they might be communicating. We listen with all of our senses and pay attention if we feel particularly pulled to something. If I were to walk around and say, "This plant is so-and-so and it does this," I would rob students of this valuable sensory exploration and they might overlook plants that their intuition and instinct are pulling them toward and that have much to teach them because they aren't interested in what they "do." They would be in their heads and removed from their bodily senses as they walked around "knowing" these plants that it takes lifetimes to know and whose medicine is multifaceted.

When we finish the walk together, I give them time to wander through the garden and everyone, without fail, is called to a particular plant. I often use the analogy of walking into a party crowded with strangers. Without speaking to anyone, there will be certain people we gravitate toward, and it's the same with plants. There are plants whose unique architecture and energy will attract us if we give them a chance. I've approached plants the same way I approach people: I'd rather get to know a few deeply than know many on a surface level.

One of the most common questions I and other herbalists get is "What is this plant good for?" While I understand the question and why it is asked, and I try never to make anyone feel bad for asking, the question betrays a very one-dimensional way of looking at these complex life forms. If I were to simply answer that question, I would be influencing the person's relationship with that plant, and there are so many ways to work with a plant's medicine. Imagine how rude it would be for me to walk around a party introducing people like this: "This is Susan, she's good for making you feel sad and sometimes sick to your stomach with her stories. This is Dan, he's good for making you numb, then angry, and then numb again with his patronizing monologues." Or alternately: "This is Kim, she's good for making you feel happy and worthy with lots of compliments." If you trusted my opinion, however on point or well-meaning it may be, you'd probably begin a conversation by looking and listening through those skewed lenses or steer completely clear of someone like Dan who might drone on and waste your time, yet who might also have something valuable to share. As my friend Matt likes to say, "Your triggers are your teachers."

On a recent retreat, my friends Boyuan, Akilah, Jahan, Cara, Natalia, and others sat, meditated, and communicated in their own way once they found their plant, or in some cases, once their plant found them. Everyone had ample time to derive their own information using all their senses. Some chose to write stories about who the plant is and how it gave its medicine to the people, some gathered information through meditation, seasoned herbalists looked at the plant through the lens of the doctrine of signatures, and others just asked the plant directly. Boyuan was the biggest skeptic of them all but told me she felt her plant staring at her. She walked toward flashy and colorful trees and flowers, but something kept pulling her back to the spiraling fern. Well, it was the fern that kept calling her to the fern. She told me, "The mischievous little fern fiddlehead kept on flirting with my line of sight. I wanted to ignore it because it was plain and unexceptional, but the plant kept taunting me. It was buoyant and chatty when I really quieted my mind and slowed to listen, and the message for me was, 'Don't take yourself too seriously.'"

On these retreats, after everyone's chosen a plant ally, we regroup, share a refreshing hibiscus infusion, and, one by one, each participant guides us to their plant and shares their story, why they were drawn there, and what their instinct and intuition told them. This is always my favorite part. It is so interesting to see which plants people have been drawn to, and I love their amazement when they find out that what they observed, intuited, and felt is often accurate and somehow what their mind, body, soul, and spirit need.

Once we all explore together, Ancel and I reveal what we know about the plants and the ways they are traditionally used as food or medicine. Ancel asks more questions, like "If this plant were in a cafe reading a book, what book would they be reading? If they were going to a party, what sort of dress would they wear? If they were a professor, what subject would they teach? If they were in a restaurant, what would they order?" These questions stimulate our imagination and intuition and tune us into the "personality" of a plant. This is another way in, as we gather to explore while truly paying attention.

The nice thing is, this is just the beginning. The relationship between person and plant can be nurtured through the entire weeklong retreat, and even for years to come. Many former students tell me that, years later, they still connect with their plant ally through meditation.

This is an exercise we can do anywhere, even with our houseplants. And I always encourage people to get reacquainted with weeds. We may have been conditioned not to like them, or even to poison them, but look again. Look at their beauty, vitality, and strength. Find a weed or wildflower you're drawn to, observe the ways that particular plant is resilient, and write down what you notice. There may be some potent information there for you, and the so-called weed is often doing important restorative work for the wild.

I'VE ALWAYS BEEN UNCOMFORTABLE SPEAKING ON BEHALF OF THOSE WHO CAN better speak for themselves. I've preferred to step out of the way and give people, plants, or the Earth a megaphone. I want people to experience the wolves, the plants, and the land firsthand and let them build their own relationship without the need for an interpreter.

I had one teacher who would translate for us and say, "The cherry blossom is happy we're here and says . . ." and I didn't like it. Knowing her, she did have that sort of relationship with the plants, but at the time, I thought the method was phony and it made me more skeptical of her. I realized later that it was because *she* was telling us what the plant was saying. I've found that communication is highly personal, unique to each person, and rarely comes through in the form of words. I've seen and experienced communication as shifts of consciousness, sensations, the language of image, bodily sensations, story, song, or sudden understandings. As a predominantly visual and kinesthetic learner, images, symbols, and hands-on experience are the way I've translated the world around me for as long as I can remember. Visual art has been my way of processing ever since I could pick up a pencil, and probably before that.

As I've developed my work and curated Sacred Warrior experiences, I've realized more and more that my job is really about getting out of the way so people can develop their own relationships with nature without my influence or interference. I suppose I'm a matchmaker between people and nature. When we develop intimacy in our own ways, we are more likely to fall in love. And that is what I'm hoping for through this work because with all of the incredible abundance she offers, the Earth clearly loves us and she needs our love, generosity, and caring in return. With a giant feather dipped in milk and the extract of eyebright, I want everyone to see how beautiful this world really is—weeds and all. Boyuan recently told me, "The amazing thing about your teaching is that once you start to teach, you become invisible." I couldn't think of a better compliment.

ELECAMPANE

Inula helenium

Family: Asteraceae

Elecampane's warming, pungent roots can reach deep into the lungs to move, clear, and release old infected mucus. This movement makes way for new secretions to arise along the respiratory membrane that contain fresh and newly adapted immune cells. The root helps the air inside our bodies flow more freely, and her bitterness moves stagnant energy in the digestive system. With more space, our inner flames can come into balance to process and assimilate nutrients. The herbal actions and inulin of the root help support beneficial bacteria to help us compost and release what our body no longer needs.

    The botanical name, *Inula helenium,* honors Helen of Troy. The beautiful sunflower was said to have sprung from the places where her tears touched the Earth when she was kidnapped by Paris at the start of the Trojan War. Like the story, the flower essence is used to overcome long-held fears or feelings of grief, helping us move through and move on, and ease deep longings for home. As the roots reach deep into the darkness of earth, the plant's bright sunflower-like blossoms express fiery medicine as they grow three to six feet tall toward the sun.

HEALING PATHS

Two roads diverged in a wood, and I—
I took the one less traveled by,
And that has made all the difference.

ROBERT FROST

The most valuable items in my home are the jars of herbal tinctures, vinegars, and oils in process. Valerian root, elecampane root, mullein leaves, mugwort, goldenrod, burdock root, echinacea root, lobelia, calendula, ghost pipe, reishi, wild rose, and chaga are submerged in apple cider vinegar or 80–100 proof vodka. Some spirits I bought, but the special ones were made from fermented ginger and cacao on Ancel's farm in Costa Rica, or local grain in the Scottish borders by friends at Highland Boundary. There are dried herbs hanging upside down: tulsi, lemon balm, spearmint, and more goldenrod. Some of the plants in my apothecary were grown in medicinal gardens, but most were wildcrafted.

I look at the goldenrod tincture and remember the time and place I harvested the medicine. My partner and I were on a deserted Fort Tilden beach in New York in autumn as monarch butterflies fluttered around the bright yellow wildflowers growing along the dunes. I thought of my grandmother and my mom, who often reminded me that *Vanessa* means "butterfly": "Metamorphosis. Grace. Complete transformation, like you." I asked permission from the plants to gather the medicine, stated my intent, listened for an answer, and gave an offering of gratitude. Goldenrod appears in autumn as the days get shorter and nights get longer, a potent medicine for difficult transitions. As I harvested, I reflected on the ways I have come out of darkness transformed. That moment and all its medicine is contained in that jar and in each drop of tincture, and each jar has a story.

I would have been fascinated by my homemade apothecary as a child. I was always seeking something in the woods behind our house on Summer Street. I made potions and concoctions from pine needles, glittering mineral-rich soil, fresh water from the nearby stream, and special stones. I knew nature possessed secrets, mystery, something deeper than I could possibly under-stand, and while I was encouraged to explore the outdoors and enjoy nature, I thought my potions were just play. I had no idea that there was real medicine under my feet and all around me, and neither did my family. The pharmaceu-tical monopoly has brought about the abandonment of traditional plant use for many, and though herbalism is making a comeback, for many years the practice was reduced to the realm of old wives' tales and folk knowledge.

LIKE MOST IN THE WESTERN WORLD, I WAS RAISED ON THE SYSTEM OF ALLO-pathic medicine. Also known as conventional medicine or the scientific tra-dition, allopathic medicine relies on a process of reductionism, focusing on symptoms exhibited rather than the organism as a whole. Typically, this sys-tem separates the mind from body and individual from the environment. While it can be a life-saving system that shines in moments of trauma, like my car accident, on a day-to-day level, it can distance us from our bodies and our interdependence with the body of Earth.

Growing up, I could get prescriptions with a phone call, and at the time, I was grateful for it. My maternal grandfather practiced medicine profession-ally and was our family healer. I always felt cared for in his presence, and though his Russian Jewish background connected him to a strong lineage of herbalism, his family abandoned their folk knowledge when they immigrated. Growing up in Massachusetts, he had been incredibly close to his mother, who became sick when he was ten years old. No one knew what was wrong with her and she died one year later. In solace, he buried himself in books and told me her death was why he had been determined to become a doctor. He received early acceptance to UMass Amherst (Massachusetts Agricultural College back then), but his goal was Harvard Medical School. For some reason his professors told him he would never get in, and if he did, he would never be able to keep up with everyone else. I guess they didn't have much faith in a poor Jewish kid, but his mind was made up. He studied, applied, and got in with a scholarship and graduated at the top of his class. To him, conventional medicine would keep his loved ones safe. And in many ways, it did.

My grandfather made me feel safe, and so did my medicine. My inhaler was always in my pocket, I took my daily dose of theophylline pills, got weekly allergy shots, and often took steroid inhalers, and of course antibiotics were there to save the day and kill everything off when all else failed. I was given shots of adrenaline when asthma attacks were out of control, hooked to ventilators when my lungs grew weary, and tethered by IVs to theophylline drips in intensive care too. While I practiced breathing techniques and had to be conscious of my breath, I had few tools to manage my asthma, allergies, and weakened immune system other than prescription drugs. For years, I was absolutely dependent on pharmaceuticals to help me breathe and get by, and with constant outside intervention, I looked outside myself for healing.

As my grandfather grew older, years after his retirement he developed Zenker's diverticulum, an upper esophageal sphincter dysfunction that made it difficult for him to process food. By the time he was eighty years old, his daily meals were Boost drinks—since liquid was all he could keep down. While his mind remained as sharp as ever, he became physically dependent on others and his body slowly withered away. Years after he died, my mom started to exhibit the same symptoms and needed to have surgery. I was nervous. I dreaded the thought of anything happening to her, especially after losing my grandparents.

The night before her surgery, my grandfather came to me in a dream. We were in a large empty parking lot and pulled up in identical cars at opposite ends. I watched him stride toward me, strong, healthy, and in his prime. My grandfather, the loving, caring patriarch of the family, smiled and said, "I'm glad you've embraced the path of the healer." I didn't consider myself a healer then, and really, I still wouldn't describe my work that way. But in my dream, my grandfather spoke to me, healer to healer, about my mom and her condition. He assured me she would be okay, and before he turned around to leave, he said, "It's your turn to take care of the family now."

When I woke from the dream, I felt he was with me, and the dream is still as vivid as any memory. It felt like a real transmission, a passing of the torch and his embrace of my woodland path. When I began to make my own medicine, learning to identify plants in my environment and wildcraft, it felt like a rapid recall of something I already knew how to do. After years of teaching students how to read the language of nature and make their own medicine, I hear many of them say the same thing: "It feels like a deep remembering." Wild medicines like dandelion, burdock, nettles, and elecampane are safe, powerful, abundant, and free. Herbs can never be patented and owned by any individual or corporation because they are, and always will be, the people's medicine.

I OFTEN WONDER WHAT IT WAS LIKE FOR THE WOMEN IN MY FAMILY IN THE Middle Ages in Europe and Russia. If I were an independent woman practicing herbalism then, there is a good chance I would have been burned as a witch. According to the *Malleus Maleficarum*, or the *Hammer of Witches*, the guide to conducting witch hunts throughout Europe, "when a woman thinks alone, she is evil." This sadistic book was written in 1484 by the Reverends Kramer and Sprenger and led to the death and persecution of thousands of healers over three centuries. Some argue that it was in the millions.[1] Two thirds of those killed were women, and the highest proportion of men were killed in Russia and Iceland.

In the Middle Ages, a time of rapid social, economic, and religious transformation, the Roman Catholic Church influenced the direction of healing, stating that illnesses were punishments from God.[2] Prescriptions became faith in *him*, confessions to priests, and prayers. Long before the witch hunts began, the male-dominated medical system was actively engaged in eliminating female healers through the exclusion of women from universities, and university-trained physicians were not allowed to practice without calling a priest to advise them.[3] People became obsessed with the spirit and often neglected their bodies. Burgeoning urban doctors had to prove that their attention to people's bodies didn't jeopardize the strict doctrines of the soul and were not allowed to treat patients who refused confession.

Whether practiced by wise women or Druid healers in the countryside or priests or doctors in the cities, healing often involved ritual and ceremony in addition to plants and practices. The bean feasa, as they are known in Gaelic, or wise women, served their communities not only as herbalists, but as mediators between people and spirit.[4] They often lived on the outskirts of villages, or at the edge of the forest, where they weren't disturbed by as much energetic interference. I imagine that these respected healers were highly sensitive and attuned shamanic practitioners. In addition to using herbs to heal physical imbalance, the bean feasa might conclude that a person's dis-ease was caused by offending a water spirit or other guardian of the land. The cure might include an offering to mend discord with the spirit of the Earth, in addition to herbal treatment.

As male, upper-class healing grew in urban areas, female healing as part of the peasant community, and especially the rural community, became suspect. Those living on the edges of community—the country folk—were usually the last to be converted to monotheism and were called pagans, which simply means "country dwellers," or heathens, meaning "those who live among the heath." The bean feasa were easy targets, and women gathering in groups, likely to share and pass down herbal knowledge, were seen as consorting with the devil and often faced persecution. The "flying" and shape-shifting into animals that became the witches "familiars," part of later lore, likely referred to the use of entheogens for visioning, a common practice for medicine men and women of traditional cultures throughout the world.

Since it was thought that witches were incapable of speaking scripture aloud, the accused were made to recite selections from the Bible—usually the Lord's Prayer—without making mistakes or omissions. While it may have simply been a sign that they were illiterate or nervous, any errors were interpreted as proof that the speaker was in league with the devil. Gruesome confessions that "proved" the women's malevolence were extracted through horrific torture, and others could prove their innocence only through absurd and now infamous water tests where the accused were tossed in to see if they would sink or float. An innocent person would sink, but a witch would simply bob up to the surface because they had renounced baptism when entering the devil's service. Or they would float because water was so pure that it repelled the guilty. Of course, many of those who sunk and thereby passed the water test still wound up dead.

There is much scholarly debate as to the details of witch hunts and the social and political reasons behind why they happened, but the result was a dissolution of solidarity in peasant communities, gradual severing from Earth-based knowledge, and a mistrust of community healers. Feminist scholar Silva Federici argues in *Caliban and the Witch* that the witch hunts were directly connected to the attempt of the wealthy military class to gain control over the commons—natural resources like water, wild medicine, and fertile ground—accessible to all people, and begin to privatize and control the use of land.[5]

As the witch hunts stole trust from community healers, the study of medicinal plants and the written records were put into the hands of monks who, in their famous physic gardens, renamed many of the plants, like *Hypericum perforatum* (St. John's wort), after their saints. In some cases, folk medicine and Christian practices intermingled. There were those who tenaciously held on to the old ways and passed them down through families and oral tradition. Witch hunts took place not only in Europe, but all over the world. And in many places and in many forms, they still do. In recent years, the term "the witch wound" has been used to name the fear that traditional healers of today, especially women, have of sharing their work with the world, being seen, and standing in their power.

LISTENING

The wind was howling and rain lashed against the windows so intensely last night that it entered my dreams. I dreamt that the spirits of the land were angry, frustrated that we no longer understand their language. "You don't listen to the whispers in the wind anymore," they told me. So they rattle the foundations of our homes and scream through every crack and crevice in our walls with an overpowering force to make us pay attention. But still, we don't understand. In dream time, I spoke with the spirit of air and promised to do my best to learn, and to remember.

When I awoke, I walked outside and took a deep breath. I exchanged breath with the land, listening to the voices in the wind the way I listen to the subtle nudges inside my body before physical symptoms scream at me. I looked out along the mountain slopes and soggy grasslands here in the Scottish Highlands and felt grateful to know many of my green neighbors. Scots-pine stands tall in the distance and the bright yellow flowers of the porcupine-like gorse, whose essence is used to overcome feelings of hopelessness, were scattered among the hills. I saw heather, and Scots broom. Yarrow, St. John's wort, thistle, wild mountain thyme, red clover, eyebright, nettles, and self-heal would reappear soon too. Inside, I had a pot of fresh rosemary and thyme boiling on the stove. Both are full-spectrum antimicrobials. Their aromatic steam was warming and cleared the air as I breathed in their healing volatile oils. I drank a warm infusion of elecampane root, a plant that has been incredible for my congestion-prone respiratory system.

I arrived in the Scottish Highlands in early March 2020, not long before the coronavirus pandemic hit and the frenetic pace of the human world was forced to pause, and eventually lock down. From the perspective of traditional Chinese medicine, coronavirus manifests as a damp, cold, depressed condition in the body. I wrote a lengthy explanation of this on a shared document for my herbalism students. While I meant a depressed tissue state, one of my students, Sia, said, "Perhaps this is a manifestation because of sadness and grief that we as a species have been walking with. Maybe that's what we're being asked to confront right now. That coldness, that dampness, that depression." She paused. "For myself, that is definitely something I'm being asked to confront—the grief of Mother Earth." Elecampane, that plant that reaches deep into our lungs to clear old, unshed tears, was the first plant that came to mind.

It's mid-March 2020, and I've received more queries about herbal medicine in the last few days than I ever have. I just got off the phone with my brother. He has an ear infection and hasn't been able to get a doctor's appointment so I gave him a strict herbal protocol. Students—past and present—have called and emailed, my mom ordered herbs, so did colleagues, my father and his wife, friends, acquaintances, people who follow my work on social media, my partner's friends, and even the skeptics who thought my work was quaint, antiquated, and weird. What was seen as an alternative lifestyle might not seem to be alternative now.

If we can connect recent epidemics like Lyme disease, SARS, and even aspects of COVID-19 to ecological imbalance, destruction, and the abuse of wild and domesticated animals, we may see more holistic ways to not just rid ourselves of the danger of the disorders themselves, but to heal our species and ourselves more wholly. Lyme disease is named for its epicenter in Lyme, Connecticut—an area with an imbalanced predator-to-prey ratio. As in the Scottish Highlands, there are no wolves there to manage the overpopulation of deer, and ecologists have linked that ecological gap and its domino effect with the rampant spread of the disease.[6] Decreased habitat is putting us in closer contact with animals that would certainly prefer the cover of forest.

As science writer David Quammen explains in his book *Spillover: Animal Infections and the Next Human Pandemic*, the abuse of wild and domesticated animals and living ecosystems is bringing animal pathogens into contact with human populations at greater numbers, while our behavior is spreading those pathogens more widely and quickly. Epidemics and pandemics can be great collective teachers. They allow us to see just how interconnected we all are.

ELEMENTAL HERBALISM

Both trees and human lungs are composed of a central trunk or trachea that divides into increasingly smaller branches to become either leaves or alveoli, ideal for respiration. This beautiful interrelationship often goes completely unnoticed, but it is the foundation of all existence. Our neurons reflect the shapes, structures, and functions of underground fungal networks. The veins that carry our blood resemble the waterways of the Earth, and our digestive system, which transforms, composts, and transmutes, resembles the Earth's core and inner fire.

Each of us has a unique elemental makeup of earth, water, fire, air, and ether that influences our physical, mental, and emotional landscape. We can look at qualities of each element as they express themselves on Earth to understand the balance of earth, water, fire, air, and ether within our bodies. We can think of the elements as masculine or feminine, the primal forces of nature that merge to create life and transform material and nonmaterial reality. While we might think about masculine and feminine as gender, we all have masculine and feminine energy within us, and we need both. In holistic herbalism, we might observe all the symptoms of the body, mind, and spirit to see where there is excess of a particular element and where there is deficiency. Then, we can choose plants and practices to restore balance and facilitate healing.

When I was studying in Costa Rica, one of my teachers gave healing prescriptions like planting, gardening, getting one's hands in the soil for those with a depleted earth element, in addition to working with root medicines. Those with depleted water were told to take more baths, go swimming, drink fresh water, invoke water spirits, give offerings to water, and get involved with water protection. For me, this was validation. I had been working to restore and release my fire through boxing, balance my airy tendency to overthink and overanalyze through meditation, and create space for my fifth element, ether, through creative exploration.

We find elemental theories in nearly every holistic model of medicine—traditional Chinese medicine, Ayurveda, European alchemical tradition, in Greek and Egyptian medicine, and on and on.[7] Masculine elements are more volatile, less material, penetrate, and have an upward and outward motion. The solar energy of the sun is masculine, or yang, in nature as it illuminates, penetrates, and sometimes burns. Air is masculine in nature, penetrating our pores and blowing seeds throughout the land. On its own, air is cold and drying, so needs to be balanced by moisture and heat. Air is omnipresent and connects us to the plant kingdom and each other.

The feminine elements have an inward and downward motion. They include the fertile darkness where we plant seeds and the in-dwelling spaces where healing and creation occur. Feminine elements are symbolized by the waxing and waning of the moon, the fertile soil of Mother Earth, and the downward pull and cascade of water. Water relates to the dream realm, our subconscious, and our emotions. Water is our blood, our reproductive system, our body's filtration systems, our sweat, and our tears. When water stagnates it can become swampy, stinky, and unclean. When it's overflowing it can become a tidal wave crashing through everything we know.

Ether is the space that all the other elements fill, and to some it is the vital force. Vital herbalism, or vitalism, is akin to the understanding of animism, or panpsychism, a belief that everything material has individual consciousness. Vitalism is a doctrine that says the same elemental intelligence, energy, identity, and instinct courses through all life—plants, animals, stones, water, fire, air, and earth. Vitalism goes back as far as ancient Egypt and was developed into medical doctrine by Greek philosophy.[8] Hippocrates credited the vital force as the natural, inherent healing quality of his patients and called it *physis*—the root of the word *physician*.

THE ROOT CAUSE

I often ask my herbal apprentices how they define *healing*. Is it the absence of discomfort? The absence of a symptom? Most students agree that healing is much more dynamic than that. The absence of pain and the process of healing are two very different things. In one class, we defined physical or emotional discomfort as navigation tools, directing us to our true north. Whether we're straying from our life purpose or simply stressed out and sleep-deprived, these symptoms are messages that something in our life is out of balance and needs our attention. It's natural to want to resolve our own pain quickly, and to find solutions for others. I'm uncomfortable when others are uncomfortable, but I've learned to hold space rather than interrupt someone's tears. I've learned from my own journey that we must confront and move through our shadows in order to grow.

Holistic herbalism is not a "this for that" approach to medicine (take this plant for this symptom) or a tool to eliminate acute discomfort, though that can be done; it is preventative medicine and a daily, ever-evolving practice of self-care. For me, the most powerful aspects of the practice are working in direct relationship with the land while learning more and more about the incredible ecosystem of my body. When we work with plants and corresponding practices, we may want to treat a symptom—headache, intense menstrual cramps, insomnia, or anxiety—because it's expressing itself, and at the same time explore the reasons why that symptom is occurring. It could be as simple as dehydration, a lack of exercise, or an unhealthy diet, or more complicated issues of repressed emotions and layered walls of tension that have built up over time to protect us. Often, it's a combination of factors, and if we're willing to do the work, healing is a process that can find us when we're lost, help us grow, and elicit necessary change. In my own experience and as a teacher bearing witness to hundreds of students, the root causes of imbalance can be found within us as long we don't stay stuck trying to avoid discomfort.

The wise woman tradition of healing is often called the invisible tradition because it is a practice of constant nurturing that cares for the whole self in relationship to our environment instead of punishing the body or fixing broken parts. Whole-body prescriptions may include changes in lifestyle; practices like meditation, journaling, and talk therapy; in addition to the help of plants. I drink infusions (medicinal teas) made with plants like nettles, burdock, dandelion, or hawthorn every day and choose them based on what my body, mind, spirit, and soul need. Sometimes the changes in my health are subtle, but when I look back after a number of months, I often realize that I've been feeling better and symptoms have subsided. It's easy to notice when we're sick, in pain and an intervention radically alters the way we feel. While medical interventions such as surgery can be vital for acute symptoms or injuries, if someone is always there to save us, we may ignore and even fear our bodies, ceasing to listen to and understand the incredible ways in which they function, communicate with us, and ask for our support. Most of us have become accustomed to going to "experts" who know more about our bodies than we do, which is disempowering and leaves many of us ignorant. If we always rely on being saved, we give away our power and centuries-old ancestral knowledge of healing in collaboration with the Earth. This is not about romanticizing the past or going backward; we can honor and learn from the past while integrating the medicine, science, and practices that have brought us to the present. We can, with knowledge and awareness, create our own embodied paths of healing.

I see rewilding the self as a powerful form of holistic healing that may ask us to examine our belief systems, peel back layers of conditioning, shed tears, release trauma, and reintroduce aspects of our mind, body, spirit, or soul that have become endangered. When we learn to navigate the inner and outer wilderness, we may realize much of what we seek is already within us and directly under our feet. When we fall in love with ourselves and with the land, we come home to our true nature and engage in a peaceful act of resistance. Where our energy and nervous system may be scattered and short-circuiting in the mind, Mother Earth holds us against her body where we can plug into fertile ground. Despite our trespasses against her, she is always holding us close.

It took some time for my family to trust the practice of herbalism, but after seeing the profound changes in my own health and well-being, many do turn to me now. Just as my grandfather foretold in my dream.

In the universe, there are things that are known, and things that are unknown, and in between, there are doors.

WILLIAM BLAKE

PART TWO

Liminal Realms

T HE WORD *LIMINAL* COMES FROM THE LATIN WORD *LIMEN*, MEANING "a threshold." When we enter liminal space, we start to see ourselves and our environment differently. Liminal spaces are the veils between worlds at times of birth, death, dreaming, and waking. Plants like rose and poison ivy are boundary keepers that live at this edge. They're gatekeepers of the forest. In fairy tales and folklore, protagonists are given riddles or tests before they can cross bridges or enter sacred land. The plants that grow on this boundary line may test us in similar ways. Wild rose protects with climbing vines and thorns, while shape-shifting poison ivy forces us to watch where we're going and be mindful. These plants provide a protective thicket for wildlife and a mystical gate before the forest realm. They are fierce medicine that can awaken us if we choose to see.

PUMPKIN
Cucurbita pepo

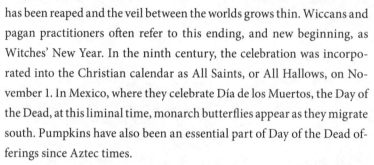

Family: Cucurbitaceae

Samhainn is a Gaelic word used to describe the ceremonial time in late October and early November when the last of the harvest has been reaped and the veil between the worlds grows thin. Wiccans and pagan practitioners often refer to this ending, and new beginning, as Witches' New Year. In the ninth century, the celebration was incorporated into the Christian calendar as All Saints, or All Hallows, on November 1. In Mexico, where they celebrate Día de los Muertos, the Day of the Dead, at this liminal time, monarch butterflies appear as they migrate south. Pumpkins have also been an essential part of Day of the Dead offerings since Aztec times.

One of the earliest known food crops in the Americas, pumpkins are believed to have originated in Mexico at least ten thousand years ago.[1] The pumpkin is a member of the Cucurbita family, which includes squash and cucumbers, and along with corn and beans (which were domesticated much later), pumpkin is one of the legendary "Three Sisters" of Native American agriculture. The Iroquois planted the three crops together, as they nurtured each other's growth, and believed they were "guarded by three inseparable spirits and would not thrive apart."[2]

SHAPE-SHIFTING

The world is full of magic things patiently waiting for our
senses to grow sharper.

W. B. YEATS

My mother and father met at a Halloween party at Trinity College in Hartford, Connecticut. When I asked my father a few years ago about their first encounter, he said, "I hung out with her the whole night and had no idea what she looked like, but I knew I would fall for her." According to my father, my mom, dressed as a lion, mentioned she had an extra lion costume. He put it on and, in the middle of the night, they drove to his parents' cottage in Norfolk, Connecticut, to frolic as two lions in the woods. They were enchanted with each other.

Two years later, in November 1972, my mom was twenty-one years old and falling asleep by a roaring fire in the same Norfolk cottage. In the liminal space between waking and dreaming, she noticed a luminescent figure in the distance. It was moving through the woods outside her window. As the figure came closer, she realized it was a woman—a floating, Botticelli-like figure with long flowing hair who gracefully wove in, out, and around the trees. My mom watched, mesmerized, as the faerie woman came closer and closer. As she neared the window and grew more clear, my mom saw that she was holding a baby in her arms. "She seemed serene, somehow wise," my mom tells me. "She floated into my room, part aberration, part earthly, and handed me the beautiful baby." When my mother woke, she could feel the woman's presence in the room and the weight of the child in her arms. Several weeks later she felt changes in her body and found out that she was pregnant with me, her mysterious woodland child.

I was born August 24, 1973, during a waning crescent moon in Cancer. I was two weeks late and didn't want to leave the womb. My mom tried shaking, dancing, hysterical laughter—anything to induce labor. What my mom intended to be an unmedicated home birth wound up a long, painful labor and eventual C-section at the Wesson Women's Hospital in Springfield. Apparently, the doctor was exhausted and after countless hours of labor and with a vacation to get to, he carved me out and I emerged banged up, with a black eye. I looked like I'd been in a brawl. (Perhaps this was an omen for things to come?)

When the nurse placed me in my mom's arms, my mother was overcome with bliss. Turning to my sweet and loving grandfather Sam, she said, "Isn't she beautiful?" He looked at me, with my black eye and pruny face, and said, "Give her a few days."

A TRUE CHILD OF THE WOODS, I LOVED FAIRY TALES, ESPECIALLY SNOW WHITE. Living in the woods with gnomes and talking to animals seemed like an ideal existence to me, so at three years old, I decided I *was* Snow White. My name was Snow White and no one could tell me otherwise. My mom thought my alter ego was cute, the sign of a healthy imagination, but my role-playing embarrassed my grandma Dorothy. "That's not her real name," she assured anyone who asked me. As three became four, I grew tired of being Snow White and decided the strength and self-determination of the Bad Queen was more compelling, so I became the Bad Queen instead. "I think you were just trying to be controversial," my mom told me recently. Or maybe I was getting more interested in powerful women, because when it came time to dress up for Halloween, I dressed as Wonder Woman.

My mom and I went to the fabric store in Mountain Farms Mall to find shiny gold, silver, blue, and red cloth for my bulletproof armbands, boots, headband, and leotard. We walked through the huge bolts of fabric until we found the perfect colors, and when we got home we sewed, pasted, cut, and glued a headband adorned with stars and re-created the leotard with all the fixings and, of course, the tall shiny red boots. I was transformed. I was so proud of my costume. I felt I embodied the strong, feminine archetype. I couldn't wait for Halloween.

Excited, but breathing heavily, I suited up on Halloween, ready to hand out candy. My favorite time of year was often the most triggering for my sensitive, asthmatic lungs. So that night, and on many other Halloweens, I would answer the door. "It was the leaf mold," my mom tells me. I must have a selective memory, because I rarely remember being sick or struggling on Halloween. I remember dressing up, even when I didn't trick-or-treat, and my mom and I immersing ourselves in arts and crafts. In all the fun and excitement, it didn't occur to me to be embarrassed when kids came to the door. Not yet.

I couldn't help but absorb the creativity of our eclectic household on Ridgecrest Road. With its revolving door of musicians and spontaneous jam sessions, art was everywhere, including the kitchen. My mom allowed me to experiment with ingredients to create magical potions and concoctions, like my famous chocolate cake made with Quik hot chocolate mix. It was the first thing I baked and I was so proud. I served it to a table of musicians and they ate it, saying how delicious it was. My mom only recently told me it was disgusting. But I was happy and oblivious back then, and that sensory exploration set the stage for the way I cook and create now. Home was a creative hub.

I felt confident and in my element amid the adults in our house, but I was petrified when the school bus pulled up for the first day of kindergarten. I didn't want to get on the bus, to leave my mom or our artsy cocoon. I cried in our driveway and took a long time making my way up the bus's steps, away from my mom and into the stares of strange children. When the bus finally pulled away with me inside, the kids made fun of me for not wanting to leave my mommy. I shrunk against the seat. Some of the adults in this new school world laughed and called me "space cadet" because I was capable of zooming into my own universe. I hated being the butt of even innocent teasing. I wasn't blank; I was creating new creatures in my head or contemplating things like infinity. The concept of infinity drove me nuts. *How can numbers go on and on and on and on and never end?* The things I wanted to ask—like "What do you think we're doing floating on this planet in the middle of outer space? How did we get here?"—turned out to be things people didn't know how to answer and questions they didn't really want to hear.

After a while, my mom couldn't afford our house on Ridgecrest Road, and as we grew older, she outgrew the revolving door of communal living. So after a short stint in an apartment, we moved to the pale-green duplex on Summer Street where the woods, and our garden, would become my wonderland.

LITTLE PEOPLE

The soil on Summer Street was ridiculously fertile. You could drop seeds on the ground and plants would soon sprout. We had a big garden in the backyard where broccoli, squash, beans, and tomatoes thrived, and across the street was a cornfield. The house was surrounded by wild raspberry bushes, and I picked the sweet fruits every summer. Along with poison ivy, these thorny bushes in the rose family acted as our natural boundary keepers. Just beyond the backyard was Mill River Conservation Area, a forest complete with secluded trails and endless nooks of discovery where invisible spiderwebs glistened in just the right light and I found rocks that seemed to be covered with gems. The voices of meandering streams cleared all the noise from the outside world. I got lost in time and came home covered in mud, soil, or pieces of fallen leaves.

I climbed the patient and kind white pine tree in our backyard and was proud when I reached the very top. But getting down was always a problem. Looking down from my high perch, the branches suddenly seemed flimsy. Nervous, I grasped the rough outer bark, wove through the soft aromatic needles, and touched the sticky, wound-healing resin. It was during these slow, careful descents that I grew to know and love the gentle spirit of white pine. With freedom to roam outside and in the woods, I learned early on that nature was a friend and endless source of wonder—something I'm infinitely grateful for.

As my porous little self navigated social realms, Halloween continued to be a time when I blossomed. I always loved the ritual and pomp of the fall, seeing the misty pumpkin patches in autumn and the orange glowing creatures on doorsteps. I entered Halloween pumpkin-painting contests and Amherst's annual window-painting contest, where all the stores in town gave up their windows for Halloween-themed painting. I relished anticipating which store I would be assigned to, and spent weeks beforehand working on my design. I sketched and drew jack-o'-lantern faces, copied them onto my chosen pumpkins, and my mom and I carved away. Sometimes we took the seeds out and put them in the oven on low with a tiny bit of salt to roast them. When my mom asked what I wanted to plant in our garden, of course I chose pumpkins.

I REMEMBER GOING TO THE HADLEY GARDEN CENTER TO PICK OUT THE SEEDS. As soon as we got home, I planted them on a hill just to the left of our back door. Every day after that, I walked out with excitement to witness their progress. Rain and sunshine took on a whole new meaning. My pumpkins and I were dependent on the weather. I understood why our ancient ancestors prayed to the sun and danced to attract the rain.

After a few weeks I began to see small sprouts. Then every day they grew a little more until huge leaves began to unfurl and flowers began to bud and then open into star-shaped golden blooms. For pumpkin blossoms to bear fruit, they have to be fertilized by bees, which move pollen from the plant's male flowers that produce nectar and pollen to the female flowers that offer higher quantities of nectar but no pollen. Bumblebees, honeybees, and squash bees are the most efficient pollinators of pumpkin. My little patch was a work of community.

And one day, when the work of the soil, sun, moon, rain, and bees was complete, beautiful orange pumpkins began to arrive. I was amazed that these small seeds contained all of the intelligence and information needed to give birth to pumpkins. I learned early on that Earth is amply generous and completely magical, as long as we do our part to take care of and pay attention to her. By putting those seeds in the ground, I initiated the incredible collaboration between the seed and the soil, rain, sun, and bees that nurtured the pumpkins' growth. We did it together.

Whether inspiring me to grow pumpkins or moving me to paint them, creativity seemed to be an animating force of nature in me, with its own agenda. As I wrote, painted, and drew, I opened gateways to other worlds. Sometimes

I felt like I had to catch words or images and put them down on paper before they disappeared, and sometimes I felt the urge to release something from inside me and make it visible. We may think of imagination itself as being something other than the earthly senses, a realm of free-flowing images that exists within our heads, but where do these images and ideas come from? What was the animating energy that coursed through the soil and called the pumpkins to grow?

With a telescope perched next to my pumpkin patch, I spent hours outside at night, looking up at the planets and constellations, searching for shooting stars, and tried to wrap my head around the fact that I was floating in the middle of outer space. I was lucky to have sweet neighbors with an open door on the other side of our duplex: Karen, a schoolteacher, and Ron, an astronomer. Karen taught me how to bake wild raspberry pies with elaborate latticework crusts, and while our art was in the oven, I stared at the photos of planets that lined their walls. I was captivated by Saturn's rings, thought to be a collection of ice, dust, rock, and moons attracted and then torn apart by Saturn's intense gravity.

At home I drew the many moons that circle Jupiter and began to look for signs of alien life and meteorites, broken pieces of outer space in the forest. It seemed to me that it would be far more strange to believe we were the only ones in the universe than to believe there were others out there. We can't observe the rings of Saturn or the moons of Jupiter without a telescope, or the countless microbes that inhabit our bodies without a microscope, but they float above us and exist within us nonetheless.

There is a window in childhood, before we are mired in social conditioning, when we can easily engage with mystery: life in outer space, plant spirits, faeries, elves, and other creatures beyond the veil. Many of my students recall talking to flowers, trees, and elemental beings before being told that they can't talk back, or that it was "just" their imagination. When I was about seven years old, we had to leave Plumbley's, a fancy restaurant in downtown Amherst, because I was distracted by creatures that I insisted were floating around me. I was excited, smiling at them, pointing and looking up, and I kept trying to show my mom and everyone at our table, but no one else could see them.

Eventually, the disturbance was enough that my family abandoned the plan to dine out.

While my mom had an open mind and nurtured my imagination, most of the adults around me seemed sure that we were it. No faeries, no aliens, no plant spirits. And yet, we didn't even know what we were doing floating in the middle of space! Their assuredness seemed truly crazy. Of course nature was animate and alive! It seemed intentionally arrogant for humans to presume we were the only conscious ones and everything else was propelled through scientifically explained biological processes.

In any event, everyone agreed to imagine another realm on Halloween. We all dressed up, moving among the disguised so ghosts wouldn't recognize us. We placed fierce pumpkins on our doorstep for protection and to keep watch, making sure unsavory spirits stayed away.

It's interesting that pumpkins, a squash used in many cultural traditions to repel ghosts and potential spiritual parasites, is also used as an anthelmintic to repel physical pests as well. Native Americans used the seeds to treat intestinal worms and urinary ailments, a remedy adopted by American doctors in the early nineteenth century.[3] This treatment is also used in traditional Chinese medicine for the treatment of the parasitic disease schistosomiasis and for the expulsion of tapeworms. I'll never forget the day when Mickey, our cairn terrier, threw one up into his dinner bowl after a treatment from the vet. Thinking about the long glassy, ghostly worm that he left writhing around in his bowl still makes me shiver. The complete pumpkin seed, together with the husk, is prescribed to remove these invasive creatures: some treatments recommend grinding the seeds into a fine flour and making it into an emulsion with water, while others say that the part of the seed that helps release these invaders is the bitter and resinous envelope that lies just under the shell.[4] However it is administered, a laxative like psyllium or senna is taken after a careful dose of pumpkin seed to expel tapeworms and other unwanted creatures from the body. The mythical, storytelling significance of plants is often woven into the way they were used by humans for centuries.

The custom of making jack-o'-lanterns on Samhainn or All Hallows' Eve began in Ireland and Scotland. Turnips or beets were hollowed out to act as lanterns and were carved with creepy faces to keep wandering spirits away. When settlers arrived in America, the custom continued with pumpkins. But this fruit does not only protect and expel; the edible flesh, flowers, stems, leaves, and seeds also build. In Mexico, pumpkin seeds are called pepitas, and with their high levels of protein, magnesium, copper, and zinc, they are an essential ingredient in recipes like mole sauce, ground into flour to make hearty and nutritious breads, and consumed the world over for vitality and endurance. The flowers offer bright, beautiful, and tasty garnishes for salads, and the young, tender leaves can be tossed in too. The Maya baked whole pumpkins in pit ovens and the shells were carved into drinking vessels called xicallis.[5] Their cosmology was animist; they believed that everything was imbued with a spiritual essence or force to be honored and recognized. The gods, like Yum Kaax, protector of plants and animals, were the supreme spiritual forces, but the spiritual essence of water or a rock also deserved respect. Every Mayan had a spiritual guide, a wayob, that could appear as an animal or in a dream in order to guide the person through life.

Every culture that lives close to nature has stories of intermediary beings like plant spirits, elves, trolls, and faeries. Are they the genius loci, the spirits and guardians of place? Or perhaps do they simply exist in their own right just beyond the veils and through the mists? Faeries we're familiar with are often depicted as tiny butterfly-like humans, but in Scottish lore, faeries can change shape and size and the female of the species is known to be particularly malevolent. In 1691, Scottish clergyman Robert Kirk handwrote the notorious *The Secret Commonwealth of Elves, Fauns and Fairies* that was found and published a century later by author William Scott. Kirk writes that the faeries—or the Sleagh Maith, as they are known in Gaelic—are "intelligent fluidious Spirits, and light changeable bodies, (lyke those called Astral,) somewhat of the Nature of a condensed Cloud, and best seen in Twilight."[6]

Traditional lore in Scotland ascribes animistic beliefs to certain hills, islands, rocks, trees, caves, springs, and wells whose energy is most potent at threshold times such as dawn and dusk or Beltane—the fertile time of birth and bloom in late spring—and Samhainn.[7] As sacred spaces, those places were (and many cases still are) treated with reverence. I have friends who still leave milk for the fae in hollowed stones, and refuse to pick plants like foxglove, let alone bring them inside. I encounter hawthorn and elder trees, especially those near healing wells, that are filled with clootie ties—a custom of placing a wish into shreds of one's clothing and tying them to branches, the wishes to be granted by the nature spirits who dwell there.

In pre-Christian Slavic lore, the leshy is the protector of wild animals and forests and one of the primary nature spirits.[8] This being is often depicted as part man, part tree, with a long white beard, tattered clothes, and overgrown bark, who can easily shape-shift into women, wolves, plants, or mushrooms. As a forest guardian, the leshy punishes humans who enter the woods without reverence.

The huldufólk, or hidden people, are elves: small, humanlike beings in Icelandic and Faroese lore that live in nature and can make themselves visible at will. In the Reykjavík suburb of Hafnarfjörður, elf shrines and sacred elf rocks adorn the yards of houses, particularly those surrounding Hellisgerdi Park, which is said to be populated with the town's largest elf colony. Neo-paganism scholar Michael Strmiska writes that these hidden folk are "not so much supernatural as ultranatural, representing not an overcoming of nature in the hope of a better deal beyond but a deep reverence for the land and the mysterious powers able to cause fertility or famine."[9] In a 2007 study by the University of Iceland, it was estimated that over half of the Icelandic population believe that elves exist.[10] The reverence and fear of beings like faeries, huldufólk, or leshy often leads to the conservation and protection of the spaces they inhabit, until such stories are discarded as mere superstition.

Scottish writer and activist Alastair McIntosh recently spoke about the realm of the faeries or little people as an analogy for the realm of our imagination.[11] When people disappeared into the realm of the faeries, it meant they had disappeared from everyday reality, and if they didn't go mad, they usually returned with poetry, painting, or song. He says, "It is through the gifts of the arts that we can come to know and respect nature not just in our heads, but embodied in our hearts too. In this sense it may be appropriate for us to relearn respect for the faery realm."[12]

It is no coincidence that many cultures honor the dead at the end of October and in early November. It is a liminal time to connect with our ancestors, to dive through generations of our familial past to find the old stories that know nature as conscious, animate, and alive. As the nights get longer and we spend more time in the soothing dark, we can also conceive. The liminal space of creation in all its forms—whether painting, making love, or planting pumpkin seeds—opens doors to spirit. In those spaces of infinite possibility, when we align with the swell and sparseness of our own seasons, we know exactly when to sow seeds in the rich, fertile soil of imagination.

MULLEIN
Verbascum thapsus

Family: Scrophulariaceae

Like the cilia in our respiratory system, the hairs that cover mullein leaves protect them from cold, harsh, and drying winds, allowing them to stay moist and green when many of the other plants are bare and brown. They are some of the first medicines I harvest in springtime and the last I harvest in autumn. The first year, rosettes of this biennial plant often remain green through the winter. Also known as blanket leaf, feltwort, Our Lady's flannel, velvet dock, velvet plant, and lungwort, this multifaceted healer, a native to Eurasia and now naturalized in Canada and the Americas, soothes and comforts. Though I rarely need treatment for asthma now, mullein is one of the first plants I turn to when I do.

Mullein seeds are incredibly resilient and can maintain their germinative powers for up to a hundred years, sprouting from bare, overgrazed ground or after the scorch of a forest fire. The plant's subsequent growth can heal the worst of soil problems, breaking up dry, compacted soil to bring minerals to the surface. Harsh conditions in our bodies can benefit from this medicine too. Tincture, tea, and even smoking the dried herb can help expel mucus by loosening it from the walls of the lungs to be coughed up. I also turn to mullein to dislodge unshed tears and soften sorrow.

COMFORTERS

"Real isn't how you are made," said the Skin Horse. "It's a thing that happens to you. When a child loves you for a long, long time, not just to play with, but REALLY loves you, then you become Real."

"'Does it hurt?" asked the Rabbit.

"Sometimes," said the Skin Horse, for he was always truthful. "When you are Real you don't mind being hurt. . . . [and] once you are Real you can't become unreal again. It lasts for always."

MARGERY WILLIAMS, *THE VELVETEEN RABBIT*

When I came upon my orange Raggedy Ann and Andy sleeping bag at my mom's house over ten years ago, a surprising swell of emotion rose within me. As a child, I spent days, weeks, and months snuggled inside that cozy cocoon. So I brought it home to Brooklyn. I hadn't thought about the sleeping bag for years, but seeing it felt like a key to my younger self, helping me color in blank spaces of memory.

Raggedy Ann and Andy lay folded on my bed in Brooklyn for a few years and brought me comfort. Whether I accessed deeper wells in dream time or significant memories because of the sleeping bag, I can't say. But it certainly stirred my emotions and showed me snapshots of the past, as though merging me with my younger self.

Then, during a period of intense change, I decided to leave New York City indefinitely and study plant medicine in Costa Rica. The orange comforter was put in storage along with other nonessential items that didn't fit in my suitcase. It sat there in that cramped space, forgotten again, for over a year.

But as New York City does, the city magnetically pulled me back. With a renewed sense of purpose, I was determined to grow my fledgling business, Sacred Warrior, within its energetic hub. While the vision was clear—to deepen people's relationship with the living Earth through hands-on learning—I vacillated between self-determination and self-doubt. I was not on firm financial footing. And yet I was still paying to keep half-forgotten belongings in a room out of sight. The emptying out of that space was a hasty endeavor triggered by an argument with my partner, Alex. I dreaded going through everything and didn't know what to do with it all. I had already pared down and made donations when I put my belongings in storage the first time. But the unit had been eating away at my meager finances. So I agreed to tackle it, bring only essentials into our apartment, and donate the rest.

We separated things into piles: Keep, Donate, and What is this? And when he came upon the sleeping bag, Alex had a firm opinion. "What are you going to do with that? Get rid of that old thing." I started to cry, a moment of emotional pause in the overwhelming reckoning of my life in stuff. My tears surprised both of us, especially since I don't cling to much. He tried to stay with me in the moment and suggested, "Maybe those tears are a sign to let it go." Alex assumed it was attached to painful memories. But that wasn't it. The sleeping bag was a portal to my childhood self. Still, I thought, *Maybe he is right.*

After two days of sorting and having way too many things in our apartment, I circled back to my sleeping bag. *Why cling to it? I hadn't thought about it until I saw it again. Let it go. Let someone else use it.* So I put it in a donation bag of old clothes, sheets, and other items I could live without and gave it away.

But today, six years later, I woke up thinking about it. I don't remember anything else I put in the huge bag for donation. I just hope it was loved by someone else and provided as much warmth for them as it did for me. And maybe it's the loss of the sleeping bag that is helping me access more memories. Sometimes we don't realize how much things matter until they're gone.

SLEEP WAS A PRODUCTION WHEN I WAS YOUNG. MY MOM FILLED AND TURNED on the humidifier, slathered my chest with Vicks VapoRub, and propped me up with at least two, sometimes three, pillows. My inhaler was always within arm's reach and my mom was just a room away if I needed her. I slept with the infamous sleeping bag and my stuffed animals piled around and on top of me. I didn't feel sorry for myself; my situation was just the way things were for me. Kids are remarkably resilient.

When I got my results from the cursed allergy test that said I was allergic to pollen, cats, mold, dust, dairy . . . it was even more clear that I needed to be careful in the world. At the time, we lived on Ridgecrest Road with Daphne, a Newfoundland; Elsa, a Samoyed (who had five puppies); Alexander, a Great Pyrenees; and five cats. My favorite cat that I carried everywhere looked as though she'd been dipped in a puddle of mud, so I named her Mudcat. I loved Mudcat, but cats were now on "the list" and I had to say goodbye to her. I was devastated. I had to distance myself from some of the things I loved most because of my allergies and asthma.

But we always had at least two dogs as family members, and Daphne, aptly named after the naiad in Greek mythology associated with fountains, wells, springs, streams, and other bodies of fresh water, was a gentle soul and born swimmer. Newfoundlands are massive dogs bred to accompany fishermen in the icy Atlantic waters off the coast of Newfoundland. The dogs have partially webbed feet and specialize in water rescues. What the Saint Bernard is to the Alps, the Newfoundland is to the cold Atlantic ocean. And like the Saint Bernard in *Peter Pan*, Daphne was my Nana.

Patient, gentle Daphne taught me how to walk. I would grab on to her thick black fur, slowly stand, and stumble as she led me around. When I became more confident, I held on to her tail. And when I could finally walk on my own, I waddled right out the front door and down the street in my diaper. Daphne followed behind and gently herded me to the side of the road. Eventually, my mom got a call from a neighbor: "Um, did you know that your daughter is walking down the street in her diaper?" My mom ran out and, along with Daphne, maneuvered me to safety.

ONCE A MONTH DURING ELEMENTARY SCHOOL, I WAS EXCUSED EARLY TO VISIT with Dr. Franklin, an asthma specialist two hours away in Boston. My mom made the journey fun, and I looked forward to the monthly doctor's visits where I blew into a cardboard tube so they could test my lung capacity. We always followed the appointment with a trip to the Boston Aquarium. I was fascinated by the octopus, the sharks, and the iridescent fish, and loved picking up the starfish in the shallow pools. I can still feel their strange sandpaper-like outsides and tickly tentacles. Then we went to eat at the famous Union Oyster House.

I adored animals and read books like *The Velveteen Rabbit, Horton Hatches the Egg,* and *Charlotte's Web,* and yet there was an increasing dissonance between the books I was reading in which animals were friends and had voices, and the way they were treated in the "real world." They were the food on my plate, floating dead in my soups, worn as fur coats, sectioned off into bits of flesh in Styrofoam trays in the grocery store, hunted for sport, kidnapped and kept in cages, and mistreated as companions.

A pivotal awakening came at the Central Park Zoo with a visit to the polar bear. I didn't know much about polar bears at the time and couldn't wait to meet one in person. But when we turned a corner in the park and came upon her, I felt like I'd been punched in the chest. I looked at the huge, beautiful bear stumbling around behind glass in a much-too-small artificial environment and knew she was not supposed to be there. But people ate popcorn and pointed, laughed, and stared at her. It was a sickening humiliation for this majestic beast, and I felt her sadness intensely. Then, in a moment that seemed like an eternity, she looked me in the eyes and it was as if we were the only two creatures on the planet. In those seconds, I felt she was pleading with me to set her free. I yearned to; I wanted to set her free more than anything in the world. I wanted to set *all* the animals free, undo the grave, shameful injustices of their kidnapping and imprisonment. But I could do nothing but stare back, helpless and complicit. I left with her sadness, and a confusing anger toward humans, stewing inside of me. The innocence of my ignorance was shattered in that single moment. I was five years old and it is a moment that will be imprinted on my emotional body forever.

As I became more aware of the abuse humans waged upon the planet, my insides felt like they were being trampled. I'll never forget seeing an image on a Greenpeace ad of a baby harp seal clubbed for fur. Those big, sweet eyes pleading, and then, the brutality. Sleep became even harder as I lay awake in horror, worried about the seals, the polar bear, the octopus swimming in circles at the aquarium and other creatures suffering at the hands of humans as I reclined comfortably in bed. I tried to sleep and piled my stuffed animals around me, but they also made me sad. They also seemed trapped. Bricks of grief were set upon my already heavy chest. I thought of the Velveteen Rabbit and how when he cried, he became Real.

STONES OF SORROW

I wish I'd known about mullein then. Not only would the plant have helped my asthma, helped me process sorrow, but putting a mullein leaf under my pillow at night might have soothed edges between realms and brought sweet dreams.

This altruistic plant is rarely found in undisturbed communities. Sunny, open sites created by heavy grazing, severe storms, logging, fire, or other devastation are ideal for the plant's growth and reproductive success. Mullein heals the worst soil problems and arrives on the scene as an early pioneer plant. Once the soil is rich again, mullein moves on. In a similar way, this healer can shift and transform wounded spaces in our bodies so we can also move through, and move on.

Traditional Chinese medicine and other holistic realms of herbalism are based on the principles that mental, physical, and emotional well-being are intricately entwined and our lungs are where we hold tears that haven't been shed. Grief and sadness directly affect the lungs, and if we are unable to express these emotions or are overwhelmed by them, the lungs can become weak and respiration can become compromised.[1] A healing prescription may include plants to support us, a movement practice to dislodge stones of sorrow, a blank page for letting go, and loved ones to comfort us while we cry. Tears can moisten, soothe, and soften us. When water is flowing freely, it can turn rocks into sand.

Whenever I mention this theory in my herbalism classes, it inevitably strikes a chord. One student shared, "I developed a horrible cough after my father died." She told me there had been no conventional medicinal explanation and went on to say, "I haven't been able to grieve him and I don't know why. I feel like tears are stuck in my chest."

When emotions are listened to and acknowledged they often point us to our deepest truths. Sometimes emotions are navigation tools, pointing us in the direction of what matters most to us. Sometimes they simply help us process the inevitable sadness and injustice in our lives and the lives of others. There is nothing wrong with any emotion, and uncomfortable emotions are meant to be felt, not denied. I know that allowing deep grief to emerge has emptied my inner wells, released tension where I was holding back, and allowed for greater receptivity of joy.

Mullein is easy to identify. The first-year plant grows in the form of a rosette, a circular arrangement of leaves that wear a thick coating of hairs to soften the force of surface winds and prevent water loss to evaporation. During the first year of growth, the large leaves store energy to rise up into a long, leafy stalk the second year with a spike of yellow five-petaled flowers at the top. The stalk, which can grow up to eight feet tall, stands erect with perfect posture, exuding the same gentle confidence on city streets and edges of mountains, pastures, fields, and forests. The soaring second-year stalk resembles an upright spine and has reminded me to stand tall and breathe deeply. It's difficult to take a deep breath when we shrink to protect ourselves or are collapsed into our chest. In rare cases, when the first-year plant can't muster the energy to complete its second-year growth cycle, mullein will turn three years old. These are some of the most mystical plants I've seen, twisting, turning, and spiraling.

Yellow five-petaled flowers that appear in the second or third year are an incredible remedy for ear infections. They are densely arranged on a spikelike terminal inflorescence and open to pollination for a single day, from just before dawn to midafternoon. They attract a wide variety of pollinators, including bees and butterflies, but by the end of the day if an open flower has not been visited by a pollinator, they pollinate themselves.

GRIEF INTO ACTION

One of my favorite recent news stories is about Inky, the octopus who escaped from his tank at New Zealand's National Aquarium.[2] He escaped his enclosure through a small opening, slid across the floor during the night, and squeezed his body through a narrow pipe leading to open waters and freedom. The staff was able to figure out his disappearance by following the wet trail he left behind. Inky knew he belonged in the ocean, not in a strange glass bowl with a collection of neighbors who were also held captive. Inky is a hero; all wild animals deserve to be free.

In fifth grade we had a class assignment to write a letter to a corporation in order to right a wrong. The example my teacher gave was writing a letter to a cereal company stating you didn't get the promised toy in your box. This idea burned inside of me, and I knew exactly what wrongs I wanted to make right. When I sat down to write the letter, feelings that had been incubating finally became words. As I poured them out onto paper, I became a fiercely protective mama bear rising from her slumber. The sadness, anger, and frustration I felt about animal abuse and cruelty, about people's greed and ignorance that made me feel pulverized inside, went onto that paper. Finally, I could say something, maybe do something about the animals' exploitation, and I aimed right for the top. I wrote a letter to the president. I figured he was the person to talk to about these grave injustices. I wrote to President Reagan about the killing of seals for fur, the cruelty of keeping wild animals in cages, and the injustice of stealing them from their homes. I wrote page after page (I wish I had a copy of that letter!), and it was catharsis.

When we handed our letters to my teacher, who helped us find addresses and was tasked with sending them out, he thought it was cute that I had written *The White House* on my envelope. While he praised me for speaking out, he made sure I knew not to expect an answer. It was disappointing to hear, but I felt better for writing the letter anyway.

After a few weeks, my teacher excitedly called me over to give me a large envelope. I saw the words *Environmental Protection Agency* on it! He announced the envelope's arrival to the class, which I hated. I hated attention being drawn to me, but this was a big deal apparently. Inside was a letter and a savings bond from the EPA. Someone in the White House had read my letter and forwarded it to the right agency. I was heard. And not only was I heard, but I was encouraged. The letter told me that the Earth needs people like me to speak on [her] behalf. I decided then and there I would always be a voice for the voiceless. Like the Lorax in Dr. Seuss's infamous children's book, I decided, as much as possible, to "speak for the trees." While they do have a voice, most people can't seem to hear it.

UNREAL

One of my most cherished childhood memories is bringing Ebony home. She was the runt of the litter and I fell in love as soon as I saw her. I have mixed feelings about dog breeding now and would always adopt, but at the time, when I was seven years old, I wanted another Newfoundland like Daphne. When Daphne passed away, I missed her terribly, and while what we shared will never be replaced, Ebony became my beloved companion for the next phase of my life. We went everywhere and did everything together. When we went to the beach in summertime, she wouldn't let me swim. Every time I went out into the water she followed and circled me until I grabbed on to her tail and she swam me to shore safely. While it was a game for me, Ebony—bred to rescue— was genuinely concerned. We went for walks in every kind of weather and she slept most nights in my room, though sometimes my asthma was too bad to allow her in. I usually tried to endure in order to have her around. She was not only my rescuer, but my comforter.

I WAS THIRTEEN, SHOPPING AT MARSHALLS WITH MY GRANDMOTHER, WHEN my asthma was triggered from out of nowhere. She rushed me back to her house where I sat in the room among the AMA journals, in my grandfather's leather chair, and practiced my breathing exercises. I had already taken as many puffs of my inhaler as I was allowed and my heart was racing. My mom arrived; my grandfather gave me shots of adrenaline to open the airways in my lungs, and my heart raced even more. But I still couldn't breathe. It's a horrible mix of sensations to be unable to breathe and panicked at the same time. Also called epinephrine, adrenaline is a crucial part of our body's fight-or-flight response, the stress reaction that causes air passages to dilate, providing muscles with the oxygen needed to either fight danger or flee. The body's ability to feel pain also decreases as a result of adrenaline, which is why we can continue running from or fighting danger even when injured. I can't help but wonder if these frequent asthma treatments and the constant use of my inhaler impacted my unusually calm response to danger (that led to delayed trauma responses) as I got older. When the adrenaline didn't work, my grandfather said, "We have to get her in the car and take her to the hospital right now."

We rushed to the emergency room. I told my mom, between labored breaths, "I think I'm going to die." I was placed in ICU for about two weeks. Two weeks that are lost to me apart from waking occasionally in a dark, sanitized room encased in plastic while the inhale and exhale of machines breathed for me.

When I was moved to another room and could receive visitors, the doctor forgot to unplug me from my prescribed IV drip and my theophylline levels became dangerously toxic. My mom was with me when I began to slur my words, my eyes rolled back in my head, and I passed out. She called her father, he rushed to the hospital, and when they realized what was wrong, he raged at the staff. Now I not only had asthma, but had to detox from a drug overdose. My soft-spoken grandfather called them "incompetent idiots" and all sorts of things that were incredibly out of character, and though I was completely out of it, I loved having him stand up for me.

My body was exhausted, and after those weeks in the hospital and given my fragile state, I had to be quarantined. It was the second year of junior high and I was out of school for months. I had a home tutor and hardly left my bedroom.

A professional worrier, I was convinced then that I landed in the hospital because I had smoked weed. I had recently started hanging out with the cool kids in junior high and that's what they did in the morning. So, what the hell, I tried it. I don't remember the feeling of being high, only the feeling of being subversive, which gave me a rush that I liked. I had been introduced to alcohol by my father's parents earlier that year on New Year's Eve and it was a revelation too. These experiences liberated me from my incredible self-consciousness.

There were countless times I wanted to speak up and out but couldn't find my voice. In class, when I wanted to raise my hand, I rarely did. I put pressure on myself to say the perfect thing so said little and moved about ninja-like. But it took a toll on me internally.

I'd sung the praises of alcohol to my friends at that tender age and maybe that was how the "bad" kids and I found each other. We were all misfits in one way or another. And though I had incredible close friendships in those tumultuous teenage years, as I attempted to navigate the strange social world of junior high and grappled with my developing female body, I began moving away from myself. I was capable of fitting in, but never felt like I did. I wish I'd understood then that, as the Krishnamurti is supposed to have said, "it is no measure of health to be well adjusted to a profoundly sick society."[3]

Lying in the hospital, I was convinced the doctors would find marijuana in my blood and I would be in big trouble. To my family, I was always "good," and I didn't want my reputation ruined.

FOR YOUNG WOMEN, WE MUST GRAPPLE WITH OUR BURGEONING FEMALE BODIES and find an identity that corresponds with cultural notions of the feminine, which often fall into polarizing categories of the good girl/bad girl, as we journey toward adulthood. And smoking is one of the props in the stereotypical representation of the bad girl. But the history of smoking, dating back to as early as 5000 BCE, shows that smoking was first used as a way to connect to spirit—for shamans to achieve trance or for a tribal community to engage in ceremony and come into contact with the spirit world.[4] Purification rituals throughout the globe use smoke as a part of the process. And though we have negative connotations around smoking, smoking mullein can be a treatment for damp, cold congestion in the lungs.

For those weaning off of tobacco, lobelia might be included in smoke blends to counter the addictive aspects of nicotine and help rid the lungs of toxins. But tobacco was also a sacred plant in Native American ceremony and in most tribes was used sparingly—until the Europeans arrived. Cannabis was more common in Eurasia before the arrival of tobacco, and is also known to have been used since at least 5000 BCE.[5]

In tribal cultures throughout the world, ceremonies were performed to mark the transition between childhood and adulthood and act out separation, transition, and reincorporation. Until recently, scientists thought that teenage angst was all about raging hormones. But as we lean into more comprehensive and inclusive definitions of history, scientists and psychologists have realized that our brains are going through another stage of rapid maturation and many have speculated that "antisocial" or rebellious behavior is a result of lost rites of passage. Without ceremonious ways to mark significant life transitions, we are left to find our way in confusion as we sort through messages from media, family, and culture and rely heavily on peer groups for feedback. Hence the anxiety and shape-shifting many of us undergo to "fit in," and sometimes it's hard to find our own unique shape afterward, or even to know what it is.

In this confusing, liminal time, I denied the intensity of my sensitive nature, which I didn't have the necessary tools to deal with. I began to grow numb and build a brittle boundary around me. As I pushed away from myself, I pushed Ebony away too. Somewhere inside I must have known that she would soften my thin shell, and at the time, I didn't want to be seen. When she tried to come into my room, I shut the door. When she came up to me for affection or to comfort me, I turned her away. It makes me intensely sad to think of it now; I turned away from my childhood companion, my dear friend, and also from myself. For all unconditionally loving Ebony knew, I simply, suddenly rejected her, and that pains me.

Ebony died when I was seventeen while I was away for a semester at Simon's Rock, an early acceptance college. I was slowly thawing then and when I finally felt her loss, my tears seemed like they wouldn't stop. But as I released the pressure of my inner dams over the years, they cleansed me and brought me back to my original, albeit newly revised, form. Ebony is long gone now, but I still tell her spirit I'm sorry. Maybe it's for her and for Daphne that I work on behalf of their wild ancestors, the wolves.

IN THE AGE OF "REASON" IT WAS DECLARED THAT ANIMALS DIDN'T HAVE SOULS and didn't feel pain.[6] With the rise of patriarchy and organized religion, the world beyond white men was found to be either deficient, soulless, or dead. Until Pope Francis declared that "Paradise is open to all of God's creatures,"[7] Roman Catholic theology said animals could not go to heaven because they had no souls. But to anyone who has spent time in nature, it is obvious that other animals feel, have emotions, build connections, experience trauma, and feel pain. Science is now "proving" that animals feel, but we didn't need a formalized discipline to reveal that information to us.[8] The history of animals is full of heartbreaking examples of the empathy and emotional reach of the full animal kingdom: when a member of a wolf family is stuck in a brutal snare that rendered them unable to move, but also left them slowly bleeding to death, the entire pack will relocate—even to a dangerous area—to be with, feed, and care for their family member until he or she passes away.

But despite the obvious fact that animals have emotions and innate and ethical rights, a war is consistently waged on them in name of profit. In 2017 the Tory government in Britain voted that all animals (apart from humans, of course) have no emotions or feelings, including the ability to feel pain.[9] All animals that are not pets or companion animals are threatened by this change in law that encourages those who benefit or profit from cruelty to live in an alternate reality, comfortably numb.

After years of working on behalf of animals, I've come to realize that in order for many people to care about and consider the lives of wolves, bats, and other essential creatures in their actions, my argument must address not just what's best for the animals in question but how such efforts benefit humanity. The principles and science of ecology can help illuminate those benefits, and so can herbalism. When we learn that a wild plant like mullein can help us heal, we might see and treat the land differently. I believe that falling in love with the Earth will help us take better care of her. It was this notion, the idea that people needed to reconnect on an emotional level in order to care, that inspired me to create the hands-on, immersive experiences I have offered over the years through Sacred Warrior. I wasn't sure if mindful, experiential learning in nature would move people the way it has for me, or change anything, but as I fell into my emotional and visceral pulls, the mission and sense of purpose—to facilitate healing through intimacy with nature—was clear.

REAL TO EVERYONE

The boy in the story of the Velveteen Rabbit becomes sick with scarlet fever and has to let go of the things closest to him because they may harbor germs. The rabbit that slept with him every night is especially contaminated and is put in a garbage bin with other items to be incinerated. The Velveteen Rabbit, discarded, feels so much grief that he sheds a real tear.

His tears touch the ground and a flower grows in its place. And from that flower, the nursery magic Fairy emerges. She tells him that she is going to make him Real. "Wasn't I Real before?" he asks. "You were Real to the Boy," the Fairy says, "because he loved you. Now you shall be Real to everyone."

When the Velveteen Rabbit finds himself in the company of real rabbits he is at first self-conscious and embarrassed about his weak velveteen legs, but when he looks down, he finds that he has been transformed: "he had brown fur, soft and shiny, his ears twitched by themselves, and his whiskers were so long that they brushed the grass." He was so excited and caught up in his new form that when he finally stopped to look for the Fairy, she had gone.[10]

AS AN AUTUMN BABY, BORN AS THE SUMMER WAS WANING, GRIEF IS THE EMO-tion I've tended toward. The tenderness I feel has been a tool for navigation, mobilizing my activism and pointing me in the direction of what matters most. As I have explored modes of healing and worked through the water-logged landscapes my grief has sent me to, I've vacillated between tension and tenderness. With integrated practices of therapeutic movement, meditation, creative exploration, and herbalism, I've cultivated the internal strength to stand tall like the stalk of mullein, so I can soften without steeling myself for protection. Over the years, especially as an athlete and fighter, I have come to know my sensitivity as my strength. I relied on the Raggedy Ann and Andy sleeping bag when I was soft, before I could build any armor of my own. I've come to realize it takes courage to be sensitive; I no longer need a soft object to muffle my reactions to our sometimes harsh world.

Somehow it helps to know that mullein seeds are ready and waiting beneath our feet, quietly anticipating their moment to rise again. To soften the hard, rigid spaces, it often takes our tears.

WILD ROSE
Rosa multiflora

Family: Rosaceae

The rose is a symbol of beauty, love, joy, and silence, and has long been associated with the mysteries of the Rosary. There are over one hundred wild species of rose across the northern hemisphere in Asia, North America, Europe, and Africa. Each has delicate five-petaled blooms, and most of them flower only briefly in summer.

Rosa multiflora was originally brought to the United States from Japan as a natural fence for livestock, a way to keep sheep, cows, and other creatures contained while predators were kept out. But the living fence couldn't be controlled; this force of nature spread and flourished in cities, towns, and woodlands throughout the country and is now considered a fiercely invasive species. Cultivated rose may be perceived as a tame, delicate flower of love, but the multiflora rose is tenacious, wild, and free.

BOUNDARIES

The sharp thorn often produces delicate roses.

OVID

I do my best to care for and protect the porous, vulnerable spaces in my emotional, spiritual, and physical body, but even as I've grown comfortable exploring and advocating for all the parts of myself, I still sometimes struggle to know where my boundaries are. There have been times I hardened to the point of painful tension, built walls that obstructed my vision, or hid inner wounds away before they healed. There have also been times that I remained too open, leaving my tender spaces at the mercy of others' wants, needs, and desires. But as I grow in wisdom and experience, I learn when and where to soften while remaining clear about areas of my life and body that require safekeeping, like the fences around fledgling trees at Alladale Wilderness Reserve that protect them from voracious deer. Without the physical boundary of the fence, or the protective presence of wolves being reintroduced to the area, the tiny pine, ash, rowan, aspen, and birch wouldn't stand a chance. But once the trees grow tall enough and wide enough to assert themselves, the deer are no longer a threat and the barrier can be removed. Ideally, this is how our own boundaries work too: they work with us, protecting sensitive spaces as needed while fluctuating and changing shape as we grow.

Knowing my limits has been essential to my mental, physical, and spiritual well-being. I know what disturbs me, hurts me, and wreaks havoc on my nervous system, but even with that knowledge it has taken extra time to learn to say a clear and assertive *No. Enough. This is where I draw the line.* Though it may seem contradictory, setting boundaries allows me to take up more space. When I say yes too often, I back myself into a corner where eventually I have to close myself off from everything to regenerate.

Boundary confusion is a subject that comes up in my herbalism courses and retreats all the time, especially for women. Some students share that they work themselves to the point of depletion and say yes to avoid conflict when they really want to shut the door and say no. When does ongoing compromise begin to strip away the framework of our fences, and how can we rebuild them without closing ourselves off? We explore this together, and as we do, assertive plants like wild rose act as our allies, reminding us that we all need our thorns. The physical medicine of rose is astringent, an action that tones slack tissue to strengthen the boundaries of our womb, throughout our veins and arteries. Rose helps to draw together and heal anywhere skin is torn and blood overflows.

IT TOOK ME FIVE YEARS AND LOTS OF THERAPY BEFORE I COULD CALL WHAT had happened to me rape. I had agreed to meet him that night and went into the woods with him willingly, so I assumed the violation was, at least partially, my fault. I was fourteen. I was young and naive, I didn't put up much of a fight, and I left my body while the act happened. I didn't tell anyone.

In the days that followed, I beat myself up for not fighting back. But when I spoke to my therapist about the incident years later, she asked, "What would you have gained by fighting back? Was it even possible at that time in your life? Did you feel safe enough to tell people?" If I fought back, I might have broken free or made the moment of trauma more violent. But I didn't know how to fight, and I hardly knew what was happening until it was too late. In hindsight, I wish I had told my mom and my best friend, Tonya. But I didn't. The impulse to hide the experience, hoping I would forget it or make it go away, was strong. I was afraid that sharing the events of that night would expose me, make me feel naked, and make the shame expand. And I wanted it to shrink.

My only romantic experience at that point had been in eighth grade, and innocent indeed: I held hands with a classmate. We'd been flirting in our way for months, but after we held hands, we were so embarrassed that we hardly spoke again. So when a handsome older student from a private school showed interest in me, I was thrilled. We first met when I was out with friends on Halloween, and we made a plan to meet again the following night.

It was dusk when we met up outside the college campus and walked together along a familiar paved path where wild rose vines protected a small forest. We lingered among the oaks and, suddenly, he kissed me. I'd never been kissed before. It was strange. No one told me what it was supposed to be like, so when he stuck his cold, minty tongue in my mouth, I was jolted. I didn't know if I liked it, but I was happy that he was showing interest in me. We continued walking farther down the path. We talked and we walked into the woods, beyond the boundary of thorns, and underneath a canopy of oak and pines where I'd always felt at home. I began to breathe the fresh air of the forest, take in the trees, and then his energy suddenly shifted. We were alone in the woods and the next thing I knew, I was on the ground.

I dissociated. Like I would during the car accident a few years later when my body experienced physical trauma, I left my body, separated somehow, and floated away into the forest. Afterward, as I came back into myself, I remember stoically gathering my things and walking to a public bathroom where I sat staring at the blood between my thighs. In retrospect, I realize I was in shock. In the moment, I cleaned up as best I could and waited until it was time for my mom to pick me up and take me home.

A strong infusion of rose petals and leaves could have healed those areas of forced entry, but instead of tending to the damage of the assault, I locked the emotions away and quietly coped with the physical pain until my body healed on her own. The term *sub rosa* literally means "under the rose," and since ancient times, the rose has been used as a symbol of silence. This connotation of secrecy dates back to Greek mythology when Aphrodite gave a rose to her son Eros, the god of love, who in turn, gave it to Harpocrates, the god of silence, to ensure that his mother's indiscretions were not disclosed.[1] Decorated carvings of roses have hovered over gathering spaces like council chambers and confessionals ever since to remind guests that what was said there, stayed there. So instead of invoking the rose's healing powers, I channeled the plant's relationship to guarded spaces. In my commitment to silence, I began to tell lies.

At first, I tried to process my confusion by writing letters to him I never sent, and telling the few friends that knew I'd met him a romantic tale—excluding of course the fact that I was deflowered by force. But when all was quiet, the truth emerged from my subconscious wells. I blamed my body, my stupidity, and my perceived weakness for the pain I was enduring and soon memories of earlier abuse arose in the form of nightmares. As everything surfaced, I began to separate further from my flesh and dwell in the realm of spirit. My mind and spirit grew strong while my body withered.

ONE OF THE MOST PAINFUL REALITIES WE ALL MUST FACE IS THAT WE CAN'T always protect those we love. My mom kept me alive when I was in the midst of an asthma attack, breathing through what felt like a crushed straw, when I thought I might die. Her love kept me going and willed me to live when I felt overwhelmed and as though I had nothing left after the car accident. But despite all of our victories, her ignorance about the abuse I suffered will always haunt her. I know she would have made thickets of wild rose grow up along the door to my bedroom and guarded it with fire-breathing dragons if she had known. And yet, as close as we were and are, my first experience with abuse happened under her nose.

As my stifled memories escaped through nightmares, the lived experience began to come into focus in waking life: my age at the time is still vague to me but the prelude to the night it happened is strangely vivid. I must have been about seven years old, and I remember shopping at Steiger's for the special Easter pajamas I wore. I was excited to pick out something special and wake up to a celebration. The one-piece, short-sleeved, high-collared pajamas were striped with pastel colors and had beautiful buttons down the front, and the elastic bottoms hugged my calves. I loved them. The Easter Bunny would visit us in the middle of the night and I would wake in the pajamas to hunt for treasures she left behind. Instead, that night I woke in a dark room with a figure hovering by my bed, hands touching me in places where no child should be touched.

I couldn't see the person clearly and I froze in fear. I didn't understand what had happened, but when I woke that morning, I felt different. My body felt dirty and I went to the bathroom to change out of those pajamas. Somehow, in my mind, they were the culprit. If I could just rid myself of them, I could rid myself of the whole experience. I put them in a paper bag, shoved it to a far corner of my dresser drawer, and never wore them again. But it happened again when he came to visit. Until one night after dinner, I looked at the silverware in the dishwasher and considered taking a knife upstairs to my bedroom. I don't recall if I actually took one, but something shifted that night. He didn't touch me again. And like the paper bag shoved out of sight in my dresser drawer, I buried the memories.

There is a survival instinct in wild animals: they hide when they are injured or weak since they know physical weakness makes them easy prey. So perhaps it was my young animal instinct to hide my trauma. I was able to forget—an act of survival that allowed me to have a happy childhood. But as my body began to develop during adolescence, I felt the urge to reject its changes. My silence made my inner conflict all the more insidious. When we try to hide our wounds without tending to them, they become infected. No one spoke openly about sexual abuse when I was young, and so I had no context for what happened to me. Telling my mom and others close to me may have begun to air out the stench of my wounds, but I feared my pain would only shape-shift into a new form and become their pain too. Abuse doesn't just torment the one whose boundaries have been crossed. Once revealed, the transgression torments everyone they love and who loves them.

CONSENT

Last summer after teaching at Sawmill Herb Farm, I harvested wild rose with my mom in an area I call "the pretty place." It was late June, and wild roses were spilling out everywhere. I knew if we didn't harvest the rose soon, we would miss her ephemeral moment of bloom. As we walked among the thickets of thorns, petals dropped right into our paper bags as though we'd caught them on the cusp of falling. Still, we asked permission from the plants and the land before harvesting medicine.

I always ask permission from the land before harvesting. It can take time to hear or feel the intuitive yes or no, but it's there. The answer might come to me in the form of a bodily sensation, an image, or a feeling in the space around me. Sometimes the response is simply a moment of surveying the environment and realizing the wildlife and surrounding land need the flowers, berries, roots, and seeds more than I do. When the answer is yes, there is an openness in the air as though I am walking through a door, and I am immensely grateful. But when I sense a no, I might feel an invisible barrier between me, the plant, and the land. I respect that feeling, and understand not to cross. Even the most skeptical of my students have learned to communicate with nature. In doing so, we learn to take only when we have permission, and learn to sense and heed the answer no.

Gorgeous thickets of *Rosa multiflora* teeming with pollinators once grew alongside a small community pond near my mom's house in Echo Hill. I went there to spend time amid the rose and abundance of plants and wildlife every time she was in bloom. I know the pollen is a valued food source for vital insects, including our beloved bees, and rose hips are a nutritious winter food for birds and mammals such as rabbits and coyotes. But one day, I arrived and the land was stripped of her boundaries and thorns. I was heartbroken. All one had to do was look at the land and see that the so-called invasive species was not displacing other plants and was in fact preventing soil erosion. Though wild rose is a multifaceted medicine and has ecological value, the plant is now considered to be one of the USDA's "most wanted" invasive plant species or "noxious weeds" and is often torn from the ground or poisoned, a process that harms the surrounding environment as well.

Since they removed the rose and other so-called invasive species, the soil has eroded and the water in the small pond has slowly dissipated. The boundaries are gone. With the loss of water came loss of the species that relied on that water and, I imagine, those that appreciated the bounty of food the wild rose provided. We need to ask ourselves if some so-called invasive species may really be harbingers of future ecosystems, protecting places where native species are struggling to thrive. Resilient plants like wild rose might be better adapted to thrive in this era of massive environmental disruption and climate change.

Tearing plants from the Earth and, worse, poisoning them without spending time with areas to build relationship with the land and see who might be benefiting from their presence creates trauma, and in the case of pesticides, makes wild communities sick. This abuse is just one example of the countless connections that exist between women and nonhuman nature. Both have suffered, and continue to suffer, nonconsensual extraction, penetration, and claims of ownership in the throes of capitalist and patriarchal systems of exploitation.

WHEN MY MOM AND I WALKED OUT FROM BETWEEN THE ENCHANTING ROSE bushes, I noticed a man coming toward us. Something felt off about him and my spidey senses were on alert. As he got closer, I scanned him, deciding how I was going to take him down and defend my mom if I needed to. Once he passed, I asked her, "If you were walking here alone and that guy tried to attack you, what would you do?" She looked at me, uncomfortable, and said, "Go for his throat? I really don't know."

Even if we haven't been attacked or violated, the fear of being preyed upon can keep women imprisoned. When walking alone through a forest or city street, we must be hypervigilant, and though there are accounts of warrior women through the ages, it still strikes many people as strange when women choose to fight. We are taught that being "ladylike" means being restrained, delicate, and gentle, but when we're seen as prey, doesn't it make sense to learn how to defend ourselves? While yoga and exercise that keeps our bodies fit have their place, I believe that self-defense is an essential skill for all women. We need places to allow the more primal part of ourselves to be and to breathe without having to be on guard, and without a chaperone.

Recently, I was warned not to go into the woods of Prospect Park, one my favorite areas in Brooklyn: "Women were raped there recently. Don't walk in those woods unless you're with a large group or with a man." But I love to walk in the woods alone, and now I was forced to question my comfort, knowing all too well that if something happened, I would be blamed for going somewhere I shouldn't. When I was in Costa Rica last year, I was told not to go to my favorite deserted area of beach alone and definitely not to walk the beautiful path adjacent to the beach. Stay on the road, because "there have been a series of rapes recently." Friends told me, "Better to go to the areas in town or to Cocles where everyone hangs out if you're alone." But I wanted to be alone in nature. If I chose to go anyway, I knew I wouldn't be able to relax or let down my guard and I would be chastised for having gone against everyone's warnings. When I finally decided to visit an area of beach that was populated enough, a man came and sat next to me uninvited, and when I told him I wanted to be alone, he was offended. I added it to the exhaustive list of times I've been called a bitch for not accepting unwelcome advances. When I was a teenager, lying on the beach relaxing and soaking up the sun, I opened my eyes to find a man staring at me. He walked over and told me to spread my legs farther so he could get a better look. I left the beach and didn't return for the rest of our family vacation. With others around, maybe my physical body was safe, but my psyche and spirit were still violated.

The fear of rape can rob us of the pleasure of solitude and our innate right to roam. With no chaperone, we are advised to stay home instead of going out at night, to be wary, cover our bodies, keep our heads down, and make sure we are not in the wrong place at the wrong time. I hear similar arguments made for animals in zoos: *They are safer in their cages than in the wild.* But at what cost to their purpose, their souls, the environments that depend on them? I had many late nights in my twenties when I debated whether to take the risk and walk home from the subway or spend my last twenty dollars on a cab. When I was alone, my safety felt out of reach because I couldn't afford it. But even in cabs I have been uneasy, on alert when a male driver turns down a wrong street.

More and more, women are coming together to say no. Enough. This is where we draw the line. Even if society makes us feel unsafe, or tries to tame and sanitize powerful wild spaces, we can at least escape from our self-imposed prisons and create boundaries that are not inflicted upon us, but that make us feel free. As we do, wild rose can help us fall more in love with ourselves and get clear about where our boundaries lie. And if forced entry happens, wild rose can help to mend spaces in our body, mind, or spirit that have been crossed without our consent.

RECLAMATION

While I had to acknowledge what had happened to me, I didn't need or want to take on the identity of victim. As James Baldwin wrote, "The victim who is able to articulate the situation of the victim has ceased to be a victim: he or she has become a threat." I believe that's true; it was for me. When I finally spoke out about the abuse I endured, I released it and began to fully reclaim my body. Righteous anger began to boil and bubble in my inner cauldron.

I confronted both of the men who abused me, and so did those close to me. I was terrified, but I knew it had to be done to prevent them from harming and abusing others. Even though I felt weak and incredibly vulnerable before facing them and asserting my boundaries, Tonya recently told me, "There was a fierceness coursing through you even when you were struggling." With each confrontation something shifted in me, and I have been one to guard sacred space and confront trespassers ever since.

THE RECLAMATION OF MY BODY WOULDN'T BE COMPLETE WITHOUT MY LEARNing to embrace the power of pleasure, and in my twenties, like many of us, sex and passion sparked creative energy and took center stage in my relationships. I couldn't imagine a partnership without blazing desire. I did the necessary work of dismantling self-blame and rising above my own walls so I could soften. It took years of conscious self-care and clearing of trauma before my body understood that she was safe and could trust me. Early on, I had occasional flashbacks, but I'm fortunate to have chosen men who helped me move through my trauma. My long-term partners listened and understood that our consensual sex was entirely separate from those who did not ask permission, though there were lovers who handled me like I might break after I confided in them. This only made me conscious of why they couldn't let go, and made it more difficult to get lost in the throes of passion. The pleasure I experienced with men I chose had absolutely nothing to do with the violence of those who'd abused me. Letting go and exploring my sexuality was an essential part of my healing.

EIGHT YEARS AGO, A BELOVED PARTNER AND I TOOK A TRIP TO AMHERST AND drove by the place I was raped. My body clammed up. That's when I knew there was another layer of healing to be done. I needed to heal my relationship with the small stretch of wood and reclaim the fragments of my spirit that fled at fourteen. I decided that on my next visit, I would go back there alone.

I WALK ALONGSIDE THE WILD ROSE THAT GROWS BETWEEN THE PAVED PATH and forest and step into the woods. The space seems to hum with knowing when I enter. A beautiful old oak stands tall, keeping watch. I wonder if the tree remembers me. I see mushrooms growing along the base of the trunk and recall my body lying against that ground. Do the mycelium remember? I sit, meditate, write myself a letter, and invite my fourteen-year-old fragment of spirit back. I've forgiven the young girl who was just trying to cope, forget, and survive. I've got her back now, and she no longer needs to be afraid. I meditate, burn purifying herbs, and wait until the ground that had scared me feels sacred.

As I walk out of the woods, I notice a new sign: the college is now reforesting the dead spaces. There was a blight among the non-native red pines, so they're removing them to rewild the landscape and turn the space into a sanctuary. "Later this spring, after the pine trees have been removed, a mix of native deciduous and coniferous saplings will be planted and will begin the long process of growing to maturity. Instead of plantation-like rows of doomed, non-native trees, the new tree mix will be reflective of a natural forest. Unfortunately, these areas may look barren for a few years until the trees grow beyond the sapling stage." That's how transformation is, isn't it? The process of evolution can look bleak and barren for a while, even though hard work is being done beneath the surface.

Though it has taken me decades to heal various layers, every time I do, I expand. And when I find another raw place inside, I can use rose to help me heal the tender tissue. After years of writing letters to those who have violated me, and who have abused the beloved Earth, I wrote a simple letter to myself:

Dear Vanessa,

Your body is, was, and will always be yours. Your innocence is intact and your right to pleasure has not been robbed. You have nothing to be ashamed of. It was the illnesses of those men, the illnesses of patriarchal society, and the illnesses of misogynistic religious doctrines that perpetuated shame. I'm sorry you were trapped in the cage of your silence. You didn't want people to see you as a sexual object, to think of your body in a sexual way. You understood this even then. I get it. I still have that fear. You didn't want the story and the telling to grow big before you could make sense of it. You know what? You were brave. And look at us now. We've done all right.

MILK THISTLE
Silybum marianum

Family: Asteraceae

Vanessa cardui, the "butterfly of the thistle," is an insect that can thrive almost anywhere thanks to the tenacity of her host plants—mugwort, red clover, goldenrod, and thistle. These resilient plants can flourish in abandoned city lots, sunny meadows, gardens, cracks in sidewalks, forest edges, or windswept dunes. Thistle is a supreme liver and gallbladder tonic and, like the butterfly, a symbol of transformation. In traditional Chinese medicine, the liver and gallbladder are related to the wood element, one of the tradition's five main elements used to understand the root cause of symptoms. Wood is an element that can rot when too damp, burst into flames when depleted and dry, or flourish in every direction, like the growth of a tree, when in balance. Increased blood pressure, frequent rashes, a prickly constitution, anxiety, inflammation, heartburn, or panic attacks might indicate disturbances in the wood element. Milk thistle can support these vital organs and steady our inner flame to process food, emotions, and experiences as we learn to grow.

Outlined in black, *Vanessa cardui* wears abstract splashes of brown, white, and sometimes blue on her orange inner wings. When she rests with wings folded together, her four circular eyespots can be seen. As a caterpillar, she is more difficult to identify; her appearance changes from a gray wormlike creature to a long, spiny one that liquefies during chrysalis. Twenty-four hours after attaching to her chosen plant, likely the prickly, protective thistle, she will turn inside out into a beautiful bronze casing, the caterpillar self melting away.

METAMORPHOSIS

In order to change, people need to become aware of their sensations and the way that their bodies interact with the world around them. Physical self-awareness is the first step in releasing the tyranny of the past.

BESSEL A. VAN DER KOLK, *THE BODY KEEPS THE SCORE*

Six months after the car accident shattered three of my vertebrae, I emerged from my fiberglass back brace. The cream-colored cocoon that had encased me from the small of my back to my collarbone and dug into my armpits was now on the floor in front of me. It looked like the severed torso of a less-buxom Barbie doll. I felt incredibly vulnerable without the now-familiar armor. But I was free.

While relentless asthma attacks forced me to be aware of my breath, and the car accident taught me to deal with intense pain and discomfort, I was still estranged from my physical body and was absorbed in the realms of my imagination. With drawing, I could enter into hours of meditative focus where my subject and I—usually lionesses, wolves, panthers, and ungulates—were all that existed. While I struggled inwardly, my art was a world all my own and the hold it had over me was so strong, it captivated me for days on end. I often felt my art released and expressed sound, and that the pencil and paper brought me into my own sort of prayer.

Now, no longer encased in my strange plastic corset, I was staring down at my flesh again. I was forced to stand tall where, in the past, I had shrunk to protect myself. Through the rigid physical healing process, I was now formed straight like a second year mullein stalk.

In his book *Waking the Tiger*, somatic therapist Dr. Peter Levine considers the ways wild animals overcome trauma and applies it to his work with humans. He describes trauma as a highly activated incomplete biological response to threat, frozen in time. When our adrenaline prepares us for fight or flight, muscles throughout our body tense in energetic readiness. But if we are held down, immobilized and unable to fight or flee, the energy generated by our survival instinct stays stuck in our body. Dr. Levine says that the traumatized person "stays in a state of acute and then chronic arousal and dysfunction in the central nervous system."[1] I had become stuck in an aroused state, and though I managed to keep it caged, I was now desperate to release pent-up energy. I wanted to unlock my restrictive physical gates, run, and never stop.

In one of my long-standing inner narratives, I had the starring role as the weak asthmatic girl sitting on the sidelines, incapable of participating in gym class. Growing up, I felt like there was a spotlight on me showing everyone I was incapable. When my elementary school gym teacher insisted I run around the perimeter of our school for the annual fitness test like everyone else, I had an asthma attack that landed me in the hospital. It was absolutely humiliating, one of the many moments that strengthened my narrative. The need for my inhaler and the fear of pushing myself too far without it shadowed my every move. I began to feel a split between the reality my asthma would let me inhabit and the way I wanted to appear on the outside.

As I grew older, I found myself using my asthma as an excuse to opt out of situations where I didn't feel confident or sure of myself. I sat with temporarily sick and excused kids, and the delinquent kids, but I was the only one consistently absent from gym class. When the activities were mild, I had to participate, and that was even worse. I was incredibly self-conscious and felt that, given my absences, everything I did was subject to double scrutiny. My defense and coping mechanisms were to act like I didn't care. But the truth is, I *desperately* wanted to be an athlete.

Soon after the brace came off and I became more mobile, I began going to therapy twice a week with a wonderful woman named Joan who specialized in anorexia and bulimia. Once I was "found out" and the secret coping mechanism of my eating disorder was exposed after the car accident, I could no longer use the potent distraction of starvation, avoidance of meals, or purging to avoid more painful truths. My family and close friends were onto me, but more than that, I was sick of it. I could no longer fool myself with the self-destructive tactics; I was too aware, too much truth had surfaced, and I was ready to heal. With Joan I spoke about the sexual abuse I experienced as a child—the rape at fourteen that made me remember and other traumas I didn't even know I harbored.

At seventeen years old, driving home from therapy with my mom, in the throes of dysmorphia, I would point out women on the street and ask, "Do I look like her? Or maybe her?" I was sincerely at a loss. As I sought to integrate my mind, body, and spirit, I began to crack open and erupt.

Without the obsessive rigidity of starving myself, I was hit with raging panic attacks. My panic would arise out of nowhere, triggered by the smallest indecision but quickly picking up speed, leaving my heart thrashing against my chest. My body was a source of unpredictable storms and I could no longer escape in the ways I had before.

It would take a year of rehabilitation before I could move in the unbridled way my body wanted to. Physical therapy was the first step of that journey. In the first few days after my brace was removed, the most I could do was lie on my stomach, barely lifting one arm off the ground, then the other. I eventually added each leg to the routine to strengthen the soft muscles along my spine. These and other painfully boring exercises went on for over an hour; as much as I hated them, though, I learned more about my body through those subtle movements than I ever had before.

But my most powerful barriers were not the brace or anything to do with the body I was rebuilding. The strongest, most intensely fortified gates were in my mind. I was convinced I was physically deficient.

WHEN I DROPPED OUT OF HIGH SCHOOL AFTER THE CAR ACCIDENT, HEALING WAS my full-time job and I was blessed to have close training grounds. Hampshire

Fitness Club, a gym with Nautilus equipment, free weights, cardiovascular machines, pool, and sauna, was within walking distance from our house in Echo Hill. As soon as my body was ready, I walked down the hill to the club every day and channeled the stringent self-discipline I cultivated through starving myself into strength-training regimens. I began to push myself with cardiovascular training, learned how to use free weights, and did calisthenics and interval training. Sweating things out was a revelation. It was pure catharsis. I began to release the fires I had been stifling inside.

Slowly, my relationship with food and my body began to heal. Every day the weather allowed, I grabbed a big blanket and walked to a large, grassy meadow near our house where I wrote in my journal, gazed out at the fields of white and red clover, and found shade under the surrounding maple trees. I was slowly stumbling beyond the psychological safety net of my body dysmorphia and seeing a world outside of my distorted perception. As those beliefs were dismantled, I began to see past their peaks and valleys, and I wrote: *There's no way I could feel fat today when yesterday I was just right, there's no way I could feel helpless today when yesterday I felt invincible, there's no way I could be so hungry today when yesterday I was satiated.* I read voraciously—books on natural healing, medicinal foods, healing from sexual abuse, self-care, and self-development. Food became medicine and fuel. Later, when I learned to eat for optimum physical performance, food became my ally. I began to nourish myself and become more grounded, more embodied. As wonderful as it was to begin to feel safe and strong in my human form, the exhilaration of growing as I moved beyond my comfort zones would soon catalyze a new addiction, and unfortunately this thrill of potential transformation would trip me up again, and I became unilaterally focused on pushing my body to perform beyond perceived limitations.

TWO YEARS LATER WHILE TAKING CLASSES AT UMASS AMHERST, I WAS INVITED to try out for the rowing team. I had been training my body full time for two years by that point. My relationship with food was continuing to shift, and I was strong. *Yes,* I thought, *this is the next step. This is the challenge I need.* I wanted to know what my body was capable of.

THE TRYOUTS ARE BRUTAL. AFTER AN EXHAUSTING ROUND OF PHYSICAL TESTS, I am lying on the grass outside the UMass gymnasium with fifty other women in agony and my would-be coach tells me to do thirty push-ups. She doesn't know about my asthma, my car accident, or the stubborn insecurities still embedded in my body. I am just another woman trying out for the UMass crew team. She waits. I've never done a push-up in my life. I tell her, "I'll try, but I can't do all of them." "Yes you can," she says. "If you want to make the team, you'll do thirty push-ups." So I lie there facedown in the grass, muscles exhausted and in pain. Somehow, though, I will myself to do them. They are incredibly lame, but still, this overcoming is a turning point. I make the team and I am ecstatic. "You have heart," the coach tells me.

I WOKE UP AT 4:45 A.M. SIX DAYS A WEEK TO PRACTICE ON THE CONNECTICUT River. We carried our heavy wooden longboat down the hill to the dock as the sun rose. The skinny boat sped across the water, leaving circular pools in our wake. I was starboard in an eight boat, which meant I set the pace for the four women behind me. I still struggled with breathing and lagged behind with running, but I made up for those deficits with my rowing technique. A perfectionist (often to my paralyzing detriment), I was a technician. As a team, we worked in synch and glided across the water. Pushing my body in those early mornings was pure bliss.

My respiratory system was still a daily challenge, but I was learning to manage it. I would suffer from wheezing initially, but if I took my inhaler or even a moment to focus on breathing after the onset of the symptoms, they would subside. And when they passed, I discovered incredible endurance. My asthma was never a problem out on the water. I began to wonder if the illness that had defined my childhood was simply a mental block. I'd had so many bad experiences with running as a kid, so my fears then were not unwarranted, but I wanted to move beyond them.

Mental Toughness Training for Sports introduced me to meditation and visualization. When I felt like I was hitting a wall during rowing practice, I did meditations from that book that included visualizing a golden light illuminating and animating my body, giving me newfound energy. I practiced visualization when I wasn't training, or couldn't. I wrote and repeated affirmations that I posted to my bedroom walls. I imagined myself, in as much sensory detail as I possibly could, conquering the dreaded ergometer (rowing machine) test and sprints, and winning races. And of course, I became obsessed with conquering the push-up. Eventually, I could do fifty, no problem, and began to merge the expansion of my mind with the performance of my body. I invited the young me sitting on the sidelines to finally come down off those humiliating bleachers. I became an athlete, and it changed my life.

STING LIKE A BEE

In Gaelic, *Vanessa cardui*, butterfly of the thistle, is called "a' bhaintighearna-dhreachmhor," which roughly translates to "the noble painted lady." Her favorite plant, the spiky purple thistle, grows throughout the Scottish countryside and is even more ubiquitous as the plant emblem of Scotland, adorning everything from shop logos to kilt sporrans to embroidered tea towels. While there are different stories about why thistle, a so-called weed, became the country's national symbol, the most famous is the story about the Battle of Largs in 1263.[2] The invading Norse army were sneaking into the Scots' encampment barefoot, creeping quietly under cover of darkness until a Norse soldier stepped on a spiny thistle. The sharp prickles caused him to cry out in pain, alerting the Scots to the Norse presence. Thanks to the protective plant, the Scots were victorious, and the plant has been honored ever since.

When thistle leaves are stroked from front to back, the young, undeveloped spines are soft. But when approached from above, whoa, do they warn you to keep back. I understand why the butterfly would choose such a harsh protective space for the vulnerable time of her transformation. Since I've been working with plant medicine, spiky, thorny plants have also been my allies. I suspected my sensitivity and empathy were liabilities. I felt too much. I felt the pain of the Earth and of species that couldn't speak for themselves, the pain of loved ones, the overwhelm of social injustice, and on and on. My understand-

ing of the ripple effect was strong at a young age. Growing up with my anten-
nae so tenderly attuned was not an easy way to be in the world.

And while it's easy to point to the sexual abuse as the reason for my eating
disorder, I also, in retrospect, feel that a combination of factors contributed to
my intense desire for control. It's comforting to locate a root source, but in
truth all of the shame and confusion and lies I felt myself weathering were
eating away at me. The eating disorder was a potent distraction from my sensitivity, my sadness, as I tried to make sense of a world that contained so much
cruelty; from having my heart broken; from being called a slut when I was trying
to process being taken advantage of; from growing up in a culture that shamed,
judged, and objectified the female body. When I allowed myself to feel all of
the things boiling away inside of me, it was like being punched in the gut. Like
my power was being taken away. Disconnecting from my hunger and instinct
and those animal knowings provided a pathway to transcend the pain of my
feelings. I attempted to navigate a world that contained such intense suffering
that the more my awareness grew, the more overwhelmed I became. It was too
much to digest and to feel, and so I sought to cap my consumption.

AS I GREW STRONGER PHYSICALLY THROUGH ROWING AND LATER THROUGH
competitive boxing, I was learning to assert my will, take up space, and create
boundaries. To some, I seemed hard and prickly on the outside, but I was
simply giving my gooey inner sensitive self much needed strength and support. Thorny plants know how to define their boundaries. It's a skill I've always had to work on.

Thistle, a supreme liver and gallbladder tonic, can help to create balance
and initiate transformation. The gallbladder is an emotionally charged organ
and can easily be affected by events or the surrounding environment. Being
easily startled and having a general feeling of fear, especially in regard to decision making, are symptoms associated with gallbladder insufficiency. A quick
return to normal after a physical or emotional shock represents a strong gallbladder.

Gathering thistle requires thoughtful, attentive movements at indirect angles; storming the plant head on will never get the job done. That same agility and deftness is vital in fighting. When someone or something is barreling toward you, blinded by rage or ready to attack, step quickly to the side to gain perspective, then make your first move.

Sports, though often fraught with their own problems, can provide us purpose and focus when approached mindfully. They can help us dig deep and develop skills, in contrast to noisy gyms and treadmills teeming with televisions that not only waste electricity but distract us from our bodies. Like hamsters on a wheel, we eat and run, chasing calories away.

WE'RE A PRODUCT OF OUR INNER AND OUTER ENVIRONMENT, ALONG WITH OUR ancestors' belief systems and those of our culture, friends, and the environment we live in. So, how do we access our intuition and inner knowing when a cacophony of voices vie for our attention? Our body can be the key. Though we hold infinite wisdom within, for various reasons most of us have been conditioned to mistrust our body. The disconnect may stem from spiritual traditions that believe our body will lead us astray, fear of illnesses we don't understand, or power structures that convince us we must look a certain way to be likeable and accepted; separating us from our innate beauty and strength.

TO CELEBRATE STARVING ONESELF—IN ANY FORM—IS TO CELEBRATE A LACK of hunger for life. And there are many who believe it is not ladylike to be hungry. But Naomi Wolf puts it perfectly in her book *The Beauty Myth*: "A culture fixated on female thinness is not an obsession about female beauty, but an obsession about female obedience."[3] Obsessing about the surface keeps us far from our untapped, infinite wells of inner strength. My rigorous training and creative release, and later, the support of wild weeds, revealed my true hunger underneath all of my suppressed anger and frustration.

My friend Encar, a primatologist and founder of the Jaguar Rescue Center in Costa Rica, says that if a wild animal is caged or tied up for too long, they lose their instinct and become dependent on humans, placing a burden on all. When I visited the rescue center I was moved by the rehabilitation of a traumatized hawk whose wings were weak after being shot. With the help of food placed at stations farther and farther away from her open cage, she was gradually getting stronger and coming out to fly. But still afraid, she flew back to the corner after she retrieved her food and her exercises were over. Slowly, she grew stronger and less dependent, until one day, after getting her food, she was ready. As her wings grew stronger, so did her spirit. Mustering up her courage in the corner of that cage, she flew away into the unpredictable freedom of the wild. Some never feel equipped to reenter the wild, and others have shaken off their trauma and reclaimed their freedom.

For years I saw my body as a cage to escape from, but like the hawk, I slowly learned to nourish my animal body, all the while digesting my experiences through writing, art, and movement. As I integrated my mind, body, and spirit, I came down to earth and began to embrace my physical form. And as I became stronger and more whole, I was gathering the strength to fly free.

POISON IVY
Toxicodendron spp.

Family: Anacardiaceae

Poison ivy is a shape-shifting medicine of attention. Her "leaves of three" and camouflaged climbing vines demand that we watch where we're going
and be mindful. Poison ivy belongs to the Anacardiaceae plant family that includes mango, pistachios, and
cashews. She blossoms in June, and her flowers are followed by clusters
of small, globular, berrylike fruits. The root of the plant is reddish and
branching, growing into the earth as inconspicuous winding vines blend
up into tree trunks and extend branches and leaves that morph into the
tree they intend to protect.

Today, as more forest and land are destroyed for agriculture, subur-
ban sprawl, and general consumption, Poison ivy's potency and presence
increases. According to research by Dr. Jacqueline Mohan and colleagues
from Duke University, this plant will become more widespread and aggressive in the future.[1] As atmospheric carbon levels rise, not only does
the amount of urushiol, the toxin in the plant, increase, but poison ivy's
chemical balance changes, meaning that the plant's potency has doubled
since 1960, and will continue to intensify with more atmospheric carbon.
If that isn't a defensive act from the Earth herself, I don't know what is.
The more humans destroy the environment, the more poison ivy becomes
a warrior.

NO TRESPASSING

We both strive to see evildoers punished. But while you have
your gallery of rogues, I have my grove.

POISON IVY, ECO-DEFENDER OF GOTHAM CITY

After a late-morning rowing practice on the water, I bolted from my
dorm to get to an exercise physiology class. My body was so exhausted
that my muscles felt like rubber but I somehow willed myself to move.
On my way down a steep set of stairs, my ankle twisted and I fell. When I tried
to get up, I realized I had sprained it severely, and it didn't take long before my
ankle and the top of my foot swelled into a disturbing round glob, all shades
of purple and blue. I had survived intense training and injured myself running
to class! I was so aggravated. I was laid up again, and all the more frustrated
because I had made the A boat and wasn't able to row in a race I'd trained incredibly hard for. I was going nuts not being able to move. In that moment, I
had all the traits for the homeopathic poison ivy remedy, Rhus tox: I was restless
and agitated, and I felt better when I moved. Typically administered in a small-
dose tincture made from the leaves and diluted many, many times, or in pellets
that dissolve under the tongue, the treatment is used to treat stiffness and
strain, and is also for people who can't get comfortable and need to change
position frequently. I was definitely feeling that way in more ways than one,
but all I knew about poison ivy at that point was to avoid the plant at all costs.

By the time I recovered, my perfectionist ego couldn't handle how far I'd fallen behind my fellow rowers. The season was almost over anyway, I reasoned. I was antsy being in Amherst, the town I grew up in. I was studying exercise science and environmental science at UMass but I didn't want my head in books anymore; I wanted to be outdoors and to test my knowledge. I wanted to learn about my body by pushing her further, experience the wild firsthand, and try something new. In rowing practice, we often ran up Mount Skinner, the highest peak in the area, and once my ankle healed, I hiked the mountain and continued on past where our training had stopped, exploring the vast Seven Sisters mountain range. Scrambling up rocks and boulders was my favorite part of hiking, so it was only natural that I ended up drawn to rock climbing.

Outward Bound wilderness training school had been a rite of passage for my father and his brother, so when I told my grandparents that I wanted to go, they helped me pay my way, agreeing it would be a character-building experience for me too. I was ecstatic. I looked through the catalog of experiences: rock climbing at Joshua Tree, canoeing in the Everglades, camping, solo time in the wild. I wanted to do the Joshua Tree rock climbing experience but it was booked and I didn't have the patience to postpone my plans. The only trip available was the sailing and hiking trip in the San Juan Islands off the coast of Washington State. I wasn't all that interested in sailing but I did like the idea of being on the water again. Once my mind was made up, I was anxious to get out there. I headed to Seattle a couple weeks later, in the early weeks of the summer of my twentieth birthday.

I spent one night in a hotel and when I was picked up, I joined the young men and women who would be my wilderness companions for the next three weeks. I hadn't really considered that part—that I would be in a group—and was surprised to find that I was one of the few in attendance by choice. Most participants had been forced by their family—to get their shit together and toughen up. In our group of ten, the three of us oddballs who were there by choice became quick friends. The van dropped us at a grassy area adjacent to the dock, and after introductions were over, we dumped the contents of our backpacks out onto the grass to be sure we had our essentials—tent, compass, Swiss Army knife, bandana, etc.—and also so our instructors could be sure we weren't cheating by carrying anything deemed nonessential. This scrutiny—learning what really mattered and doing away with our creature comforts—was part of the experience we were paying for. Our instructor came around and grabbed any frivolous items we might've tried to bring along, including the mirror and makeup case of a young woman sitting next to me. She freaked out. *What a sissy,* I thought. I judged her, but of course, deep down I understood. We women are so conditioned to define ourselves by what we look like.

Soon we loaded onto the small sailboat and were off. We sailed and rowed along the gorgeous San Juan Islands, an archipelago in the Pacific Northwest between Washington and Vancouver Island, and for most of the trip we were the only people in sight. Still programmed by my rowers' schedule to wake up before dawn, I was always up first and watched adorable sea otters float on their backs and play near the ocean shore. Together with the other students, I learned to track nautical miles. Orca whales swam alongside our small sailboat, free the way they should be instead of kidnapped and forced to do stupid, humiliating tricks for our entertainment. We rationed food, camped outside, and took turns sleeping on the sailboat under the stars. There were no roads, no clear boundaries, and yet we learned to find our way. We read the wind, watched the movement of birds and marine life, and became intimate with every ripple and every wave. When I did my solo day of camping and self-reflection, I thought, *This is what life is supposed to be.* With few external boundaries and no concern about earning external praise, it became easier for me to dive inside and solidify boundaries of my own. My experiences and challenges were integrating and I was recalibrating in the wild. We didn't see our physical reflections for weeks and it was absolutely liberating. Eventually, the girl who freaked out about her mirror saw beyond her appearance and forgot about it too.

While we abided by the "leave no trace" principle, we weren't taught to identify plants and trees. The only plant our guides made sure we knew how to identify was poison ivy. Most people are warned about poison ivy's shiny reddish leaves of three at some point in their lives, even if they have no idea how to identify any other plants. Jewelweed, a soothing natural remedy for poison ivy's sting, often grows alongside her, ready to help those who are aware. But a lot of time, people pay very little attention to where they are going or what is happening in the ecosystem, and so see neither poison ivy nor jewelweed.

Poison ivy doesn't tolerate such blindness and makes us pay with an irritating rash and, for some, an extreme blistering burn. The plant's message is specific to humans—birds and other creatures eat the berries, and goats, cows, and deer can browse the foliage with no problem.

WE WORKED TOGETHER TO PLAN MEALS AND RATION OUR FRESH FOOD OVER three weeks of sailing, hiking, and camping. Being outside and eating when I was intensely hungry made everything taste amazing. But by the end of the trip, even though we restocked once, we were down to dried food and cans. I cut my hand opening a can with my Swiss Army knife tool and was also oblivious to the fact that I could have used yarrow or plantain to help stop the bleeding and prevent infection (seems like this would have been a good thing to teach us in wilderness training school). We could have foraged but weren't taught about the abundance of wild food around us.

Like goats, cows, and deer, by the time I was fourteen I had become an herbivore and then a (somewhat flexible) vegan. These weren't hard transitions because I was lactose intolerant and, apart from the occasional slice of pizza or dish of ice cream, had avoided dairy from the time I was a child. Food was one of the first places I asserted self-control, and when I recovered from my eating disorder, food was where I asserted boundaries once again. By the age of nineteen, my food obsession became less about restriction and more about optimum health, athletic performance, and, most of all, ethics. I didn't want to perpetuate suffering and wanted to know what my food had to endure to arrive on my plate. I felt that eating without awareness not only perpetuated practices that didn't align with my deep-seated beliefs, but that I would also consume the energy of fear, horror, and enslavement of factory-farmed meat.

From the age of eighteen, I worked at the Raw Carrot Juice Bar in Amherst and learned how to make delicious, nutritious vegan meals. I could easily argue with the many people who said I wasn't getting enough nutrition or protein without meat and, like all good vegans, I learned about the impact of factory-farmed meat on climate change, and about the hormones and antibiotics that were pumped into animals to keep them alive in inhumane conditions. The industrialized Western culture I grew up in has turned the gifts of nature into "resources," and the way we consume meat feels a far cry from the indigenous cultures' practice of using all of the animal. I was trying my best to align my belief systems with my actions, yet an overwhelm of suffering and exploitation seemed to be woven into the fabric of existence.

Apart from being a college town, Amherst and the surrounding area is also a farming community. *Agriculture* means "the science, art, or practice of cultivating the soil,"[2] but most farming practices have departed from that elegant definition. I worked on an organic farm for one summer and spent most of my mornings there picking beetles off of lettuce planted in unnaturally straight lines. Most other farms in the area were monoculture farms that also planted rows and rows of the same crop, leaving depleted soil crackling in its wake. Growing one crop on a massive scale necessitates chemicals and fertilizers that get into our bodies and into Earth's waterways. Resources are drained to keep production going, securing our dependence on fossil fuels and chemical companies, and to maximize profits; many farms also exploit human labor. Though this way of growing and consuming food might be all that most people know, it is not the only way.

I didn't know anyone at the time who was tending the soil, and where in nature do you see perfectly straight lines of just one plant? Nature does not wish to expose her soil to the elements and is always attempting to shelter herself with plants; weeds do her a service by covering wounded landscapes. With their resilience and quick spread, people mistake weeds for evil intruders when really each plant has a special talent and function, and many of them help rehabilitate and heal wounded land.

George Washington Carver was the first Black American to earn a bachelor of science degree, in 1894, and was a pioneer in regenerative farming. He went on to get his masters in agriculture, and through his work on soil chemistry he understood that crop rotation was essential for healing soil. Born into slavery a year before it was outlawed, Carver knew all too well the generations of trauma that abused people and depleted land. Instead of trying to take more from the Earth, he gave back to the land with nitrogen-fixing plants like red clover, peanuts, soybeans, and sweet potatoes. And when he planted cotton a few years later, the land was revived.[3]

Masanobu Fukuoka, traditional farmer and philosopher, illuminated this in his 1975 book *The One-Straw Revolution*. He wrote, "If nature is left to itself, fertility increases. Organic remains of plants and animals accumulate and are decomposed on the surface by bacteria and fungi. With the movement of rain-water, the nutrients are taken deep into the soil to become food for microorganisms, earthworms, and other small animals. Plant roots reach to the lower soil strata and draw the nutrients back up to the surface."[4]

The recognized father of organic farming is Sir Albert Howard. While working with indigenous farmers in India in the early 1900s, he realized that traditional methods of farming were necessary to keep crops and people healthy. He argued that all farming must not fall prey to the temptation of turning the reserves of humus into a short-term profit at the expense of later generations of people, plants, and land. He saw the variety of life above and below ground as expressions of the "successive and repeated processes of birth, growth, maturity, death, and decay"[5] that feed and sustain life. He learned that diseases and insects are not scourges to be wiped out with poisons but are teachers and friends that can show us where the processes of growth and decay are out of balance. While I admire him for bringing these ancient ideas forward in time, his renown is also another instance of a white man being credited with wisdom that already existed. Farming can be simple. But we have made it complicated.

When compared to monoculture, regenerative or ecological farming can include many systems—biodynamic, permaculture, traditional ecological knowledge (TEK)—that share core holistic tenets to create fertile soil, decrease erosion, and deliver stable yields. These systems protect topsoil with cover crops and require only minimal plowing, rotate the plant species grown in one area, and recycle all animal and vegetable waste back into the land.[6] Many of our ancestors and indigenous people throughout the world evolved these methods through observation of nature and the study of relationships between plants, insects, fungi, and animals. Increasing plant biodiversity makes these approaches more adaptable to extreme weather, offers a more balanced diet to communities, and cultivates more natural resilience to so-called pests and diseases. We can take advantage of symbiotic relationships and grow kale next to a plant like dill that attracts the insects that feed on kale. Then "pests" are simply food for beneficial insects; the web of life is perfectly designed already, and we can decide to nurture instead of overhaul it.

Ladybugs, whose name was coined when European farmers prayed to the Virgin Mary as pests decimated their crops, are some of my favorite beneficial insects.[7] When ladybugs came to save the day and wiped out the invading insects, the farmers named these saviors the "Beetle of Our Lady," which, of course, was eventually shortened to ladybug. And this is what regenerative farming does at its best. It looks at all of the incredible creatures we share this planet with and asks: "Who are you? What do you need to thrive? How can we work together?" The more regeneratively we farm, the more nutrients and beneficial bacteria we harvest. A recent study by agronomists and microbiologists at Washington State University confirmed that soil teeming with bacteria, fungi, and nematodes produces more nutrient-dense food.[8] A balanced and diverse soil microbiome fosters a healthy and diverse human microbiome. This makes perfect sense since cooperation between all these creatures is responsible for transferring carbon and nutrients from the soil to the roots of plants that will eventually enter our bodies. Microbiologists have also noted that soil bacteria exposed to antibiotics and other chemicals can develop antibiotic-resistant genes that can be transferred to our the microbiome in our gut, where 70 percent of our immune system resides, wreaking all sorts of havoc on the ecosystem within our body.[9]

I NOW KNOW THAT A VEGAN DIET DOESN'T GUARANTEE A LACK OF SUFFERING, and as my body's needs and my awareness have shifted, I've adjusted. I used to eat poison ivy's cousin, cashews, by the handful. Cashews are actually seeds (called drupes in botany) native to Central and South America. While touted as a healthy snack for vegan and paleo diets, and as a "cruelty-free" alternative to dairy milks and cheese, much of the world's cashew production exploits workers in Asia, where the trees are most abundant, to ensure the lowest export prices to supermarkets in the West. In 2011, Human Rights Watch coined the term "blood cashews" because of the brutal cost of cashew production.[10] The same irritant, urushiol, that causes blistering soreness from exposure to poison ivy is present in the two layers of the hard cashew shell, and it too can cause vicious burns. Since the process of shelling cashews is complicated, most of the work is done by hand. In India alone more than a million workers shell cashews as their full-time job. This often includes entire families with children, who endure excruciating pain in their hands and upper body from chronic contact with the cashew shells for as little as £2 a day.

GOTHAM CITY

Coming home after Outward Bound was a culture shock. Everything felt noisy after being on the ocean, sleeping outside, breathing in the fresh salty air, and taking in a horizon that didn't include buildings. Even rural Amherst seemed overcrowded now. I remember hiking and looking down at the land, at the eyesore of UMass, and feeling like the land was overdeveloped. I wanted nature to take over and I wanted to get back out into the wild as soon as I could. I wanted to be an Outward Bound instructor or maybe a marine biologist like my heroine, Rachel Carson, or a primatologist like Jane Goodall. I was also getting into photography and thought that maybe I could merge my desire to create art with activism and become a *National Geographic* photographer.

Not long after those thoughts took hold, I met a well-known documentary photographer at my grandparents' house in Norfolk. I showed him my portfolio and he said if I ever found myself in New York City, I could assist him. I had never considered NYC, but the idea nagged at me. So when my friend Dawud moved to Brooklyn and said I could stay with him, I jumped at the chance. I felt the city was something I needed to experience while I was young, and I liked NYC more than I expected I would.

THOUGH THOROUGHLY INSPIRED BY NEW YORK CITY, GOTHAM CITY IS THE fictional place in the DC Universe—the shared universe of most of DC Comics' American comic books—that antiheroine Poison Ivy is constantly attempting to rewild, and where the corporate hero Batman rules. Poison Ivy started out as Dr. Pamela Lillian Isley, a botanist, biochemist, and environmentalist from Seattle. While studying advanced botanical biochemistry at university, she was seduced by her professor and injected with plant poisons as part of an experiment. She nearly died from the traumatic ordeal, but underwent a radical transformation. When she emerged from a comatose state, she was reborn and physically transformed. With plant extracts coursing through her veins, she was immune to all diseases and one with nature. Isley dropped out of school and left Seattle, eventually settling in Gotham City, ready for revenge. Now she uses plant toxins and mind-controlling pheromones for her "criminal" activities, which are usually aimed at protecting endangered species and Mother Earth. She is ruthless toward most humans but is compassionate toward women and children who have been victimized. In the DC Universe, she's become known as an ecoterrorist—using her powers to stop by any means necessary those who harm nature—with a famous poisonous kiss that can kill.

Batman's alter ego is Bruce Wayne, an heir of Wayne Industries, a business conglomerate modeled after the standards of a multinational corporation. While it may be fiction, constant messaging in blockbuster movies and comics get under our skin and some superheroes in the Marvel and DC Universes are modern-day gods and goddesses. Positioning Poison Ivy as an ecoterrorist and Batman as the wealthy "hero" with a garage full of fancy cars and overall gross extravagance perpetuates the idea that wealth and consumption are good. To me, Poison Ivy is a combination of Artemis, defender of the wild, and Hecate, the Greek goddess associated with the boundaries between worlds. As the holder of the keys that unlock the borders between realms, Hecate can open the gates of death. She is the goddess of poison plants and liminal realms. In the first century CE, Roman poet Virgil described the entrance to hell as "Hecate's Grove."

Poison Ivy has a mystical connection to nature known as "the Green," an altered state of consciousness that allows her to become one with nature and sense everything that plant life is experiencing. With this profound connection, she is able to communicate with the floral life, giving her instant allies of climbing vines, sharp thorns, carnivorous plants, and nettle stings. The Green is an elemental force that interlaces all plant life and has chosen protectors to fight off threats to the Earth.

While plant consciousness may seem like fantasy, science is now "proving" what many indigenous people have always known—that plants are sentient. Of course they are. How else would they survive? In his book *Plant Intelligence and the Imaginal Realm*, herbalist Stephen Harrod Buhner explains that "when you look at the interconnected network of plant roots and mycorrhizal mycelium in any discrete ecosystem, you are looking at a neural network much larger than any individual human has ever possessed."[11]

IN THE COMIC BOOK *A WALK IN THE PARK*, BATMAN #751, GOTHAM CITY IS destroyed in an earthquake and declared No Man's Land and Poison Ivy holds dominion over Robinson Park, turning it into a tropical paradise.[12] Sixteen children orphaned during the quake come to live with Ivy. She cares for them as though they are her sons and daughters and they live in bliss for a time. But that winter, the villain Clayface pays Ivy a visit, hoping to form an alliance: growing fruits and vegetables, having the orphans harvest them, and selling the produce to the highest bidder. She wants nothing to do with the plan, and attempts to kill him with a kiss. But Clayface overpowers Ivy and imprisons her and the orphans for six months in a chamber under the park's lake. Eventually, Batman rescues them and they work together to take Clayface down. Batman, originally intending to take the orphans away from Ivy, recognizes that staying with her is what is best for them, and they remain in her care until the city is restored.

But when Gotham City reopens to the public, the city council wants to evict her from the park, as they are uncomfortable with a "psychotic eco-terrorist controlling the equivalent of 30-odd square blocks." So the Gotham City Police Department threatens to spray a toxic herbicide that would kill every living plant in the park, including Poison Ivy, and more than likely do harm to the children. Ivy refuses to leave the park to the city and let them destroy the paradise she's created, but Rose, one of the orphans, is accidentally poisoned by Ivy. Grief-stricken, she surrenders herself to the authorities in order to save the girl's life.

DANDELION, NETTLES, GARLIC MUSTARD, SORREL, VIOLET, AND JAPANESE knotweed shoots are among the abundant wild plants that have chosen to be where they are, and there is a level of vitality to the act of consuming them that I don't feel after buying food, even from the farmers market. When I forage plants with permission from the land there, I sense a true feeling of reciprocity;

I always make sure the population is thriving before I harvest anything. In my own way, I tap into the Green when I ask permission. The plants were here long before we were; they are our elders and can be our teachers if we open our hearts and minds and let them. We wouldn't take without asking from people we wish to learn from, and the same should be true with plants.

But instead of tapping into the Green and using city parks as perennial food forests and areas for abundant wild foraging, most so-called weeds are killed out of habit, turning valuable land into semi-toxic playgrounds. New York City sprays toxic herbicide as a regular practice, as many cities do.[13] Glyphosate is sprayed hundreds of times a year onto public green spaces to treat so-called weeds that could otherwise be free food and medicine, and that would attract beneficial insects, bring up minerals from the subsoil, and sow fertility. Like George Washington Carver said, "There is no need for America to go hunger as long as nature provides weeds and wild vegetables."[14] If only we had listened. Nature is generous and abundant as long as we stop making her sick.

While chemical companies run television and internet ad campaigns claiming the safety of their weed-killing products, it is not hard to do a bit of research and learn that this is a lie. More than eleven thousand cancer victims have sued Monsanto (acquired by the Bayer corporation in 2018) alleging that exposure to Roundup and other glyphosate products caused their non-Hodgkin's lymphoma.[15] Even more insidious, lawsuits claim that the company has known about the cancer risks all along but worked hard to keep that information from the public, in part by manipulating scientific data relied on by regulators.[16] The first two legal trials have ended in unanimous jury verdicts in favor of plaintiffs. And trials continue to mount. In one recent case brought by a husband and wife who both have non-Hodgkin's lymphoma due to Roundup, evidence was introduced about the ease with which the weed killer absorbs into human skin. Our skin is our body's largest organ and we often forget that it is permeable, and that what we come into contact with matters.

The decline of monarch butterfly populations in North America since the mid-1990s has also been linked to the use of glyphosate-containing herbicides, the same used copiously along city streets and on genetically modified maize and soy crops. Monarch caterpillars are dependent on milkweed as their primary food source, and Monsanto's guidance for farmers specifically mentions that its glyphosate-containing herbicide Roundup WeatherMAX "will provide suppression and/or control of . . . milkweed, quackgrass, etc."[17] These same poisons get into the waterways, seep into our skin, and are directly responsible for cancer and species decline. And we still see ads urging us to pour chemicals on our lawn to get rid of plants like dandelions that are actually valuable food and medicine. This practice is a result of massive social conditioning and corporate propaganda that needs to transform immediately. And we *can* transform it. Every choice we make has an impact.

We all have to eat. Food justice is one of the many loaded issues that affect all of us, and our everyday, seemingly mundane choices matter. Just as we look to the root cause to determine symptoms in our bodies, we must look to the root causes of injustice to determine what ills and inequities are symptoms of bigger sins. Our hearts may break over and over again because of injustice, but as long as we don't numb ourselves, they can open even wider with greater empathy every time they do. My teacher Robin Rose Bennett always said, "The only heart that can't be broken is the one that's open." And when we honor our ethical boundaries, we must also honor our personal boundaries. The Earth has poison ivy to guard areas of overuse, and we need ours too.

THE GREEN

When I began to integrate herbalism into my life's work, I was invited to join the Nettle Patch, a community of budding and professional herbalists in the New York area. Nettles are another fierce boundary keeper, taking up space, springing from fertile soil like green flames that sting, and causing numb spaces to vibrate when touched. The sting is formic acid, the same fiery sting of red ants when we get in the way of their path and their work; in the same way, nettles have helped me steer clear of those who want to dampen and obstruct mine. I've come to love the buzz of their sting, which can stimulate places where we've been asleep, awakening sensation. And that's what we need to do to spark change: become aware.

My partner at the time joked that the Nettle Patch was my gang, and though we laughed about it, herbalism is subversive in its own way. An herbalist skilled in wildcrafting has self-reliance and awareness of their environment that most have forgotten. The study of plant medicine gave me another level of confidence, that, like fighting, has given me sovereignty over my body and reconnected me to animal instinct and the ability to feel confident and at home in the wild.

The belief that we are powerless is a myth that keeps many of the wrong people in power. His Holiness the Dalai Lama says, "If you think you are too small to make a difference, try sleeping with a mosquito." We can all, in our own ways, tap into the Green and be voices for the plants and land that we depend upon to breathe, eat, heal, and thrive. And beyond that, we can be positive remediating forces. We can harvest wild medicine and, at the same time, help the plants flourish. Grassroots movements begin from the ground up and weeds can teach us a lot about resistance. They cluster together, grow everywhere, adapt to change, and never give up.

So with all of this in mind, the next time you sit down to eat, I invite you to sing this sweet little song of gratitude that I learned from my friends in the Nettle Patch: "Blessings on the blossoms, blessings on the fruits, blessings on the leaves and stems, blessings on the roots."

The Earth would die
If the sun stopped kissing her.

HĀFEZ-E ŠĪRĀZĪ, *THE GIFT*

PART THREE

Solar Energy

THE SUN PROVIDES THE INITIAL ENERGY THAT STARTS THE CYCLE OF photosynthesis, the method by which plants turn light into food. Without the sun, plants would not be able to live, and with no plants, there would be no oxygen for us to breathe.

HAWTHORN
Crataegus spp.

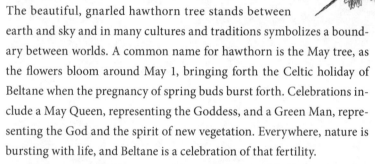

Family: Rosaceae

The beautiful, gnarled hawthorn tree stands between earth and sky and in many cultures and traditions symbolizes a boundary between worlds. A common name for hawthorn is the May tree, as the flowers bloom around May 1, bringing forth the Celtic holiday of Beltane when the pregnancy of spring buds burst forth. Celebrations include a May Queen, representing the Goddess, and a Green Man, representing the God and the spirit of new vegetation. Everywhere, nature is bursting with life, and Beltane is a celebration of that fertility.

There are over 280 species of dense, deciduous hawthorn trees that thrive in temperate climates. The Latin for the genus, *Crataegus*, is derived from Greek, *kratos* meaning "strength" and *akis* "sharp," in reference to the tree's fierce thorns. The serrated leaves, white flowers, and bloodred fruit are used in tinctures and teas to strengthen the physical, emotional, and spiritual heart. This powerful medicine can normalize both high and low blood pressure, promote circulation, offer courage, heighten pleasure, and ignite passion. Hawthorn is a mystical tree that is especially sacred to the faeries; some say that hawthorns mark a gateway to the faeries' world. Like the spell of love, this tree is sometimes misunderstood and viewed warily, because of her intimidating thorns and enchantments.

LOVER AND A FIGHTER

O see ye not yon narrow road,
So thick beset with thorns and briars?
That is the path of righteousness,
Tho' after it but few enquires.

"THOMAS THE RHYMER,"
SCOTTISH BALLAD

L ove can appear unexpectedly and seduce us out of our comfort zones and into realms where we may choose to be held captive or struggle to break free. In a dance of surrender and self-control, intimacy with a partner can be a space of liberating depth or a caged claustrophobia. When I moved to New York City in 1995, I never thought I'd stay long. But love caught me before I could escape the city and return back into the wilderness.

One moment of being with Ernesto—a quintessential earthy Taurus—was like a month spent drinking a daily decoction of burdock root, and over the course of our relationship, I dropped into my body in a way I never had before. I gave in to a feeling that went far beyond attraction; it was recognition of a compatible soul. We lived on the same frequency and found it was easy to lose ourselves in each other, and by that point in my life I knew that I wouldn't fully find myself unless I was willing to risk falling, and getting lost.

We met at XL, the Beastie Boys' former clothing store on Avenue A, where both of us, struggling artists, had part-time jobs. It was early 1996 and I was assisting photographers, going on shoots, and painting the occasional mural, waiting for my imagined big break to arrive. I often sat outside of XL or in Tompkins Square Park drawing in my sketchbook and found work when nosy people looked over my shoulder. A talented DJ, graffiti artist, and aspiring hip-hop producer, Ernesto had just finished art school in Chicago. We were filled with creative fire and I loved the city then. Everything felt full of possibility. Every day there was someone exciting to meet, art to see, things to create, and streets to explore.

After work, Ernesto and I wandered through the East and West Village. We roamed up to the gallery district in Chelsea and down over the Brooklyn and Williamsburg Bridges. We spoke about everything—our families, past relationships, our dreams, aspirations, and fears. An original member of The Hash Crew and OT and TME graffiti crews, Ernesto tagged telephone poles, walls, and signs as we walked, and in some places, I can still see his signature on the streets where we fell in love.

Our love was a slow and steady burn. We wanted to see each other again, and then again, and then again. We had both just ended relationships so we were hesitant, but our friendship smoldered and quickly caught fire. As we struggled separately to save money and find our own way, we stayed with friends and crashed on couches until I found a place in the East Village where, without much formal conversation, he moved in. We slept in a loft bed, our friend Omar slept underneath us on the floor, we had a roommate in the next room and a steady stream of friends stopping by. It was fun, but crowded. We painted occasional murals, and I walked eleven blocks down to Spoon in the evenings where he spun records and I sat at the corner of the bar by his turntables. We kissed as records played, and when he finished, we strolled by the water until the sun rose.

Ernesto had a way of bringing all of my fear, insecurity, joy, pleasure, and loneliness to the surface when we made love. When our bodies were tangled together as one, I entered into spaces of transcendence that opened the gates to my creative energy and made me feel free and painfully attached all at once.

His healing hands touched all the right places. I said "I love you" first, and I meant it like I'd never meant it before. I couldn't hold the words back; they emerged from my body and flew out of my mouth before I could stop them, and in response, he physically crumpled, afraid of what returning the sentiment might mean. He didn't say the words for weeks and I was terrified. But when he did return the words and open up to my love, the feeling was boundless and hypnotic.

With a turntable and mixer under our bed, next to Omar's cot, we lived amid a soundtrack of Roy Ayers, the Ohio Players, the Jones Girls, and Stevie Wonder and listened closely for sounds and rhythms that moved us as we sampled records and made beats. We passed drawings back and forth to create strange, imagined worlds and cautiously began to envision and create a combined future. At first, it bothered him that I was white. He never pictured himself being with a white woman, but as we fell deeper and deeper in love and he saw that his family approved of me, his worry seemed to fade. Everything seemed to be blending beautifully.

When Ernesto and I could no longer piece it together in the East Village, we moved to the Bronx where his family helped us find a decent deal on an apartment for just us two. My life was still in downtown Manhattan and I spent most of my days working part time for *Satya*, an animal and Earth rights magazine on Bleecker Street, volunteering for Friends of Animals, and earning a steady paycheck as a personal trainer at Crunch. We left each other love notes as we came and went from our apartment, and then, one day, he said he wanted to spend the rest of his life with me. I was ecstatic. I had found my prince.

GETTING LOST

In Scottish and Irish Gaelic folklore, hawthorn trees mark the entrance to the Otherworld and are associated with the lore of the changeling, a faery child swapped for a human child who is spirited away to the land of the faeries.[1] Gifted musicians might also be abducted to satisfy the faeries' insatiable desire for music and dance. And while those kidnapped musicians might feel as if only a night had passed as they entertained the faeries, they would emerge from the mound, the portal at the base of the tree, to find that years had passed. Men, women, and children were warned not to sleep under the hawthorn around Beltane, at dusk or dawn or any time the veils are thin, because of the heightened risk of being kidnapped or seduced into the alluring underground faery realm where time slipped away. When (or if) they returned, they were forever changed.

At the beginning of the thirteenth-century Scottish ballad "Thomas the Rhymer," Thomas Earlston is beneath a hawthorn tree in the Eildon Hills and playing exquisite music. His melodies attract the beautiful queen of Elfland, who rides up on her white horse, and he is immediately enraptured by her beauty. In this ballad, the presence overwhelms Thomas and he believes she must be the Virgin Mary, saying:

> "All hail, thou mighty Queen of Heaven!
> For thy peer on earth I never did see."
> "O no, O no, Thomas," she said,
> "That name does not belang to me;
> I am but the queen of fair Elfland,
> That am hither come to visit thee."[2]

The faery queen knows that Thomas desires her, so she tempts him with a challenge: she dares him to kiss her, knowing that if he does, he will be under her spell and bound to serve her in the Otherworld. Overcome by awe, he agrees, and the faery queen leads Thomas into the darkness of the hill and down below the roots of the hawthorn tree. As they venture through this underworld, they ride on the back of her horse that is "swifter than the wind." The queen explains that the narrow path, beset with thorns and briars, is the path of righteousness; the broad, smooth road leads to hell; but the third "bonny road" will take them to "fair Elfland," their Otherworld destination. Thomas dwells with her for what seems like days, but he emerges to find that seven years have passed on Earth. A stone, surrounded by gnarled old hawthorns, now marks that spot of the Eildon tree. Many still believe that the hills are hollow, and that faeryland lies inside.

Scotland is dotted with hills and mounds that are said to be entrances to these invisible lands. Stories claim that if faint sounds of music can be heard, and that if hawthorn is growing there, the area is most definitely imbued with magic. Like her sister wild rose, the hawthorn tree is an assertive boundary keeper whose two-inch thorns are easy to navigate when approached mindfully, but if approached blindly, they are unforgiving. A single tree is a presence that can live to be seven hundred years old with branches that burst forth with flowers at the time of birth on Beltane and ripen with red berries at the time of death on Samhainn. The Hethel Old Thorn, managed by the Norfolk Wildlife Trust, is the smallest wildlife trust nature reserve in Britain, consisting of one ancient and sacred seven-hundred-year-old hawthorn tree that continues to blossom and grow.

I imagine generations of birds and other wildlife living in relationship with the Hethel Old Thorn. The nectar-rich flowers attract bees, hummingbirds, and other pollinators; deer and rabbits graze on the leaves and twigs, and the rich berries that cling to branches through winter provide important food for black bears and countless birds. While most hawthorn leaves are serrated and deeply lobed, their shapes can vary wildly, even within one species. I've seen many small bird's nests in the heart of lush, dark-green leaves and tangles of menacing, thorny branches, perfect refuge from hawks and would-be predators. Often planted to mark and protect holy wells in Scotland and Ireland, many hawthorn trees are still decorated, petitioned with offerings, and venerated by those who honor the old ways.

Regular use of the sweet and mildly astringent infusion or tincture of the flowers, berries, and leaves can strengthen the heart to make it a stronger muscle and more efficient pump. In herbalism, hawthorn is known as a heart and circulatory trophorestorative, an herb that has long-term benefits to a particular system within the body when taken over a period of time. As someone who tends to have cold extremities in winter, I've learned to begin drinking hawthorn infusion in October to keep my circulation strong. Sometimes I steep the leaves, flowers, and berries in a brew with warming cinnamon chips, grounding burdock root, and my staple, stinging nettles. I always add a thorn to my tinctures—an essential aspect of the plant's expression—as long as the tree and fae folk give me permission to take one, of course. Omitting a thorn makes for a defanged and less complete medicine.

It's tempting to isolate a plant into constituents—high levels of flavonoids, oligomeric proanthocyanidins in the berry, vitamins, minerals—to determine the "active ingredients," but when we dissect a plant into "useful parts," we are getting fragmented medicine, not to mention disrespecting the life of the living being. For most herbs, it is the combination of constituents, the synergy that evolved through all of their adaptations, that make plants potential healers. As herbalist David Winston writes, "The active ingredient in hawthorn is hawthorn."[3] It's the unique blend of elements that makes hawthorn as potent as she is.

I love the scent of hawthorn flowers; they smell sweet to me. But to others, they smell of rotting flesh. Some others say the flowers smell like sex. The hawthorn is and was a symbol of sexual freedom and a symbol of fertility during Celtic Beltane celebrations. And since hawthorn promotes circulation, which increases bodily sensation, hawthorn has become famous as an aphrodisiac. But later, as Christianity took hold in Rome, Greece, and Britain, the hawthorn became a symbol of enforced chastity. What had been a symbol of life and sexual potency, and a festival that celebrated those traits, became instead a time of purification. The May Queen became white, pure, and untouchable. Hawthorn's merry month of May transformed from a wild celebration of the fertile to a sterile period of restraint. In puritan and Christian mindsets, it was considered incredibly unlucky to marry during the hawthorn month—an idea that doesn't coincide with the medicine and gifts of this abundant and protective plant at all.

Thankfully, the way we think about this medicinal tree has outgrown the confines of puritanical religion, but guilt and amorphous ideas of sin still weave themselves into all kinds of embodied pleasure. For too many years, my pleasure was invaded by hypervigilance and rules: don't combine this food with that one, exercise self-control, beware of your animal passions. Even when we listen to our inner voice and take time for self-care, we may feel guilty when we unplug to soak in a luxurious bath, tune into our deepest desires, and truly fall in love with ourselves.

CHANGELINGS

I was afraid that in order to commit and give myself fully to a partner and to the totality of love, I might also have to give up my freedom. I wanted to drown in emotional bliss and yet also desired to be free. I navigated the constant ebb and flow between the steady burn of love for Ernesto in my heart, the instinctual need for periods of solitude, and the hunger for limitless growth. The love I shared with Ernesto opened doors and tore down barriers inside me, exposing the illusion that a particular effort might inadvertently lead to a dead end—no effort can ever be wasted. Yet the world that I felt I had access to beyond our relationship began to feel small. I'd chosen to settle into a relationship that meant setting down roots in the Bronx, keeping predictable hours, being accountable to Ernesto. I wrote, *I'm addicted to being with him, it's becoming an answer to sadness, something is wrong.* I wanted to keep wandering together but he was ready to build a home, and as I became more restless, Ernesto became more rooted. When I was absorbed in our spell, I forgot about the kind of life I wanted to live. Whatever it was, I wanted it to involve him.

ERNESTO'S MOTHER ENDURED A LONG STRUGGLE WITH LUNG CANCER THAT eventually spread throughout her body. She died two years into our relationship and I felt helpless. His grieving prompted in him a craving for even more stability, and though I felt restless inside, I wanted to be his rock. I wanted to unzip my skin and let him crawl in. I wanted to make his pain go away but I could never seem to get close enough to touch or heal his tender wounds. I missed him even when he was pressed against my body.

Ernesto doubled down on his dream of being a hip-hop producer and opened a recording studio, using two of the bedrooms in our four-bedroom apartment. While that had always been the plan, the apartment became his whole world, making me feel more stuck than ever. Like the faery mound, people were drawn into our home through the alluring pull of music, and it didn't take long before musicians were walking in and out of our apartment the way they had when I was growing up. The vibration of bass and the beat of drums against my bedroom walls were familiar, but it was hard not having privacy. Ernesto was content, nestling into his chosen path, while I was still grasping for mine. In our enchanted lair, I wanted to be with him forever. But when I went out into the world, I wanted to be free.

IT TOOK ABOUT AN HOUR TO GET FROM OUR APARTMENT ON BEDFORD PARK Boulevard to Crunch in the West Village. My client schedule began at 6 a.m. so I had to get up by 4 a.m. and be on the train by no later than 4:30. I had no formal fight training at that point, but on those early-morning and late-night subway rides, I'd scan the platform and subway car and if I felt any unease coming from someone, I'd think through how I was going to take them down. I discreetly scanned potential threats for weaknesses and if none were apparent, I'd imagine going for their eyes or breaking my glass bottle to use as a weapon. Something inside me was vicious and knew I would stop at nothing to defend myself, but this ferocity was a part of me I had yet to explore.

I would emerge from the West Fourth Street station as the sun rose and watch people stumble home from partying. My routine represented a weird juxtaposition: I passed crowds whose habits were a glimpse into my recent past. Since I lived far away and trained people at odd hours, I usually stayed in the city all day. I ran along the water to Battery Park and back again, wrote and drew in my sketchbook, and hung out with Angela, a trainer from Greece who became my best friend. And Ernesto, always the romantic, came to pick me up and take me out to dinner whenever he could.

On Valentine's Day we usually dressed up and met for a special date in the city. We also made sure our apartment was clear later that night so we could go home and make love with no one else around. It was a day I always looked forward to. But one year, when I brought my outfit downtown and bought his gift in anticipation, I called him to find out where we were meeting and was surprised when he said he couldn't make it. Something had come up and I needed to meet him at home. He assured me we would still do something. I was so disappointed—I was tired of being together at home.

When I got to the door of the apartment, I heard the faint sounds of music still being played; he made me wait. When he finally came out, he blind-folded me, led me in, and laid me down onto what felt like silk. When he took off the blindfold, I saw that he'd covered the entire apartment in rose petals. The *entire* apartment. He had spent the day turning our home into another world.

THAT SUMMER, CRUNCH OFFERED A WEEKEND BOXING CERTIFICATION FOR trainers. The idea that you can learn to teach boxing, or even learn to hold focus mitts, in a weekend is total bullshit, but the prospect of boxing excited me. When we students were brought through drills and taught how to throw a real punch, my body felt a strange and deep sense of relief. I'd always imag-ined fighting but had never had a fight in my life. The coaches, two profes-sional fighters, told me to take it easy on my partner, and I was frustrated to have to hold back. I knew I was just scratching the surface of my power and suddenly knew that I needed to explore more. I had been looking for a skill with the same intensity as rowing and I knew in my bones that boxing was it. When the weekend course was through, I talked one of the fighters into train-ing me and began in earnest the next day. I slipped right back into the disci-plined training I'd learned in rowing and began boxing with the same level of dedication.

After a day of training, I was soaked in the bittersweet sweat of anger and fear that I hadn't even known was lodged in my body. It was as though I had just swum, fully clothed, in the ocean and every time I peeled those sopping clothes off and carried my heavy, waterlogged bag home on the subway, I felt a little more free. While Ernesto initially supported my training, he began to resent my passion for boxing. But something in me was being wrung out and revealed, and I couldn't stop.

After I'd been training for six months or so, a fighter and his coach came in for sparring—a rare event at my training location. Though we had a ring, it was more of a prop used for boxing fitness, not fighting. The fighter's sparring partner didn't show up, and since I was hitting the bags nearby, they asked if I wanted to get in the ring and throw punches at him. They assured me it would be a one-way fight; he just needed to work on his defense. I was nervous but agreed to step in. When I entered the ring, I transformed. I started to attack, pressure, and pummel him. Not necessarily well, but I think my intensity surprised all of us. I clearly needed to unearth my aggression. When the visiting coach and fighter told me I should consider training to fight, I knew they were right.

But Ernesto hated the idea. He worried about me getting hurt and said it would have been different if he'd met me as a boxer, but he'd met me as an artist, aspiring photographer, and environmentalist. This pivot didn't make sense to him, it wasn't the way he saw me. Like everyone else, he saw me as calm, peaceful, and sweet. "You don't even like watching fights!" he insisted. It was true, but doing the fighting felt different.

There were times he woke up in the morning, looked at me, smiled, and said, "Let's get married today! Let's just go down to city hall and do it!" And at first I loved his big-hearted impulsive nature, but the idea of marriage began to scare me. I knew he wanted a family, and though I imagined having kids with Ernesto, and the emotional pull got to me at times, I didn't really have the biological craving that women are expected to have. It bothered him that I was awkward and unenthused around babies. Though he wasn't ready yet, he knew his future included a family and wanted me to coo over the little ones in our orbit, and I just didn't.

THE MORE I TRAINED, THE MORE RESTLESS I BECAME, AND I REALIZED THAT as intimate as our relationship was, there were parts of me that couldn't let Ernesto all of the way in. I had walls to break down and I felt boxing would help me do that. I also knew I might uncover parts of myself that Ernesto didn't like or want to see. I was being pulled toward becoming a fighter, something that seemed to make absolutely no sense, and he wanted to build a home. I knew that in order to be truly content with him, I needed to be content with myself, and I wasn't there yet. I wasn't planted like he was and I didn't feel whole. While I was in love with him and couldn't bear the thought of losing him, I was even more afraid of ignoring my inner voice and living in a space where I couldn't grow. I knew it wouldn't be right for me to stay feeling this way, and I didn't know what else to do at that point other than leave him.

I'll never forget the day we walked from our apartment on Bedford Park Boulevard and hiked into the nearby forest where I knew I would say goodbye—even if Ernesto didn't see it coming. We brought my boombox and one of my favorite Stevie Wonder albums, *Fulfillingness' First Finale*, played in the background. I couldn't listen to that album for years afterward. The lyrics to "It Ain't No Use" tore into that moment, and still tear into me: "We're not each other's everything."

As we spoke, I felt like I was ripping myself from the very life force that was keeping my heart pumping. We cried from spaces so deep it seemed we would choke on our tears. I felt pulverized. But the restlessness inside me was a beast that rose up stronger and more powerfully than my attachment to Ernesto. I needed to leave the soothing comfort of his arms to fight my inner demons. If I didn't, I was afraid I might lose myself in the trance of love and longing, or that I would wake up one day and be married with kids, and that terrified me. Though I had found my prince, I never knew what happened beyond the "happily ever after" part in fairy tales and was afraid that, like Sleeping Beauty, my story might end there. So I said goodbye to our collective future. It was a decision I would battle with for years to come.

As we emerged from the forest, our spell broken, I looked out at a world that was suddenly *mine* and not *ours*. Entirely transformed by our love, I sensed that Ernesto's shadow and the overwhelming pain of our separation might haunt me for the rest of my life.

I LEARNED YEARS LATER THAT I COULD ENGAGE THE PROTECTIVE ENERGY of hawthorn when I felt naked, and nest in her thorny center. Hawthorn's potent medicine encourages us to open our hearts and fall in love wholly while helping us assert the space needed to stand our ground and fall in love with ourselves too. Whether physical, emotional, or spiritual, hawthorn's medicine strengthens our heart so that energy is flowing out from our center, increasing our ability to love from our own core. When we listen to the true longings of our hearts and allow them to guide us through our shadowlands, city streets, or narrow roads thick with thorns and briars, we are rarely led astray.

DANDELION
Taraxacum officinale

Family: Asteraceae

Dandelion is a fighter whose fiery medicine breaks through cracks in pavement and relentlessly returns to carpet-like lawns despite being sprayed. The plant's taproot has work to do; it brings minerals from the subsoil to grasses and other plants that can't reach deeply. In our bodies, dandelion roots and flowers ignite digestion and activate the power in our solar plexus, while the jagged, bitter leaves—dent de lion, French for "tooth of the lion"—flush, clean, and clear the kidneys, the organ where we store life force energy. Beyond the bitterness in the leaves, you can taste the salty, mineral-rich properties responsible for cleansing and clearing our internal waterways. As a liver cleanser, dandelion root helps move anger and frustration out of the body while feeding and supporting beneficial bacteria. And for those who deplete themselves trying to people please, dandelion is an excellent ally.

GUT INSTINCT

It is not part of a true culture to tame tigers, any more than it
is to make sheep ferocious.

After Ernesto and I parted ways, I had to ease my family into the idea
that I would pursue fighting. They thought I had lost my mind. My
grandfather, the physician, told me about the brain damage boxers
would inevitably sustain and suggested I see a gruesome exhibition at Harvard
Medical School, his alma mater, where pictures of pummeled brains were on
display. My mom, as usual, was (and is) a saint. She has always wanted me to
do whatever makes me happy. And even though boxing scared the shit out of
her, she saw the ways I blossomed and healed through training and pushing
beyond the perceived limitations of my body. She supported me, and even came
to fights—although she flinched more than I did. And she had my back when
I decided to turn pro.

After a couple of short-term living situations, I found an ideal space I
could afford. A friend occupied a crumbling sixth-floor, rent-controlled, one-
bedroom walk-up in the East Village and I told her to please, please let me
know if she ever decided to leave. Sure enough, about a year after I begged her,
she decided to move in with her boyfriend and the apartment became mine.
Sometimes after a day of training, I had to practically crawl up all of those

stairs in exhaustion. But fighting was a compulsion, and now my life revolved around boxing. I was in love and completely devoted.

LIKE HERBALISM ONE DAY WOULD, BOXING NOW FELT LIKE A DEEP REMEMBER-ing, something I already knew that only needed to be awakened in me. Martial arts, like yoga, were originally a holistic practice of self-development. And though it's generally perceived as men's domain, women are natural warriors and have been for eons. Scáthach, whose name in Gaelic means "shadowy," was a legendary martial arts teacher in 500 BCE whose fortress, Dún Scáith (Castle of Shadows), stood on Scotland's Isle of Skye.[1] Scáthach only trained warriors skilled enough to brave the fierce boundaries of her fortress. One of her students was Cú-chulainn, the earliest Gaelic hero warrior captured in written stories. Scáthach was also a formidable magician with the gift of proph-ecy, and in some accounts, became the Celtic goddess of the dead, ensuring the passage of those killed in battle to Tír na nÓg, the Land of Eternal Youth in Celtic mythology.

Women were not only solitary warriors but shaped fighting styles such as Wing Chun, a system created by the Buddhist nun Ng Mui, a master of Shao-lin Kung Fu.[2] The Dahomey Amazons, or Mino, which means "our mothers," were a Fon all-female military regiment of the Kingdom of Dahomey in the present-day Republic of Benin, which lasted until the end of the nineteenth century.[3] Lozen was a famous warrior and prophet of the Chihenne Chirica-hua Apache. According to legend, she was able to use her spiritual powers in battle and called on the favor of the gods to learn the location and movement of their enemies. She fought alongside Geronimo in the last campaign of the Apache Wars.[4]

And finally, another namesake, Nessa. Nessa was a princess in Irish my-thology who was raised by twelve foster fathers.[5] She was originally called Assa, meaning "gentle," because of her sweet nature until Cathbad, a Druid and leader of a band of landless warriors, attacked her foster fathers' house, killing them all. Gentle Assa sought vengeance and formed her own band of warriors to hunt him down. Her fighting skills and legendary band of warriors earned her the name Ní-assa, "not gentle."

But I didn't know about those women then, so I learned from men by going to fights, watching live sparring, and studying legendary battles on bulky VHS tapes. I studied the technique of Muhammad Ali, Pee Wee Rucker, Félix Trinidad, James Toney, and other fighters I'd see in the gym, like Shaun George. Muhammad Ali became my idol. He was not just a boxer but an activist and man of conviction. I read every book about him I could find. And though I didn't have female boxers to look up to at the time, I read about different kinds of fighters—women like Assata Shakur, Elaine Brown, Jane Goodall, Angela Davis, and Gloria Steinem. Their stories and struggles kept me going when I felt I had nothing left in the ring.

After intense and sometimes demoralizing tours of boxing gyms and potential coaches in New York City whose tests of my ability and heart resulted in black eyes, bloody noses, and bruised ribs, Gleason's Gym became my home away from home. I remember the first day I walked up the stairs and into the famous, grimy Brooklyn boxing gym. There was no music, just the sound of boxers hitting heavy bags, speed ropes hitting the floor, trainers yelling at their fighters, and the intense, overwhelming smell of sweat. That day, I was the only woman there to train among serious fighters and I was intimidated. I'd been training in gyms for years, mostly around men, so I was used to that, but the atmosphere here felt different. This was Gleason's. And I came because I was ready to fight, not just box for fun anymore.

Women's boxing was in its infancy then. There were few female fighters and not much of a career to be had for most, but that didn't matter to me. My compulsion came from someplace else. My body and I were still catching up on lost time together and I wanted to know the part of myself that was predator instead of prey. After years of toning down, I relished exploring the "not gentle" Vanessa.

In *Waking the Tiger*, trauma therapist Dr. Peter Levine talks about moving as an essential way to release embodied trauma.[6] By moving, we're following our impulse to literally get trauma out of our system. When threatened or injured, all animals draw from instinctive reactions to protect and defend themselves, such as freezing, stiffening, bracing, fleeing, collapsing, or fighting. But when those responses are interrupted or overwhelmed, we experience trauma. When I think about the way I dealt with my abuse when I was young—freezing, leaving my body, and playing dead—it makes sense that as I finally faced that trauma, I had to move in such an intense and extreme way to get it out. Boxing gave me a sense of purpose like nothing else at the time. I felt there was no way anyone could take me down with all I'd been through.

IN MY FIRST DAY TRAINING AT GLEASON'S, I REMEMBER WALKING UP THE stairs to the ring and climbing between the ropes with what seemed like all eyes on me. After warming up on the speed rope, my coach at the time, a friend and professional fighter, told me to climb up into the ring and shadowbox. I was onstage and I felt like a fool. The asthmatic girl who had never had a fight in her life and whose defense mechanism under threat was to freeze was fighting an invisible opponent in one of the most famous boxing gyms in the world. The first few rounds were exhausting. I was trying way too hard. But after a while, people lost interest in me and I forgot that I was performing. I burned off my nervous energy and entered my own world—what athletes call "the zone." I was in a groove, in sync with my body, though maybe, I thought, I'd lost my mind for pursuing boxing at all. But in sparring or in a fight, there is no time to second-guess your decision or to dwell on a bad one. This was a great teaching for me as an overthinker and overanalyzer. I learned to trust my instinct and act. There were countless times in the past when my instinct told me to act, speak up, speak out, and I didn't, or couldn't. In those moments my heart beat fast and my body became hot. Words wanted out. It was clear. But I swallowed them, I toned down, and they burned me.

As I trained, poetry and art poured out of me like they had after the car accident. The angst of my breakup with Ernesto and the intense boxing training dislodged tears, words, and images wanting out. I carried my sketchbook everywhere, needing to get them on paper fast so they could make their escape. When I returned home, I painted my cabinets and furniture, covering my apartment with eyes peering out from red, orange, and yellow flames. My apartment was on fire. Clearly, I was rekindling my inner flames—glaringly obvious symbolism that didn't occur to me at the time. Collages of eyes peered out from my red cabinet doors. One of my boyfriends, a professional fighter who stayed in my place to take care of my sweet dog, a husky-and-Doberman rescue named

Kobe, called me and said, "Um, your dog is doing great, but the eyes around your apartment are giving me the creeps." The place was my canvas in more ways than one; drawing on the walls felt like freedom.

After a night of creative release, I walked from my apartment on Seventh Street and Avenue B to the F train on First Avenue, ready for another day of training at Gleason's in DUMBO (Down Under the Manhattan Bridge Overpass, now an upscale, gentrified neighborhood, was a sketchy neighborhood with one bodega and affordable art studios then). I walked to the subway visualizing training in vivid detail—throwing and landing a perfect hook, precise body shots, and imposing my will in sparring. When men catcalled me on the street, I could imagine smashing their faces in. When memories of sexual abuse, rape, or feelings of frustration came through, I hammered the heavy bags. "From the ground up," my trainer always said. "All your power comes from the ground up."

Like weeds that burst through the cracks in the sidewalk, it's the roots, the life force energy of Earth, that push the weed through the pavement to break free. As I grounded myself and learned to tap into the energy of a weed, I stopped walking around in heels. Why I wanted to cram my feet into ridiculous, painful shapes to please men (many of whom often enraged me) is a mystery. Wearing high heels can also cause musculoskeletal pain, especially in the muscles running up the back along the spine, and can prevent us from truly standing tall.[7] But social conditioning is strong, and for much of my life, so was my contradictory insecurity. I wanted to look good according to society's standards and yet I found I also wanted to punch those oppressive standards firmly in their tender gut. "Kill the body and the head will fall," they say in boxing. And as the spark that boxing lit in me grew to a bright flame, I wanted to topple the system of patriarchy and the incessant messaging that told women what to look like and how to behave. But I had yet to escape the ways in which I was still a product of those cultural forces. My friends and I would rage about men who catcalled us on the streets one day, and feel ugly the next if we didn't get any attention.

A woman's power is in her beauty, we're told, and we all know that to be an attractive woman, we must contort our bodies into Barbie-doll shapes through diets, corsets, Spanx, and all sorts of bizarre contraptions—even surgery. But don't be too sexy; if you lure him in with a skirt too short, a man can hardly be blamed for what he does to you. Yet if you want to attract and keep a man, you must find some way to be alluring without crossing into dangerous territory. When I started boxing I knew that any day could be the day I got my face reconfigured. While I didn't want that to happen, I was willing to take the risk. Many of the men who were my peers at the gym insisted I was too pretty to box, but their vague definition of this superficial state didn't equate to feeling strong or good about myself, and often even compliments from that outside gaze brought me pain. I was cultivating a different kind of beauty. Boxing offered a space of raw authenticity in a superficial world.

TOOTH OF THE LION

"You're too intense" are words I've heard a lot. Balance is something I've struggled with; when I find something that I know I must pursue, I go all in. When that kind of knowing crescendos in me, it's like a buzz, and then a spark. If I pay attention, give that recognition space, and feed it with my thoughts, the knowing becomes a roaring flame. If I push that knowing or instinct down to follow what are often arbitrary rules that define balance or moderation, I betray myself and sacrifice inner space that is meant to be filled with wildflowers to something tamer and more manicured instead. When I listen to my hunger, the wildflowers of my passion and focus can break through pavement to guide me into light.

In healing traditions like Ayurveda, our center—our digestive system and inner fire—is where our seat of confidence lies.[8] This center, our solar plexus, is perceived as being yellow, illuminated like the sun and dandelion's beautiful flowers. Strong and relentless, dandelion always comes back to bloom every year, unphased by her unpopularity or contemporary categorization as a weed, to bring light to lawns, sidewalks, and city streets. These so-called weeds appear on lawns no matter how much toxic poison people douse them with. In fact, dandelions take up toxins and appear to cleanse the very toxins they are poisoned with.

I found a book called *Healthy Healing* in my twenties, a book of natural remedies that I always referred to when I felt out of balance.[9] It was because of that book that I started to use roasted dandelion root tea as part of my morning ritual. Back then, I bought my dandelion root at an expensive health food store, which now feels absurd considering this wild healer grows everywhere. These plants are available to us for free, and for a reason. Though I considered myself an activist, this is something that hadn't registered yet.

LEO TRAINED SOME OF THE MOST SKILLED PROFESSIONAL FIGHTERS IN THE gym. I loved watching his fighter Shaun George spar. Shaun had a beautiful style and seemingly effortless grace, while still being completely dominant in the ring. I wanted to be like that. I wanted Leo to be my coach. I was fighting as an amateur at the time and I was beginning to question my current trainer, who was overscheduled and always in a rush to leave. One day, while I was sparring with a guy and in the zone, I mimicked some of what I'd seen Shaun do. I'd rehearsed it in my head, and while in action I was not quite as graceful, I noticed Leo watching me, smiling. Meanwhile, my coach was upset. I wasn't following his instruction. *But I'm doing better!* I thought. I was confused and my pride was dampened. When my coach left, Leo called me over to say he was impressed, and reminded me to always "move in the path of least resistance."

I sought him out before I left that day and he advised me to get *The Art of War* by Sun Tzu: "Study it, and apply the principles to boxing." I did and every day after training we spoke about it. When I finished *The Art of War*, he gave me more books to read. Then he began interjecting while I was training with my coach, and the little nuggets of wisdom he imparted changed my approach and multiplied my power. He applied physics to boxing and taught me how to generate power based on those principles. While my trainer had gotten me started on this path, I needed to take my skills to another level.

When I approached Leo, at first he said he wasn't interested. He told me, "There is no future in women's boxing. I would be putting my reputation on the line by training you. There's nothing in it for me." Many of the trainers took on fighters as prospects, assuming the fighters would do well and not only build their trainers' reputations but make them a lot of money too. Neither could be said of me. I was crushed. I figured the interest he had been showing meant he would take me on, but I could see now that wasn't the case.

Still, I continued to show up and train even harder to prove myself and my worthiness.

Leo continued to watch me and was impressed with my level of dedication. Eventually, he agreed to train me on a trial basis. He saw an opportunity to change the face of women's professional boxing with a woman who had true skill, but I had to be willing to deconstruct and revise my style according to the way I was born to fight, not the way I'd been taught thus far. He watched me closely. What was my natural inclination in a fight? My previous trainer was a boxer like Muhammad Ali. He bounced and moved and often got frustrated with me when I couldn't perfect that style. But it didn't come naturally. As a woman, I have a low center of gravity, and I doubt anyone would describe me as being bouncy. More like a lion quietly stalking their prey and moving them into the corner, then quickly attacking. I was a "puncher," Leo said. Much more suited to the pros than amateur fighting. In each of us, there is a natural framework for fighting; it's something we were all born to be able to do. So Leo watched me shadowbox and hit the bags and took note when moments of authentic movement came through me. I wasn't good at running away, but I could stay in the clenches, pressure opponents, impose my will, and fight. I wasn't fast but I was quick. I used my low center of gravity and learned to generate power from the ground up. Leo was training me to be a counterpuncher, and I can't say I ever mastered the skill, but my body made sense of the instruction and I was able to blend my instinct with the techniques he taught me.

After six months of a grueling but exhilarating trial period, it was official. I signed a contract with Phoenix Sports Management and trained with Leo at Gleason's five days a week, sometimes six, for at least a few hours. I watched boxing when I got home, ran every day, learned to eat for optimal performance, and my body weight was public knowledge, which, believe or not, was healing. I was a lightweight. I fought between 132 and 139 pounds. Boxing became my life.

Leo was always at the gym waiting for me, dressed to the nines. There was an air of sophistication about him and he took no shit. He was a former Black Panther who worked with fighters like Davey Moore and Maurice Blocker, and whose age was a mystery. He was in incredibly good shape but had the wisdom of an old man. He was my Yoda. The fighters at Gleason's became family to me. We gave our blood, sweat, and tears to training every single day. No matter my skill level compared to theirs, or the fact that I was a woman in a man's world, everyone saw how dedicated I was, how hard I trained, how much heart I had in the ring. Even in this seemingly inhospitable environment, I was breaking through and blooming.

One of my favorite things about boxing gyms like Gleason's is that beginners mix with world champions and professionals. When boxers were preparing for fights at Madison Square Garden they came in for sparring. And there were a number of world champions who trained alongside me each day. We all hit the heavy bags and speed bags, sparred and shadowboxed on the same three-minute bell, and rested during the same one-minute period. That ebb and flow of energy became a living, breathing organism all its own, and it was impossible not to get caught up in the intensity. I felt like an urban warrior with a secret mission. My paying job transformed from personal trainer to boxing coach: I started teaching women how to fight.

ANGER AS A MOBILIZING AND HEALING FORCE

Anger can be an essential animating force of life and when we push it away, our resistance can harm us. And women especially are often taught to tamp it down. After I had been boxing for a few years, I found myself confessing to my mom, "You never modeled anger for me." She was shocked by that statement but claims that she took the loving criticism to heart. I worry that she still holds it all in, that there is something boiling inside her that has found no real release and contributes to her high blood pressure and anxiety.

I find myself thinking about my realization—about the moment I realized that I had grown up without witnessing the most influential woman in my life deal with anger—when I counsel the women I'm teaching. I talked to an herbal apprentice this spring who was dealing with anger, frustration, and anxiety around racial injustice. "I've been taught that when I speak up, I'm too aggressive, too bossy, or that I shut people down," she told me. She has been working to tone down her anger and aggression through yoga, but that practice isn't easing her anxiety. Another student shared that "I've been having so much rage and grief lately . . . bottled up. It's been coming out in hives every night since the last week of May. But ever since I started feeling the anger and letting it come out—and getting to a point where I can cry or yell—the hives get better. It's still there but the breakout is milder. It's very strange because my body has never reacted this way before. I describe my body as feeling like stagnant boiling water with lots of stuck water and fire. The energy and pressure comes out as hives unless I release some of that grief and anger."

Anger is energy that can help us to set boundaries and take steps to defend ourselves, but when we attempt to tone it down or bottle it up, it can become toxic. As we explored in the milk thistle chapter, in traditional Chinese medicine (TCM), the liver, whose job is to filter toxins, is the organ associated with anger.[10] Pent-up anger is believed to aggravate and cause imbalances in the liver and vice versa. In TCM, dandelion root is used to clear trapped heat (anger) while the leaf, a diuretic, is used to clear dampness (grief) stuck in the system. We use the terminology "pissed off" when someone upsets us, and it just so happens that le pissenlit (piss-in-bed) is the French nickname for dandelion. Like my students experienced, grief and rage—two emotions that are hard to grapple with—often go hand in hand.

THE INNER FIRE I RELEASED AND CULTIVATED THROUGH FIGHTING ALLOWED me to further embrace the depth and power of my sensitive nature. Sensitivity grants me heightened awareness and makes me attuned to my surroundings. Those of us disposed to a sensitive nature can feel when our opponent is close, just as we might feel, sense, or see energy emanating from a medicinal plant.

Boxing was not really about boxing; it was about pushing my boundaries and seeing how far out of my comfort zone I could go. How much could I handle? Could I trust myself enough to step into the ring with someone who wanted to hurt me? When my inner flames are licking my center and growing in intensity, I listen to what my body is truly hungry for.

I know that when my inner fire burns freely, I radiate outward like the sun. So instead of building walls to protect me, I can burn away what doesn't serve me and call upon the resilience of dandelion, who has the strength to burst through concrete and thrive almost anywhere, when I need to be reminded of my power. This plant that we love to hate is an incredible healer; a fiery plant can increase our own life force energy and resilience.

Joyce Carol Oates seemed to grasp the pull and obsession of boxing when she wrote, "I can entertain the proposition that life is a metaphor for boxing—for one of those bouts that go on and on, round following round, jabs, missed punches, clinches, nothing determined, again the bell and again and you and your opponent so evenly matched it's impossible to see your opponent *is* you."[11]

NUTMEG

Myristica fragrans

Family: Myristicaceae

Spices were once as valuable as gold, and one of the most coveted of them all was nutmeg. In seventeenth-century Europe, people were willing to spare no expense to acquire the sweet spice, and bitter war ensued between the English and Dutch, who fought to control the Spice Islands, then the world's only source of nutmeg. In the early 1600s the Dutch invaded and during fifteen years of horrifying colonization, reduced the Bandanese population from fourteen thousand to six hundred. Survivors were forced to work as slave laborers in the nutmeg groves, and in pathological attempts to maintain a total nutmeg monopoly, the Dutch spice cartel killed anyone caught growing the spice without proper authority, drenched imported seeds with lime to ensure their infertility, and burned their own nutmeg-filled warehouses to regulate price. But their total control of the market was kept at bay by the British, who controlled Run, a tiny island in Banda teeming with nutmeg trees. They went to battle for Run, but the British and Bandanese resisted, and after many deaths and exhaustion on both sides, they came to a compromise. Hungry for total control of nutmeg, the Dutch traded an island in the Far West that the British had already occupied illegally. While the Dutch thought they got away with a steal, that is how New Amsterdam—otherwise known as Manhattan—became New York.

CONSUMPTION

If a person eats nutmeg, it will open up his heart, make his judgment free from obstruction, and give him a good disposition.

HILDEGARD VON BINGEN

The attempt to satisfy greed is like drinking salty water when thirsty. When lost in greed we look outward rather than inward for satisfaction, yet we never find enough to fill the emptiness we wish to escape.

TENZIN WANGYAL RINPOCHE

I step across slippery layers of woven roots and dodge beneath tree branches as Ancel leads me through a narrow path in the botanical garden of Puerto Viejo. We turn left into a small alcove and come upon a large evergreen tree with shining leaves whose apricot-like fruits lay scattered on the ground. Ancel picks up a pale yellow fruit, peels back the flesh, and reveals the pit: a waxy coating of bright red mace that looks like an abstract painting, a vibrant treasure hidden inside the common-looking fruit. I'm awestruck. While all plants are a work of art, this is something exceptional. We pick up more fallen fruit and look inside; each weblike coating is different. *Why would nature hide this away*? I wonder. *What is the purpose of this artwork that no one can see?* Underneath that splash of crimson is the shell that encases nutmeg, the seed—and one of the world's most coveted spices.

I was drawn to Costa Rica by its incredible biodiversity, progressive environmental policies, and the intriguing fact that the country had never had an army. It seemed that they were doing something right. Plus, I envied my friends who ran yoga retreats in warm, beautiful places, and I knew to listen to that. I learned not to tamp out feelings of envy but to look at what those feelings were drawing my attention to—usually some sort of deficit in myself that really only my efforts could amend. I arrived in Puerto Viejo de Limón in 2008 after working with hip-hop icon KRS-One on the Stop the Violence Movement. Like the HOPE event, it was work that looked good on the outside. While I am still convinced I devoted my time and energy to a good cause, it depleted me. I needed to reset and refill. When I arrived in Puerto Viejo with no phone signal and without easy access to wi-fi, being untethered gave me valuable time and space to put life in perspective. I swam in the ocean, screamed underwater, gazed at new and beautiful plants, learned about the wildlife, and remembered what made me feel truly full. Being immersed in the jungle surrounded by lush greenery, where howler monkeys woke me in the morning with their crescendo of deep, ghostly howls, felt like home. I thought I might want to move there so I got to know people in the community, planted seeds of connection, nurtured friendships, and arranged to go back to Costa Rica to study plant medicine and have a place to live via work-trade. Relationships, perseverance, and barter systems have always gotten me by. Even in New York City.

In her chocolate-making hut in the Costa Rican rain forest, Ancel and I grate nutmeg seed into a warm cup of cacao, made from the beans and spices that grow on her permaculture farm. Talk about a savory, sensual experience! There is no way to compare the nutmeg we find in the supermarket with freshly ground nutmeg. Once ground, the volatile oils in nutmeg quickly evaporate and the seed loses medicinal potency.

What we find in the grocery store might taste like nutmeg, but the multidimensional powers and flavors of this spice can be captured only when the seed is fresh—freshly grown and freshly grated. In this form, nutmeg can make us feel relaxed, euphoric, and can ease anxiety and insomnia. The warming spice has been an integral part of Ayurvedic medicine to balance the excessive windy and airy constitution of the vata dosha that can manifest as anxiety, worry, insomnia, and high blood pressure. Nutmeg has been used for centuries to aid digestion, regulate diabetes, heighten pleasure, promote respiratory health, and treat asthma.

When taken in large doses, however, nutmeg is an unsettling hallucinogen. The seed contains a psychoactive chemical called myristicin, which is related to mescaline and amphetamine and ecstasy. And while that might sound intriguing, nutmeg-induced hallucinations often come with difficulty moving properly, vomiting, dizziness, and seizures. This small-dose medicine can be extremely toxic when taken in large quantities, while the right amount of freshly grated seed can ease people who tend to worry and be high strung. For people with low blood pressure or who tend toward depression, however, nutmeg isn't beneficial. Herbs are not a "one size fits all" cure, and nutmeg's powers perfectly illustrate that. We must all explore our unique needs before being led astray by promises of any sort of superfood.

VENICE WAS THE EPICENTER OF EUROPEAN TRADE IN THE MIDDLE AGES, MAKing the city the richest and most powerful in Europe for hundreds of years. At the dawn of the spice craze, nutmeg was sold by Arab traders to Venetian peddlers and shopkeepers as a scent, an aphrodisiac, and a medicine for exorbitant prices while the source location for nutmeg was kept a secret. As noted earlier, until the nineteenth century, the only place nutmeg grew was on the Banda Islands of Indonesia, a group of small volcanic islands near Australia known as the Spice Islands. Because the Arab traders controlled the information about nutmeg, they were able to perpetuate the idea that the spice was rare—and thus worth all of the extra expense and fuss.

Many of us still believe that the more scarce something is, the more valuable it must be. But nature is abundant, and any scarcity we might perceive is an illusion. The nutmeg tree doesn't keep her seed or medicine from anyone. In the right conditions, after about eight years, female trees flower, fruit, and produce seeds year round. One tree can produce an average two to three thousand fruits and seeds in the course of a year. This generous tree can live to be one hundred years old.

When nutmeg's location was eventually discovered by European explorers, they were interested in controlling what the spice represented—wealth, access to something rare—rather than building relationships with the people of the Banda Islands or even using or growing the spice. A cruel and bloody battle ensued over control of nutmeg for almost two hundred years, and with militarized capitalism, the Dutch East India Company became the richest corporation in the world.[1] But seeds can only be contained for so long, and it didn't last.

BEFORE THERE WAS COUNTERFEIT LOUIS VUITTON, THERE WAS KNOCKOFF nutmeg. Once nutmeg made it to America, the seed's popularity continued, and with increasing demand, traders passed off phony wooden nutmegs to unsuspecting customers. Connecticut earned the nickname the Nutmeg State because its peddlers became so skilled at these forgeries. And we continue to be duped and convinced to shell out hard-earned money for illusions all the time.

"WHAT DO YOU WANT TO BE WHEN YOU GROW UP?" IT'S A QUESTION WE ARE asked as kids and most of us are encouraged to imagine, dream, play with different identities—firewoman, movie star, veterinarian, poet, president. We learn early on that our work identity will be intertwined with our personal identity. I took that to heart. I always loved drawing, admired artists, and could easily spend days lost in the process of creation, so naturally I wanted to be an artist and, somehow, work with all the wild animals that I adored (and worried about) from afar. But as I grew older, I kept running into the question of money. Could I make money doing this? Was I good enough? My maternal grandparents, immigrants who found security in jobs like doctor and nurse, thought that art was risky. And while I was fairly good at it and my drawings were praised, the time spent creating was seen as more of a hobby since very few "make it." Like other arts, it was sometimes viewed as nonessential, and the time spent creating it, a luxury. Even when time is free.

As I lay flat on my back with three fractured vertebrae after the car accident, I found I couldn't escape myself and my passions. I learned during that time that life is too precious to squander doing work that doesn't move me. I vowed then that I would refuse to earn a living doing something "safe" because I feared failure. I was convinced there was a reason I was here on this planet, at this moment in time, and that if I followed my instinct and stayed true to myself, I would find a way to support myself. At least I would know I tried. In a world where we spent so much time working, I was determined to work on what I loved.

In the late '90s and into the 2000s boxing was what compelled me and I was struggling financially—literally fighting to fight—when I decided to become an amateur, and later professional, boxer. There wasn't much money to be made as a woman but that wasn't what had drawn me there anyway. My grandparents kept suggesting that I use my personal training knowledge to become a physical therapist; "It would be more secure," they told me. They were worried. But I wasn't searching for that sort of security, I wanted to push my limits and live life. Like Ralph Waldo Emerson wrote, "People wish to be settled, but only insofar as they are unsettled is there any hope for them."[2] That was my motto. I felt that if I gave into a "regular" job, I was settling.

Like all New Yorkers, I needed money to survive, but I also thought money was the devil and identified with "the struggle," so I was pretty bad at making it. The bloody history of nutmeg is not nutmeg's fault; in the same way, money itself isn't overtly bad, but I believed the desire for money was shallow, and it's taken me a long time to unpack my contradictory feelings about welcoming abundance.

I ADORED MY MOM AND KNEW SHE WAS DOING THE BEST SHE COULD WHEN SHE drove our green Chevy Nova to and from Wildwood Elementary School where I went to class and she taught special ed. I loved having her in the building but I was embarrassed to get into the puke-green, loud car at the end of the day. It would not go quietly, announced its presence, and embarrassed me. I never told her this, of course, but I looked at all the cars in the lot and made wish lists in my head about the ones I wanted . . . this one, and this one, and this one. But at least I could trick people by wearing cool clothes.

When I went down to Florida, where my beloved maternal grandparents spent their winters, my grandmother wanted to spend beautiful sunny days in Marshalls and other brand-name discount stores while my grandfather waited patiently in the car. Shopping was her favorite pastime. She was glamorous and loved fashion. She should've been a buyer for a department store but instead shopping was a balm for what I imagine was her boredom. Even though I didn't want to spend hours in the store like she did, I did want to go back to school with the latest brand-name clothes. So I scoured the racks on those beautiful sunny days we could have been at the beach. It wasn't the clothes themselves but the logo and the label I was looking for: Esprit, Polo, Izod, Benetton. Those were cool and, in turn, I would be cool by wearing them. I could get fully functional clothes and sneakers, but I wanted to have the brand names. I even got some stuff that was hideous because it had the right logo.

I understood that we were struggling at home, in part because my dad didn't pay child support. My mom and her family made jokes about my father's eccentric family but she still told me she didn't want to take him to court because I had a relationship with his parents and she didn't want to destroy that. It was a strange setup. There were times I was brought to Italy for a month or two and when I came back to our humble living, I felt inwardly resentful and better than everyone else. But that quickly faded. There was a part of me that lived in luxury, but it was sporadic and seemed conditional, and another part that was happy and lived with what we had, which was more than enough. My father's parents sent occasional gifts and whisked me away on trips— experiences I'll always be grateful for—but were not there in my day-to-day reality. Sometimes they remembered my birthday, and on one birthday I'll never forget, they sent me a huge package. I was so excited and couldn't wait to open it! It sat in the garage for a couple of weeks until my ninth birthday, and every day I imagined what it might be. When I finally opened it, I found a huge swan mold for an ice sculpture. What? What the hell was I going to do with that? I was bewildered. It remained in the garage, leaving me in confusion, and it's probably still there today.

LAST WEEK I DREAMT THAT I WAS ABOUT TO EMBARK ON A LONG AND IMPORT-ant trip when both my father and my deceased paternal grandfather, Robertson, appeared. Robertson smiled at me and had a bag full of gifts to give me. When he handed me the first one, a piece of meaningful, valuable jewelry that had been in our family for generations, I was wowed and deeply grateful. And then he handed me more: beautiful necklaces that I placed around my neck, heavy brooches and gems, priceless boxes and heavy metals that began to blur to-gether, tug on my neck, and weigh me down as I put them in my bag. Each gift made me heavier and heavier. They were gestures of his love but I was begin-ning to feel burdened with them. I was conflicted. What do I do with all of this? Now I have to carry his love? I was buried in stuff. Then I turned to my father, who was ashamed that he couldn't afford to give me anything but his love. But that was all I wanted anyway. Suddenly, I felt my father's energy shift; excitement emanated from him when he remembered that he did have some-thing else to give me after all. He reached into his pocket to give me three photographs: one picture of me with Daphne, our animal companion, and two pictures of me, him, and my mom when I was a child. They were weightless, beautiful, and deeply meaningful.

HYPNOTIC SEEDS

One New Year's, a good friend invited me to do the Deepak Chopra twenty-one-day meditation challenge as a way to start the year. As someone who is often holding space for others, I thought it would be nice to be guided, so I was open to it. It began with a journaling exercise, a recorded meditation, and the mantra "I am awake to the abundance that surrounds me." It was a nice re-minder as I walked around the Brooklyn Botanic Garden reflecting on the incredible abundance in nature, the abundance in my life, and the overall il-lusion of scarcity. The next day, the messaging was similar. But then it began to morph. As I meditated, Chopra's voice assured me that if I want a better car, a bigger house, or more money, it is all within my reach. A few days after that, one of our tasks was to write on receipts of recent purchases "Everything I buy is good and will come back to me sevenfold." Everything I buy is good? I doubt that is true for many of us but Chopra gave us permission to buy more stuff because it will "come back to us sevenfold." Yuck. While some people may struggle with a scarcity mentality, which is worth overcoming, I think the majority of people in the Western world do not need any justification for more "stuff." I was done after day five. According to the program, the things we don't like illuminate where our "resistance" lies, and while I admit I have had issues around money, I trusted my resistance and didn't stick around to see if the messaging redeemed itself.

Using spirituality to encourage or justify materialism is not unusual, of course. Chögyam Trungpa, Tibetan Buddhist teacher and author of *Cutting through Spiritual Materialism*, wrote, "As long as we follow a spiritual approach promising salvation, miracles, liberation, then we are bound by the 'golden chain of spirituality.' Such a chain might be beautiful to wear, with its inlaid jewels and intricate carvings, but nevertheless, it imprisons us."[3] I read Trungpa's book *Shambhala: The Sacred Path of the Warrior* in my midtwenties and it was the first spiritual philosophy that completely resonated. His teachings—synchronizing mind and body in everything we do, overcoming habitual behaviors, relaxing within discipline, and finding the sacred dimension of everyday life—validated my underlying belief systems and provided guidance for my life ways. So much so that I have a version of the Great Eastern Sun with the knot of eternity in the center (very similar to the Celtic knot) tattooed on the back of my neck. I saved money to get the tattoo at New York Adorned in the East Village on August 24, my twenty-sixth birthday. My sun, of course, has twenty-four rays. It felt like a personal power totem and a reminder of what I believed in. It felt so much a part of me that I told people I scratched off my skin and it was there.

CORPORATIONS WORK HARD TO CONVINCE US THAT WHAT WE REALLY NEED IS right around the next bend—something bigger, faster, better and more, more, more. But more is not always better. Like nutmeg, many things are healing in small doses but toxic in large ones. Equating wealth with external accumulations—whether that's money or things—keeps us spiritually impoverished and ceaselessly hungry. When I finally let go of the idea of finding the right brand or style to be loyal to—even while there are some designers using a sustainable approach—I became a lot happier than when I was scouring for clothing that I was sure would make me look like I was worth something.

Whether they consciously seek to dissuade us or not, corporations are threatened by self-sufficiency: when we grow our own food and realize the value of the plants that have evolved to thrive around us, we regain control over our perspective on what we truly need. The illusion of scarcity triggers the instinct to hoard, when there is plenty to go around. The healthiest foods we can eat tend to be the ones that grow in fertile ground close to where we are. Our local produce, and abundant wild superfoods like dandelion, burdock, lamb's quarter, nettles, blueberries, and elderberries have learned to thrive in our exact environment, under our weather conditions, and so these local plants, each in their season, can help us adapt to our homeland and the seasons. Yet many of us are still convinced that the more rare, the more exotic something is, the more valuable it is. But wouldn't it make more sense that plants thriving in abundance have the most vitality and life force energy? Why do we want to eat something scarce that may be struggling? We can reconnect to our wildness and harvest free, abundant, and nutrient-rich plants like nettles and get immediate energy instead of buying moringa, acai berries, goji berries, and other expensive products that have been processed and are shipped in wasteful plastic packaging, often from at least two places. I've had a number of students tell me they had been buying supplements like burdock, reishi, and elderberry at the store without realizing these beings were growing right around them. And for a while, I was also convinced that I had to go far to seek what I needed.

THE MORE COMFORTABLE I FEEL IN MY OWN SKIN, THE MORE EASILY I CAN shed what no longer fits. The more courage I develop, the more willing I am to brave the empty, cavernous spaces inside. I suppose in my early twenties it felt important to define myself by my answers to questions like, What do you do?

Who do you want to be? How are you going to support yourself? I was told more than once then that I should pick "one thing" and strive to excel at it. Doom myself to be a jack-of-all-trades, and I'd find I was a master of none. But I couldn't square that kind of claustrophobic focus with my desire to learn, explore. Who said I wanted or needed to be an expert? And in the intervening years I've come to suspect that experts don't really exist. I am now confident about the knowledge and practice I have the privilege to share and teach, but am I an expert? No.

My partner recently awarded me a "Bachelor of Elf Spotting" certificate that is proudly displayed on our refrigerator as a joke. It was a free download from *Last Week Tonight with John Oliver*, a skit about finance that mentioned Reykjavik's actual Elfschool. While I am actually curious about Iceland's Elfschool, I cannot stand weekend certifications or online diplomas for traditions and practices like shamanism, meditation, or herbalism. I recently saw one that anoints you a "master herbalist." The truth is, there is currently no certifying agency or licensing board for herbalists in the United States and therefore no such thing as an herbal certification or titles such as master herbalist or certified herbalist.[4] Not only is fast-tracking knowledge like herbalism dangerous, but such certifications—clearly moneymaking schemes—take credibility away from those who have spent years studying and uncovering their paths through experience. Those who seek to learn something sacred would gain much more by learning firsthand with knowledgeable elders and practitioners, and in relationship with nature, certificate or not.

I know countless talented artists who feel they can't claim the identity because they don't earn a living from their art. And there are artists who are "making it" for reasons that aren't clear to me. Success is often propelled by relationships and perseverance and, yes, sometimes talent and sometimes luck. These forces more powerfully dictate whether what we "do" can earn us a living. But underneath our angst to identify ourselves, the core takeaway should be that we don't have to define ourselves by how we make money. One reason we attempt to fill voids with stuff, or stick to our work deadlines instead of doing what we love, is because we have bought into a world that exploits our insecurities and capitalizes on our poor sense of self-worth. We are searching for happiness, and what we find is at best a steady income.

I've tried on various identities in my struggle to find a calling that will adequately answer the question society is really asking us when as children we hear, "What do you want to be when you grow up?" Our answer often does shape who we become. And the answer the world wants isn't what's your passion, but how will you earn the income by which you will be judged. As we age, the question morphs to become "What do you do?" But casually defining who we are in relation only to our work can cause a lot of problems. We are all multidimensional and so much more than what we "do."

It took me a long time to identify with labels like boxer, herbalist, artist, or writer. I trained for amateur and then professional fights for years before I felt I had the right to introduce myself as a fighter. But at some point, even though I worked to earn that title, the identity became too confining. Calling myself a boxer or a fighter limited how people saw me and how I saw myself. I earned the perspective, wore it out, then outgrew it. Letting go of hard-won identities in a world that asks us to compartmentalize or define ourselves based on how we make a living can be difficult and traumatic. Fighter became an identity I had to shed in order to grow.

THE DUTCH EAST INDIA COMPANY WAS BANKRUPT BY THE END OF THE SEVEN-teenth century.[5] Constant wars with rival powers and rebellion from the islanders eventually destroyed its sociopathic spice cartel. Then, in 1769, a roving French horticulturist aptly named Pierre Poivre, swooped into the Spice Islands and smuggled out nutmeg seeds and trees. The French planted these seeds on their colony Mauritius, and that was it. The Dutch monopoly was through. During their occupation of the East Indies, the British took nutmeg seedlings from the Bandas and planted them in Singapore, Sri Lanka, Sumatra, and Malaysia, and from there, spread them to Zanzibar, East Africa, and Grenada, making the British rich as the world's second-leading nutmeg exporter, and now we sprinkle this coveted spice on our lattes and eggnog and bake it into our pumpkin pies.

Nature continues to show me just how abundant life can be when we tend to her soil, nurture relationships, and follow our inner longings. Custodians of the land are all we can really be, and Mother Nature cannot handle any more taking without the proper energy exchange. There might always be more to grasp for, always a place inside where we feel as though we are not enough. But if we reach into that space with curiosity—before reaching for our phone, the remote control, or our credit card—we might find a place inside ourselves that is simply asking to be healed. People who feel full and satisfied make bad consumers, so the world doesn't make it easy for us, but we can't afford to stop doing what we love. While it might be uncomfortable, everyone and everything benefits when we listen to the echoes in our voids and explore what we're truly hungry for.

ST. JOHN'S WORT
Hypericum perforatum

Family: Hypericaceae

St. John's wort works to restore and repair over-stimulated and burnt-out nervous systems. The infused oil alleviates pain and can be rubbed into the skin to help with sore muscles, sciatica, and damaged nerves, while the tincture or tea can ease and enliven us from the inside out. The bright yellow flowers bloom at the peak of summer when the days are longest, and as treatment for seasonal affective disorder and depression, this plant literally lets more sunshine in. If we were to take one of the plant's leaves and hold it up to the sunlight, we could see small window-like holes that let light shine through, and if we were to crush a blossom between our fingers, the yellow flower would exude a bloodred stain.

NO PAIN, NO GAIN

There must be those among whom we can sit down and weep
and still be counted as warriors.

ADRIENNE RICH

Leo and I both loved hearing the distinct *pop* that reverberated through
the gym when I hit the heavy bag just right. As I circled the bag, I'd see
him smile and look around to note who was watching. We were proud
of my power. We were also proud of the way I could work the speed bag. I made
a lot of noise with that rhythmic, hypnotic little bladder. Growing up around
music helped me get the beat just right, and I was better at that bag than most
of the men at the gym.

I was finding a new identity through boxing and felt I needed to go the
extra mile to prove myself as a woman in a man's sport, especially as a woman
who had started in her twenties. I trained long hours, learned how to move
beyond pain, and rarely, if ever, showed mental or emotional weakness. Not in
the gym, at least. Fighters and coaches who saw me train respected me for how
much heart I gave to the sport, and I was praised for visibly moving beyond
extreme discomfort, forcing my body to keep going even when she was telling
me to stop. When Leo wasn't there and I knew I was being watched, I self-
consciously reverted to skills that showcased my power and impressed others

instead of enduring the awkward movements and tentative skills I needed to practice. A mistake I would suffer for later.

Leo always reminded me that he'd trained eight world champions from the ground up—fighters including Simon Brown, Maurice Blocker, Iran Barkley, and Davey Moore—so I had a lot to live up to. Eventually, he decided to train, manage, and promote two other professional women alongside me who had been amateur fighters: Aiko, a fighter from Japan, and Adrienne, a friend from Brooklyn. With the three of us, Leo thought he could change the game in women's boxing and that we three skilled fighters would attract diverse crowds. We signed under his fledgling company Phoenix Sports Management and some people called us "Leo's Angels" (a nickname I hated).

When Leo took her on, Adrienne was already my best female sparring partner in the NYC boxing world. We trusted each other, pushed each other, and were able to talk honestly about how we were feeling. When we had our periods, we took it easy and avoided the body shots. When we felt good, we went all-out and didn't take it personally when one of us punched the other in the gut or went home with bruises. We'd talk on the phone to debrief, praising each other when we performed well and dissecting the areas where each could improve. Only in fighting did I find friendships like this.

I trained with fighters, worked with fighters, and while I was still pining away for Ernesto, I had a couple of beautiful intimate relationships with boxers during those years. Some of the fighters truly loved, lived, and breathed the sport, while some came from boxing families so they were expected to excel, and still others were just so good at the sport that fighting was simply a means to an end. We understood the self-discipline, the level of dedication the sport required, and my fellow fighters didn't fetishize my training like some other men did. I wanted to be seen as a skilled fighter no matter my age or gender, and there was little that was sexy about my education in the ring: the long grueling hours, the pain, the bruises, and the dramatic emotional highs and lows of sparring sessions. But the ring was a space to take risks, to put ourselves on the line and see what we were capable of. We wanted to know how far we could push ourselves—how much power we could cultivate and how much pain we could endure. Few places felt so intensely raw and real to me. We were always pushing closer and closer to our physical and emotional edges, and while the fighters around me helped me become strong, I provided a space for them to cry when we were alone. But I found that while this symbiosis was energizing, I also craved someone or something that allowed me to surrender the strength that had come to define me.

ST. JOHN'S WORT IS A HEALING ALLY FOR THOSE WHO HAVE FOUGHT TOO HARD and too long and are mentally, physically, or emotionally bruised. John Gerard, author of *The Herball, or Generall historie of plantes*, wrote in 1597 that St. John's wort is "a most precious remedy for deep wounds,"[1] as the plant's antimicrobial properties help to disinfect wounds, reduce inflammation, and heal from the deepest part and out toward the periphery. This usage led to the English nickname "balm of the warrior's wound."[2] St. John's wort was, and still is, seen as a wise choice (along with plants like plantain and yarrow) for the treatment of puncture wounds, as suggested by the second part of the plant's botanical name: *perforatum*. Gerard recommended that the leaves, flowers, and seeds be stamped or pressed, immersed in olive oil, and set in the hot sun until the extract becomes the color of blood, a pigment due to the bioactive compound hypericin where much of the medicine resides. Topically, the oil helps ease conditions ranging from pinched nerves like sciatica to overall damage to the nervous system, whether through injury or viral infection, while easing the pain of overworked and overused muscles.

In the Scottish Highlands where I often seek refuge and work on conservation, St. John's wort is planted outside my cottage door for protection. *Hypericum*, the first part of St. John's wort's botanical name, is derived from the Greek *hyper*, or "above," and *eikon*, or "the picture," as a result of the popular custom in which various species of this genus were hung above holy pictures to repel the devil.[3] I watch as the wide-open flowers swarm with fuzzy bumblebees. The flowers display confidence with their bright blossoms, yet their thin stems make the plant also appear delicate. But they are stronger than they appear; that thin stem is wiry, buoyant, and surprisingly resilient. You would never know that the bright yellow flowers of St. John's wort bleed red.

———

THERE IS AN ARC TO TRAINING, ESPECIALLY LEADING UP TO FIGHTS: AN UPHILL regime, next a peak moment just before the fight, then an easing off to ensure you are strong and ready for battle. At first Leo and I abided by this rhythm, but we usually got news that, for one reason or another, my fight was canceled— my opponent pulled out and a replacement couldn't be found or it just fell through, with no explanation. I was embarrassed that my fights kept falling apart and I had little to show for all the training I had been doing. Except for the skill that too few people saw, I had no "proof" of all my hard work. When people asked, "What's your record?" I couldn't boast. So I reached my summits in "fighting shape," where I excelled physically, but deflated emotionally. When my fights fell through, I dove right back into training, didn't take the necessary breaks from the gym, and my body started to get mad at me. Staying stuck in the throes of being strong—of being ready to fight without any denouement for decompression—can be self-destructive, especially when training reinforces that toxic idea that it's dangerous to ever admit to weakness.

DEFENDING MYSELF IN SPARRING, KEEPING MY GUARD UP, AND HAMMERING away at heavy bags often left me hunched over with closed fists. It hurt to open my hands in the morning, and pain shot down my legs when I sat for more than a few minutes. My life became about pain management and I began to perform better in my training than I did in everyday life. I developed a trick that I learned from one of the many sports psychology books I read: no matter how tired I was, how much was going on in my mind, as I walked up each stair of the two flights into Gleason's, I left behind each worry, each ounce of exhaustion, each ounce of pain and self-doubt. Once I walked through the door of the gym, I was present and ready to train. This trick was great for the first few years of training as I pushed beyond my insecurities and comfort zones, but I became too good at leaving my feelings—my connection to my body's signals—behind and I was now ignoring the screams and pleas of my body. By then, I had already tried training southpaw (left-handed) so I could ease the pain on the right side of my body from repetitive movement and hitting the bags too hard, and finally the pain began to affect my performance—meaning that I could be in danger in a fight. What had been healing, and had led me to a new spiritual practice, was starting to become harmful. My body needed a break but my ego wouldn't let go. The longer I trained, the less my body trusted me.

BOXING IS A DANGEROUS PLACE TO FIND ONE'S IDENTITY. THE SPORT OFFERS at best a short-lived career at a very high cost; I witnessed iconic fighters come into the gym slurring their words. While the objective of boxing is to hit and not get hit—most training makes it actually quite difficult to hit a skilled fighter, who can deftly and swiftly move around the ring—getting hit is inevitable. Yet Leo was angry when I did. It made him look bad as a trainer and underneath his ego, he knew it was risky. A fellow boxer warned me that Leo would ask a deceptively simple question before taking me on: "Do you want to be a tough fighter or a mean fighter?" Because Leo didn't train tough fighters like Rocky, punchers with no finesse or defense that keep going even as they get pummeled. Mean fighters were elusive, like Pernell "Sweet Pea" Whitaker; they could stick, move, and attack while barely getting grazed. Though I answered the question correctly and said I wanted to be a mean fighter, I was a tough fighter. When I got hit hard, I shook it off and kept going, and kept going even when my body told me to stop. I didn't admit it to others but it scared me. I downplayed those risks to concerned friends and family but it was always in the back of my mind. When had I crossed the line? When did it become abusive? When was it enough?

IN GAELIC CUSTOM, ST. JOHN'S WORT HAS TO BE FOUND BY ACCIDENT IN ORDER to be effective,[4] and that always seems to be the way I find St. John's wort in the wild anyway since the plant is less common in the Northeast and Scotland than plants like dandelion or nettles, and I rarely set out in pursuit of them. I see this as nature's "handle with care" message since St. John's wort must be used with sharp awareness—internally, the medicine increases the activity of liver enzymes that metabolize drugs, so using this herb in combination with other medications must be done with caution, and is generally contraindicated.

St. John's wort is a strong medicine, not a tonic herb that can be used consistently. Like boxing, the medicine of St. John's wort needs to be worked with mindfully, and we need to know when to stop. If one did come across the plant, it was considered an auspicious blessing, for *Hypericum* was highly protective and wearing St. John's wort as an amulet, carrying it in one's pocket (or in Gaelic custom, under one's armpit)[5], and having the plant indoors, especially by a window, could ward off malicious spirits and the demons of melancholy.

Like stumbling upon the blessing of St John's wort, boxing and I found each other by accident and, for a while, the sport provided healing and release while helping me cultivate a strength I didn't know I had. But when I crossed over from strength to toughness, I realized it would take more courage and confidence to know when to let fighting go.

UNDERNEATH ALL OF THIS PHYSICAL PAIN, I CONTINUED TO SUFFER ANOTHER pain: I missed Ernesto, too terribly. St. John's wort might have helped me cope with the gnawing sadness I felt, as the plant has famously been found to assist in mild depression. Fighters and I found it hard to commit for one reason or another; we were more devoted to boxing than to each other. No one measured up to Ernesto and I began to worry that with him I hadn't experienced ascending to a new level of potential, one that would allow me to connect to others in a richer, deeper way, but that I had experienced instead the peak relationship of my life. And now I was going to have to live in a space of recovering from him, and from our connection. I always had the feeling of being too late for things. I would have done anything to get back together with him. I held tight to the wisdom he shared with me when I left in the first place: sometimes, love isn't enough. He wouldn't endure the pain of our relationship again, and I had to remember the piece that fighting had unlocked in me that would've always nagged me if I'd limited my earlier self.

THE SUN INSIDE

I look closely at the wild St. John's wort found by the loch in the Scottish Highlands and notice how their buds look like little flames and how the stamens of the open flowers look like vibrant rays of sun. I reflect on their intense symmetry, the angles and order of the leaves—perhaps helping us rein our energy inward and reassert order when we feel scattered. In a recent dream, I was told by a teacher (or some sort of dream guide) that St. John's wort "safeguards the sun inside of us." A beautiful message that rang true since the plant activates our solar plexus, the seat of personal power in the body. Internally, the medicine has an affinity for our enteric nervous system—the brain of our gut—and works with our complex signaling mechanisms that enable us to assimilate food, emotions, and experiences and act upon animal instinct. Being heliotropic, the flowers face east each morning to greet the rising sun, and as the light moves across the sky to the south and descends in the west, the blossoms follow—worshiping and embodying the sun.

With a photosensitizing effect, St. John's wort opens up our own light receptors and lets more sunshine into our bodies, a poetic connection as the plant is among the most recommended herbs for seasonal affective disorder in the dark days of winter when we are longing for light. Taking the tincture internally has even been reported to make some people more susceptible to burns, though this is debated. But if taking the plant does attract too much sun, a simple infused oil made from the flowers can be applied to a burn to draw out heat, reduce inflammation, and rapidly promote the healing process. And when that same oil is used topically, prior to sun exposure, the protective elements of the plant act as a natural sunscreen. The strong, bloodred homemade oil is often all I use as a sunscreen. But I tend to run out quickly, and when I've bought the oil from others, there are times I've burned. There is a balance of opposites in this plant, as in many, that can be confusing when studying the energetics. Some herbalists classify St. John's wort as a warming and drying remedy that initiates healing in damp, dark spaces, while others classify the plant as a cooling remedy that calms fires of inflammation. But like all living beings, plants and their actions on our unique bodies—that are always in a state of flux—are complex.

JUST AS I WAS BEGINNING TO ACCEPT THAT THE PAIN I WAS FEELING WASN'T anything I could truly push past, a friend in the boxing world introduced me to Ronald. Ronald is an acupuncturist who runs a small place in the heart of Chinatown that has been in his family for generations. I began to see him monthly, and sometimes weekly, to deal with my chronic pain. I learned that the sciatica that hobbled me was piriformis syndrome, an inflamed muscle in my glute that was pinching my nerve—a reaction to overtraining that I never gave the time or care needed to recover. We spoke about herbs for healing and when I couldn't figure something out myself, Ronald and his father, Ming, were the first people I turned to. It has been that way ever since.

When I stopped getting my period and the edges of my cheeks started breaking out in zits, Ronald and his father explained I had too much yang, too much scattered fire. They gave me herbs and an acupuncture treatment that brought my period back to a regular rhythm, and brought my red face back to a calm state. Midwife and herbalist Ruth Trickey explains that St. John's wort is "indicated in conditions where exhaustion and tension combine—a common finding in women who present with hormonal problems."[6] But at that point in my life, I wasn't aware of how beneficial St. John's wort would have been; all that Western culture had offered me was a pill, and I refused to alter my hormones that way. Ronald helped me track my cycles by taking my temperature and using lunaception—synching with the moon—to manage my daily life. He told me, "You American women don't know your bodies, all Chinese women know this!" I had to laugh. From what I had experienced, it was probably true. He was reliably direct and blunt, which I appreciated. He also told me I needed to rest. And since my pain was affecting my training, Leo agreed that a couple of months off would do me good too.

Suddenly, I had a lot of time on my hands.

I began to paint and draw more, and get more involved in a formal Zen meditation. The combination of familiar practices helped me get reacquainted with the parts of myself I'd put aside. Boxing showed me doors beyond pain and told me I had more to give, so I dug deep, found wells within my soul that drowned my instinct to quit, and washed away my anger. But what boxing unlocked in me also messed with my ability to recognize the power of limits. The way I fought always left me wanting more, always promised that what I needed or what would sate me was just around the next corner, through the next door. And so I stayed, and the taste of sweat purged me of my pain. In any relationship, we may cause ourselves pain by trying to fit back into an old shape that once led to bliss, but we outgrow our old bodies.

When I was immersed in boxing, I felt as though my training days would never end. When people came in to film, as they often did in Gleason's, Leo turned them away from me, saying, "She's training." But now I regret that I didn't capture those moments. Yes, we recorded my sparring sessions so I could watch them and correct my flaws, but then we recorded over them the next day. I know what I ultimately cultivated happened deep inside, but I wish I had more evidence of that transformation, and had frankly enjoyed more of the external praise, the proof that women could be good, skilled fighters with integrity.

AFTER ANOTHER TWO YEARS OF TRAINING WITH LONGER AND MORE FRE-quent breaks, I was standing on the Broadway-Lafayette subway platform after having had another three weeks off training because of an injury. During those weeks, I simply had to rest and be, and in the recent past that had made me feel incredibly restless and uncomfortable. But standing there that day, I real-ized I had been feeling good mentally and emotionally even though my body still hurt. And in that simple but pivotal moment that I will never forget, I felt deep contentment and an apologetic love for my body. I knew she had endured enough. My body was exhausted, and I was burnt out on training people too. I just didn't have the same passion for boxing anymore. I realized it was time to let it go and reintegrate other aspects of myself I had begun to yearn for. I had other things to fight for.

It was not a smooth and easy breakup. I wrote love letters to boxing as though I were a tormented lover: *I miss you, I want to go back to you. It was never about beauty, it was me you saw, it was me you revealed and you always saw more, asked for more.* But they were love letters to an old flame and old self I had already outgrown. I was saying goodbye to a version of myself I was clinging to, and I realized how much my ego had gotten caught up in it. I had been hiding behind the identity of a "boxer" for years. An identity that I had to earn and that took me a while to claim, but I knew I had to let go. Leav-ing boxing meant that I had to leave Leo too. All the time and energy he'd put in and we didn't have anything to show for it, but I also felt him stepping away. It had been a lot: five to six days a week and setting up fights and in general being there for me all the time. But outside of the boxing world, he was a difficult man to deal with. I saw the bitterness others spoke about. I needed to step away. Adrienne and I commiserated about it all, and not long afterward, she decided to leave too.

THERE WAS A LEVEL OF PASSION IN BOXING I FOUND DURING THAT TIME, ESpecially as I was uncovering and cultivating strength I didn't know I had, that I know I will not be able to replicate anywhere else. But the sport that had inspired such dynamic physical and spiritual expansion also damned me with tunnel vision. Everything revolved around my performance at the gym, and after the initial years of exhilarating growth, the training became a space of limitation that punctured holes in my vital energy.

When I didn't need training to feel good anymore, I was relieved. My wounds had time and space to heal, and I began to refill my inner reservoir, integrating and absorbing my boxer self while getting reacquainted with the rest of me. I was content, centered, and my spirit was satisfied. I could walk away feeling radiant and free.

GOLDENROD
Solidago spp.

Family: Asteraceae

Goldenrod's small yellow sunflowers bloom late summer and into autumn as the days become shorter and nights become longer. They contain the energy of the late-summer sun, offering warmth and light to illuminate dark, damp spaces within our bodies. This plant, whose botanical name is *Solidago*, comes from the Latin words *solidus*, meaning "whole," and *ago*, meaning "to make." Goldenrod is a medicine of transition, balance, wholeness, and integration.

Goldenrod is considered a weed by many in North America and is often blamed for late-summer allergies because they appear with their striking recognizable blossom at the time people begin to sneeze. But goldenrod pollen is too heavy and sticky to be blown far from the flowers that are pollinated by bees, flies, wasps, and butterflies. The inconspicuous culprit for our seasonal allergies is ragweed, with their green camouflaged flowers that bloom at the same time and are pollinated by wind.

Goldenrod tincture and tea is a remedy for the very allergies they often take the blame for, and their showy flowers can be made into a wonderful yellowish-gold dye. This beautiful North American native has naturalized throughout Europe, Asia, and parts of Africa and can help us find our way as we transform and learn to embrace change.

ILLUMINATION

The fragrance, color, and form of the whole spiritual expression of Goldenrod are hopeful and strength-giving beyond any others I know.

JOHN MUIR

I paint flowers so they will not die.

FRIDA KAHLO

Cicada songs come to a crescendo as summer wanes. With more than three thousand species around the world, these strange and magical insects rise around midsummer to sing through the passing of the season after living underground for up to seventeen years. Their appearance is catalyzed by soil warmth, and when it is time to emerge, they dig to the surface in the dark of night, crawl up a tree trunk, and anchor themselves onto the bark with their claws. The skin of their back then splits and they emerge transformed, a newly winged creature. In the right light, their wings look like iridescent rainbows.

Goldenrod blooms near the end of the season as the cicadas serenade us. These perennial wildflowers are living torches that grow from rhizomes and rise together in fields, forest edges, and beach dunes, helping us find our way back to clearings as daylight fades. They provide food for the transformation of butterflies, supporting the most species of butterflies and moths year round, and are my favorite medicine for life's inevitable changes. Transition is difficult, even if the change is exactly what we wished for; it means climbing out of our familiar shell, stepping into the unknown, and letting go. Allying with goldenrod by spending time with the plant in the wild or working with the flower essence or small vibrational doses of tincture, tea, or meditation can help us adjust to new circumstances and new versions of ourselves.

When I soak the hairs of my paintbrush or cover my fingertips in red, yellow, blue, and green to move them along blank pages, I also shed old selves, integrate prior experiences, and clear space to receive wisdom and revelation. Though the process may be silent, I have always felt that my visual art was an expression of sound. When I allow abstract images and shapes of sound to emerge from my body and onto paper, canvas, sand, or solid ground, I let go without wondering who will see what I produce, without analyzing what it's worth or why it needs to emerge.

IN PLATO'S *PHAEDRUS*, SOCRATES TELLS A STORY ABOUT INSECTS THAT WERE once human.[1] After the Muses were born, he says, some became so intoxicated by their own music that they sang and danced until they died, forgetting to eat or drink. Cicadas rose from their bodies, reincarnated by the Muses to sing continuously, without requiring food or water, their only task to make music and spy on humankind to see who honored them through the devotion of art. They tell the goddess of dance about those who have honored her through the rhythmic movement of their bodies; they sing praises of poets, especially poets of love, so that they may gain the favor of Eros; they celebrate those whose songs and voices are the sweetest and most hypnotic; and they point to the way to the paintings, drawings, and sculptures that are most alive.

The most common cicadas in the Northeast are periodical cicadas (*Magicicada septendecim*) and annual dog-day cicadas (*Tibicen linnei*).[2] Dog-day cicadas spend at least four years underground and the emergence of these solitary creatures is not synchronized, so we hear them every year. In 2020, billions of periodical cicadas, known as Brood XIV, emerged together after having been underground for seventeen years. Because of their regular population explosions, periodical cicadas have been confused with the sort of locusts that occur in crop-devastating swarms. But unlike locusts, cicadas are mostly beneficial to the ecosystem. They prune mature trees, aerate the soil, and serve as nitrogen-rich compost when they die. When the summer season ends and they have found their partner, they will leave their shells behind and return underground with the fallen leaves, providing food for the soil and wildflowers.

LIKE THE MUSES WHO FORGOT THEMSELVES AS THEY SANG AND DANCED THEIR way to death, I didn't think about how much time I spent in the act of creation, how much of me was being absorbed, or where creation would lead me until, after shedding the identity of a boxer, I decided that I wanted to be an artist. Being an artist meant that the time I spent creating mattered, and that what I yielded must be considered "good" by the gatekeepers of art's strange and intimidating world. I always felt uncomfortable when I walked around Chelsea in New York City and stepped into sterile galleries, far removed from the process of creation. I felt like I didn't belong but I wanted so badly to be accepted there too, and to be seen. The art of boxing helped me cultivate the internal strength needed to be brave and share my vulnerable inner world—my colors, my shapes, my expression that insisted on moving through me and out of my body to be born. For years, I hesitated to pursue an artist's identity since the act of creation meant so much to me. Putting art out into the world beyond my journal and sketchbook pages meant being exposed, being rejected—and I risked being misunderstood like goldenrod or the cicadas.

I often wandered through MoMA, the Museum of Modern Art, both inspired and bewildered by what the curators considered valuable work. Goldenrod is a weed to many, but was once seen as a treasure and a symbol of good fortune. How and why did that value fade? As I explored, I wondered about the materials of the masters before the advent of synthetic and petroleum-based colors in the nineteenth century, back when colors were made from plants, minerals, insects, and animals. Goldenrod flowers create a beautiful, warm, gold pigment, while their leaves make a vibrant green. How treasured was goldenrod then? During the reign of Queen Elizabeth I, the healing abilities of the wildflower were highly coveted and the powdered plant was sold for as much as a half a crown per pound. But not now.

Like my love of weeds and wildflowers, it is always the visceral works of art that move me. I'm moved by lines that are still alive, by abstract shapes that seem to writhe on the page and into me—images that could only have come from that particular artist in that moment of time. Those images unlock something inside me, opening up new ways of seeing beyond any limits to my perception. I believe that the purpose of art is not to be successful or good, rather, as Pablo Picasso said, "The purpose of art is washing the dust of daily life off our souls."[3]

Whether it is music, poetry, dance, or painting, our souls can be thrust into the present and renewed in an instant upon hearing, seeing, or creating the right work of art at the right time.

CYCLES

About a year after the periodical cicadas went underground in 2003, I gave up boxing. I knew the identity would be hard to let go of, so that was exactly what I needed to do. I was tired of people seeing me as a boxer. An identity that once felt like an honor I had to earn now felt like a mask that left my true self in the shadows. I wrote in my journal: *I've been sleeping in my clothes lately, not caring about changing. Too tired and cold to peel off the layers. My frame of mind is falling apart, unable to hold on to the pictures inside. My self-image is changing and I want to be free.* I was ready to focus on art, on beauty, on different forms of self-expression.

I was living in Williamsburg at the time of this personal transition and all I wanted to do was write, draw, and sit in the grass of a small park near my apartment, surrounded by weeds and wildflowers. I woke, wrote, and drew, and walked in trancelike circles between my apartment, the park, and the art store. Meditation practice had inspired a new style of art: pointillism with words that I called "visual verse." I let every word and thought come out of my body unedited—the good, bad, ugly, and embarrassing—in tiny, tiny sentences using Micron pens. The rainbow of colors made abstract images out of my noisy insides. I wanted to empty out and I figured if the words were tiny enough, no one would try to read them anyway. Some of my best writing is probably in those pieces and underneath piles of paint, because after a while I realized I was getting attached to the words, so I painted over them.

I didn't want to leave that hypnotic space but I was running out of money, so I decided to sublet my place and take a break from the city. I needed to recalibrate and figure out what was next. I stayed in Amherst with my mom, where I slept, meditated, wrote, and drew in my old bedroom, which was healing, uncomfortable, and strange. Some days I felt like a failure and other days I felt free. I walked endlessly in the woods and mourned all the training camps I never went to and all the fights that never happened. Most mornings I woke up, meditated, and spent the rest of the day drawing. I was beginning to move beyond the confines of what I was conditioned to believe was worthwhile art, and in turn, I created art that was visceral, real, and good. I knew I had found just the right mode of expression for this moment, though a curator who would come to see my work would later say, "I love it, but it's so personal, so detailed, I don't know what to do with it. It's like folk art."

Yet all of that effort quickly began to feel selfish and like a waste of time. Though I was healing and creating pieces I was proud of, my art wasn't being seen and I felt like I wasn't doing enough for the outside world. After a few months, I got a call from my friend and former boxing client who worked with the Norbulingka Institute in Dharamsala, India, whose mission is to preserve Tibetan art and culture. She wanted to create a fundraiser on behalf of the institute, and knowing my background in activism and organizing, my interest in Tibetan Buddhism, and the fact that I was in limbo, she thought I might be interested, and ideal. That call answered my prayers. I moved back into my apartment in Williamsburg with renewed purpose and became the coordinator for the event we entitled HOPE on behalf of the Norbulingka Institute and His Holiness the Dalai Lama.

We decided to do an exhibition as part of the fundraising effort and I found myself in touch with top photographers in the city, like Annie Leibovitz, Mario Testino, and Roberto Dutesco. It was exciting, but it didn't take long before I began to resent playing the role of an event coordinator instead of participating as one of the artists. I lamented my own pursuit of photography that led me to the city and eventually got sidetracked, and I went home after a day of work where my paintings, drawings, and collages were hidden in my apartment, filling it up, unseen.

WHEN THERE HAD BEEN A FIRE SCARE IN MY PLACE ON SEVENTH STREET IN the East Village several years earlier, my drawings and sketchbooks were the first and only things I grabbed. I smelled smoke and impulsively ran downstairs with those parts of me that were irreplaceable. I stood out on the street with my neighbors for over an hour. All was okay.

When Ernesto and I moved from our first place in the East Village, my portfolio that I had carried from place to place for years and was filled with all of my best and most meaningful work from childhood, from the time of the car accident and through my early adulthood, was lost. I drove Ernesto and myself crazy trying to find it. How could it just disappear? But somehow, it had. That archive was gone and I would never get it back. The drawings I did after the car accident, the animal studies, a drawing of a wolf that I still remember as being one of my best works—the loss of those moments and their renderings was heartbreaking. Those images illustrated periods of transition in my life that there are no words for. They were my inner world made visible. They were parts of my soul crying out in visual form. And now those parts of me were gone.

Back then, I separated the drawing and writing I did for myself from the drawing and writing I did for others. Pieces that were most precious were hidden away in black sketchbooks. They were pieces I drew because I had to, and there was so much vitality in them. They were wild and raw. When I drew from a space of being seen, there was a stiffness to my art. So gradually my style had to shift so that my doodles and inner workings became the pieces that I would show.

After the HOPE event, I went back through the same cycle again—removal from the city and dedication to art. I was chasing an idea, not something that was burning from within me. I was exhausted doing work for others, so again I went away to recalibrate, away from the city in an underground lair. And while I got away from myself at times, my periods of incubation grew shorter as I moved closer to my path. I was getting closer and closer to living with my true sense of purpose and self-knowledge the whole of the time. Like goldenrod that lights the way out of times of darkness, I traveled deeper inside with every cycle to find light and emerge in more authentic incarnations.

IT'S A HOT STEAMY DAY IN LATE AUGUST AND I HEAR THE CICADAS OUTSIDE my window. I'm in Brooklyn amid the wild, urban fecundity, watching green life break through every crack in concrete and crawl up the sides of buildings. Goldenrod is blooming on the city streets, in my community garden, and in Prospect Park, marking the transition to autumn. When I am in Scotland, I collect silence so I can endure the city sirens and cars. Sometimes I pretend the coming and going of the traffic are ocean waves, and underneath I listen to the click and hum of the cicadas. I can't imagine a summer without their song.

Coming out as an artist has been a cycle of burrowing and breaking free. There are old skins, old inner selves in stacks, notebooks, sketchbooks, and portfolios. Some are unfinished, some I feel proud of, and others I haven't looked at in years. My art is the thing I have clung to the most. I have described my pieces as snake skins—layers I needed to shed in order to grow. In a sense, the work has been both my baggage and my healing. Last fall, I considered burning my art in a symbolic bonfire but it's hard to know which ones to show and which ones to set aflame. Maybe one day some of the old images that I deemed "not good enough" will resurface, be seen, and wash the dust off someone's soul. Mary Oliver writes of goldenrod, "They rise in a stiff sweetness, in the pure peace of giving one's gold away."[4]

Into the darkness they go, the wise and the lovely.

EDNA ST. VINCENT MILLAY

PART FOUR

Going Underground

WE NEED DARKNESS AND SILENCE TO RECHARGE. DARKNESS IS RE-
ceptive, feminine. A powerful, mysterious void and source of
strength. Darkness is negative space, but not negative in the way we've
come to define it. It is infinite, universal potential and the fertile soil of
the feminine that exists in the womb and below our feet in the body of
Mother Earth. Darkness is rich, black charcoal that remains after a fire,
a substance that absorbs, cleanses, clears, and creates life.

JAPANESE KNOTWEED

Polygonum cuspidatum

Family: Polygonaceae

Japanese knotweed is a tall herbaceous perennial with the ability to thrive in toxic soils, drawing out heavy metals and poisons to detoxify damaged
land. With an extensive woody rhizome system, the plant
can set up whole underground systems that can grow inches a
day, moving beneath highways and around obstacles to set up col-
onies on the other side. Though the plant flowers in the fall, she doesn't
rely on pollination to reproduce; the extensive underground roots are
responsible for her spread.

This pervasive plant learned to thrive in the harsh environment of
Japanese volcanoes amid extreme changeability, and grows successfully
on the lava fields lining the slopes of Japan's active volcanoes. She developed the ability to store explosive energy deep underground and spring
forth through feet of ash and volcanic rock, and can break through seemingly firm foundations to create a feral instability. But as this plant dis-
mantles, she creates soil that is fertile and new. And volcanic soil is
especially fertile, its magnetism having just erupted out into the upper
world.

VOLCANIC SOIL

People will do anything, no matter how absurd, in order to avoid facing their own souls. One does not become enlightened by imagining figures of light, but by making the darkness conscious.

CARL JUNG

He took the platinum chain off his neck, wrapped it around the back of mine, twisted it, and pulled me into him. We were in a hotel on Atlantic Avenue in Brooklyn, not far from our apartments. But we each had roommates and wanted to be alone. With my growing collection of plants and potions, he was a little afraid that I'd put some sort of spell on him, even though I've never been one for spells. I've always wanted someone to desire me of their own free will, and we were magnetically drawn to each other the way I craved. We knew each other for some time before we spent the night together, which took discipline on my part—I wanted our tension to build.

The Earth herself is a giant magnet. The planet gets her magnetic field from spinning electric currents within her molten metallic core, which create invisible veins of force between the North and South Poles. All earthly matter experiences magnetism, some more strongly than others. Creatures such as bears, bees, and birds have built-in compasses for migration and are able to sense this magnetic field, using its energetic pull to navigate toward what they need. It feels to me that we humans aren't so different. We use the core of our own animal bodies to navigate and attract. I've tended to go where I feel pulled.

Jamal and I existed in a fiery shadowland where we got lost and became nothing but our bodies tangled into one endless beginning. He resonated through me, skin against skin, souls touching. He opened doors inside me until they were hanging off their hinges. When he would depart, he'd leave me wide open and I'd create art. That was our deal.

Before I met Jamal, I'd burned myself out on the city, working for others in my nonprofit job and giving my creative energy away. I needed to reset and recharge. After my beloved grandparents passed away, their house remained empty for a time, so I decided to spend months in their basement seeking communion with myself and with their spirits, in a space of my own choosing. It was my little den where I did nothing but paint, meditate, reflect, and write. My sister thought I was nuts. "Why are you staying in the most creepy corner of the house by yourself?" I craved the silent darkness, and it's where I was pulled. In the quiet basement, I let the noise and ideas that were interfering with my own transfer out of my body and into art, or quieted them through the practice of meditation. As I relaxed into my own space, the busyness of the external world began to melt away and I could hear my own voice again.

When I'd begun a formal Zen meditation practice seven years earlier in 2000 while living in the East Village, I was restless. But I could get into the zone through art and movement so I figured I could master meditation too. Yet it wasn't until I committed myself to sitting on the cushion in sangha for thirty-minute stretches that I understood how much was bubbling beneath the surface in me. I realized my thoughts had energy all their own, at times pulling me away from my center and causing me to waste my energy in wrong directions. So I decided to commit myself to a consistent practice, and there was a Zendo not far from the boxing gym where I was teaching. I went during breaks and after work. I figured if I could achieve inner stillness in the chaos of the city, I could do it anywhere. I sat for at least one intensely uncomfortable hour a day.

The Rōshi of the Zendo told me to count my breath, to "go back to one when thoughts come up and start again." I understood the premise of this practice, but at the time I didn't like it. I suppose I was scared to suppress my feelings, to keep things inside. I had weathered the pressure and the power that reared up in me when I tried to stash and store things—tension, anxiety—like a feral animal that had her primal instincts in check for too long. Those strong emotions left me no room. I asked my instructor, "If I count, aren't I suppressing those thoughts? Wouldn't it be better to just watch them and let them get tired?"

I quietly rebelled against my instruction and let my thoughts do their thing. I wanted to see them for what they were. I did try to relax and notice when I got attached to one and it became a new thought and then another, but I stayed in this space of bearing witness, hoping that with the expansion and contraction of my breath they would pass like intense storm clouds. I let them run and scream and do crazy dances until they got tired of it . . . and then there were more. But when I just stayed with it, kept watching and kept breathing, they exhausted themselves and space appeared between the clouds.

AFTER MONTHS OF HIBERNATION IN THE CREEPY CORNER OF THE HOUSE, I found access to more peace and realized with surprise that I was ready to return to the city—not as a boxer or a nonprofit coordinator; I was attracted to the idea of making my mark as an artist there. New York had pulled me back. (There are rumors that the city has amplified draw because it is built on a lattice of crystalline rock that includes some of the most common materials used in the fiber optics of our cell phones—silica glass fibers, quartz, and magnetite—that keep us connected and addicted through light pulses that transmit information down fiber lines.) While in the cave of my grandparents' basement, I had used some of the same skills I developed while working with nonprofits on behalf of my own creative drive: I made calls and connections, submitted my work to New York galleries, and reached out to the musicians in my orbit who might need album covers. That's what I loved about New York; I could shape-shift and come back into its energetic hub to "make it" with a new vision and revised self. And the DUMBO neighborhood in Brooklyn had become a thriving art center. I had my first show in the art festival at none other than Gleason's, my boxing home. From there, I landed a solo show, sold a few paintings, secured more commissions, and created art for events. It seemed like this new phase of me was taking off when the economic crash of 2008 hit. Suddenly, I was stressed out and struggling to pay my rent.

Pressured to get it together, I figured I would coach boxing again. Friends and former clients had been asking me to, but I had kept committed to my art and held the easy work at bay. Now that I was desperate, I negotiated with myself: *My body has healed and I can reenter the sweet science from a different perspective. I've missed it anyway.* But underneath it all, I felt like a failure. If I was going to go back to boxing, I wanted at the very least to explore new training grounds. I started training people in Prospect Park, and went to check out the Mendez Boxing gym in Chelsea, and that's when it happened. Guided by instinct, I walked into a fancy gym nearby and there he was. The attraction was immediate. We talked about boxing, the possibility of my working there (I didn't really want to work there), and he gave me his card. I could not get him out of my head. Days later, I invited him to one of my art openings and was totally preoccupied by when and if he'd stop by. When he finally walked into the gallery that evening, my heart beat fast and my body burned.

ACCORDING TO A VERY POETIC REPORT FROM TUFTS UNIVERSITY, "THE ENERGY-laden, electrically charged solar wind blows out from the Sun in all directions and never stops, carrying with it a magnetic field rooted in the star. Although it is exceedingly thin, far less substantial than a terrestrial breeze or even a whisper, the solar wind is powerful enough to mold the outer edges of the Earth's magnetosphere into a changing asymmetric shape, like a teardrop falling toward the Sun."[1]

A teardrop falling toward the Sun. There is such beauty in the fact that it is the Earth's powerful feminine magnetic sphere that allows her not to be consumed. And yet, I wanted Jamal to consume me. Had I not spent all those hours in my grandmother's basement fortifying my own magnetic field, my wish may have just come true.

At first, we wanted to claim each other but we struggled with our opposing wants and needs, so we would drift apart and then crash together again. When he would get possessive, I'd insist on poetry: "I just want you to consume me ... Why does it have to be so complicated?" He would vanish for a few days, and in his absence I would crave the subjugation of being claimed. Somehow, he had the keys to free and trap me simultaneously. Our senses of time and space often seemed at odds, but when we were alone, we melted together; I didn't know where his body ended and mine began.

Eventually, we found our rhythm. He gave me the kind of attention I needed—blazing intensity counterbalanced by vast expanses of nothingness. I painted the colors that came through in the way he touched me, the way he stared, the memory in my concave mattress, the exposed fruit still raw where he'd bit in. Although it frustrated me and pained me sometimes, our relationship was by design. In those in-between spaces I dove into my fertile darkness, plugged into my energy socket and recharged. He loosened something inside me and I found I had the strength to dive deeper. My senses were soothed and then heightened, able to savor the subtle.

Somehow it all felt familiar, as though we'd done this dance before. We quickly got into step, shedding masks and coming out from behind walls to share the tender places they were protecting. A stellar athlete, many of his dreams were thwarted when he got locked up on drug charges. We stayed up all night when he agreed to read me the stack of poems he'd written while he was in prison. As we sat on the edge of my bed, he conjured with his words the dehumanizing ways prison does a number on your psyche, especially as a Black man in America. His raw and beautiful writing ensnared me. He allowed me to confide in him too; I shared my art, my fears, my traumas.

So that was how it went—he helped me dive deep and access parts of myself I didn't know how to access alone, and I tried to support him with the same acceptance and fuel for life. Sexual energy is vitality, creativity, life force energy, and a partner can be the catalyst for an awakening. Volcanoes are the architects of the Earth; eruptions and the movement of tectonic plates crashing into each other create land as we know it. And as we moved inside our own shifting, explosive landscape, we shared some angsty, beautiful years, and created new terrain that is forever smoldering under my skin.

UNDER THE SURFACE

Many of the practices and rituals that dominate healing and spirituality today seem to emphasize light, but many ancient traditions spring from fertile darkness and honor light and dark in equal measure are timeless. These balanced observances are in alignment with the true forces of nature. It is in the fertile darkness that we plant new seeds and life is conceived. The mystery of darkness is where growth, healing, and transformation begin. While well-meaning, I find the expression "love and light" to be incredibly irritating. When we over-value masculine, or yang, energy, we set ourselves up to struggle with just *being* and tapping into our intuition. In the city, neon lights and street traffic keep us going all night—washing out the stars that shine in the night sky. When I take time to adjust to darkness, I begin to see lightning bugs, stars, and constellations that had been lost in the overwhelm of artificial light.

Some teachings say that we must reconfigure "negative" words with positive affirmations to hypnotize ourselves into happiness. While that may work for some, the practice never resonated with me. I want to unmask my shadows and see them for what they are. If they lure me in and grow larger in my imagination, I do my best to breathe, write, draw, and ground myself. When engaging practices that allow me to move beyond surface layers of thought, I get rid of static and am better able to receive the wisdom held in my quiet, still places.

In ancient and present-day goddess-centered traditions, people tap into the power of darkness by going into caves, the wombs of the Earth, to experience sensory deprivation. Descending into caves was and is seen as a way to achieve knowledge; they are spaces where the noise of the external world is blocked out so innate wisdom can arise. These dark, subterranean spaces are places to engage mystery, enhance psychic awareness, and, in some cases, attain enlightenment. I crave that too. The quiet dark helps me recover my spark, my voice, and my creative fire. Creating or entering spaces that mimic the natural flow of day into night can reset our circadian rhythm—our biological clock that lets us know when it's time to sleep, wake, reproduce, and consume.

JAPANESE KNOTWEED ROOTS CONTAIN NATURE'S HIGHEST SOURCE OF RESVERatrol, a botanical hormone that resembles female sex hormones, which, not surprisingly, gives knotweed fierce feminine power. Even a tiny, tiny rhizome can regenerate an entire plant, and if left to do her thing, she can spread quickly and relentlessly underground. Japanese knotweed habitats range from parking lots, roadside embankments, forest edges, disturbed grounds, and volcanic deserts to much of the industrialized world where other feminine power may be absent.

In the United Kingdom, Japanese knotweed has gotten a bad rap as something of a supervillain in some quarters, particularly with landlords who are convinced that this plant destroys homes and degrades the value of land they perceive to be theirs. Often referred to by the media as "Britain's largest female,"[2] Japanese knotweed first spread throughout the country after German botanist Phillipp von Siebold sent a small cutting to Kew Gardens in 1850.[3] All the knotweed in Britain grew from the underground rhizomes of this one single plant. But the plant's reputation as a supervillain is overblown. According to a recent report by the House of Commons Science and Technology Committee and ecologist Dr. Mark Fennell, "We found nothing to suggest that Japanese knotweed causes significant damage to buildings—even when it is growing in close proximity."[4] But because of her bad reputation and incredible resilience, people pour millions of dollars and copious amounts of toxic herbicide in the ground to get rid of her. The only true beneficiaries of this smear campaign are the chemical companies that produce glyphosate and other toxins (the real supervillains, in my opinion) that kill not just knotweed but the surrounding wildlife and have been shown to cause cancer. Meanwhile, the properties of knotweed have been shown in numerous studies to prevent and treat cancer.[5]

Like many herbalists and Earth-based healers, I have come to believe that plants appear when and where they're needed. Swiss physician and alchemist Paracelsus once said that "the same star influences or soul influences that cause diseases in people also cause healing plants to appear in the same areas they arise."[6]

It is in the plant's native Japan, where knotweed is known as itadori, whose translation is "remove pain," that people have been living in harmony with this plant for thousands of years. The roots and shoots have become an integral part of food culture and traditional medicine.[7] The young stems are eaten as a spring vegetable, with a flavor similar to incredibly sour rhubarb. The roots are used to treat a variety of ailments ranging from fungal infections and skin inflammation to cardiovascular diseases and pain, as the name suggests. Japanese knotweed has a strong immune-enhancing capacity that benefits the cardiovascular system and has been shown to have anti-cancer, "anti-aging" (I take issue with that term), and estrogen-regulating effects.

A recent study by Harvard Medical School showed that resveratrol taken from knotweed rhizomes stimulates in humans the production of a serum that blocks diseases by speeding up the cell's energy production centers, affecting the activity of enzymes called sirtuins that control several biological pathways and are involved in the aging process.[8]

Tincture and decoction of the root have been shown to kill the spirochetes (spiral-shaped bacteria) of Lyme disease that are found in difficult-to-reach areas by enhancing blood flow throughout the body. And though this organism, *Borrelia* bacteria, which we now call Lyme, seemed to appear just over forty years ago,[9] a recent study by Oregon State University found a fifteen-to-twenty-million-year-old piece of amber from the Dominican Republic that is the oldest fossil evidence of *Borrelia* fossilized in amber and shows that this bacteria has been around for about fifteen million years—long before humans walked the Earth.

In a recent interview, herbalist Stephen Harrod Buhner, author of *Healing Lyme*, said that "this disease is forcing people to break out of the allopathic medical paradigm because it doesn't work for Lyme."[10] In that sense, the disease itself—along with Japanese knotweed, the so-called invasive healer—is proving to be a valuable, fierce teacher for some. In order to truly heal, we need to examine the root causes of deeper, persistent illness and resolve the ways we abuse and exploit our ecosystem in order to reconnect to nature and access sustainable recovery practices. Healing is often about restoring balance to reset our vitality, instinct and circadian rhythms. And while it's worth talking about constituents of plants, like resveratrol, the way I really view plant medicine is to look at whole plants, their behavior in the wild, and what's happening in our bodies in relation to nature.

AS MORE FOREST AND LAND ARE DESTROYED, THE PRESENCE OF INVASIVE SPEcies and so-called weeds will only increase, so we must learn who these plants really are before attacking them. Negative perception of these plants fuels a war on invasive species, contributes to more ecological damage, and increases our adversarial relationship with the living Earth. Learning about a plant's community dynamics and species niches is crucial to helping us understand the motivation of so-called weeds or invasive species. If a plant is doing harm, we need to explore the reasons why they are thriving: Where are the ecological gaps? What species of plant or animal might be missing? If there are absences, can the missing links be safely and effectively reintroduced? What are the human practices surrounding the ecosystem? Are those practices overwhelming and killing the native plants? If so, can the community be educated and practices shifted for the well-being of all? If there is no clear underlying cause and a plant is truly overwhelming an environment, are there alternative uses for the plant such as food, medicine, or biofuel? Invasive species are not inherently evil, and the short-term "solutions" of herbicide can have dire long-term consequences that cause the greater community of plants, animals, and people even more harm than the emergence of the plant itself.

I see in knotweed a fierce feminine energy that, like wild rose, has arrived to shore up ecological gaps and burst through the foundations of our literal and figurative homes. Fear of darkness and fear of fierce feminine power—present in all species and genders—are often intertwined. Maybe this plant is a manifestation of the Cailleach or Durga, "the undefeatable goddess" in Hindu tradition—dark goddesses forged by people's experience of nature. Who knows. Maybe instead of poisoning this plant, we can pay attention.

WHEN JAMAL AND I TRIED TO PUT OUR PASSION IN THE NICE, NEAT BOX OF boyfriend/girlfriend, it was smashed. We didn't want to build a traditional partnership, and the passion and depth we shared were what we were after together. That was okay for us. Relationships don't have to fit into any kind of construct, and in many ways, those deep spaces that don't obey conventional rules can be the most real. I like to think that our years together shifted something inside us each, unlocking creative sparks that we brought out into the world.

I BELIEVE THAT THE MOST POWERFUL PARTS OF LIFE ARE OFTEN UNSEEN. WE might be afraid of what exists under the surface, yet within those voids and unseen spaces growth and healing can truly begin. While our imaginations may go wild when we're unable to see what's in front of us on or below the surface of a deep, dark loch, in order to grow we must embrace the risk and let go of our desire for control and clarity. We might plunge into infinite depth or the abyss of passion and maybe even lose ourselves for a spell, but we should trust that we will find our way back to the surface, and we'll be transformed. Our contact with fire can be explosive but with enough time in the healing darkness, the solar winds won't consume us.

At many of my Sacred Warrior retreats, we gather around a bonfire at night to reflect, meditate, write, and release what we're ready to transform into the flames. We let the purifying flames burn away old stories, habits, and patterns we've outgrown. I guide everyone through a meditation beforehand so we can get quiet and spiral into our inner caves. When we emerge from meditation we write, in stream of consciousness, until it's clear what we need to release to step more completely into our power. When everyone is ready, we throw our words into the fire, thanking those stories, habits, and wounds for all they taught us and the ways in which they may have protected us for a time. Then, since nature abhors a vacuum, we share what we will replace them with as we watch them burn.

When the fire goes out, we're left with the darkness of night and rich black charcoal—an element that absorbs, cleanses, and purifies. Fire consumes but it doesn't leave us empty-handed: we're left with a substance that literally absorbs toxins, filters the water we drink, and cleanses the water of our body. And while lava rivers spread and create bleak landscapes for a time, the elements of fire, water, and air erode those rocks so that plants like knotweed can break through the stone, destroy illusory foundations, and create life anew.

SKULLCAP
Scutellaria spp.

Family: Lamiaceae

Skullcap is a plant in the mint family that relieves tension in the body caused by the mind. Skullcap soothes tension in the jaw and can ease those of us who lay awake at night with swirling thoughts. The drops of tincture under my tongue feel like soothing hands stroking my head. This is also a wonderful ally for those like me who are sensitive to sound. The plant quiets worry and patterns of repetitive thought, allowing us to dream and vision beyond surface-level noise. This plant was once called mad-dog herb because it was thought to cure rabies, and the extract is useful when our jaw is tense and we want to growl.

Chinese skullcap has a high level of melatonin, a hormone made by the pineal gland (also known as the "third eye") that regulates our sleep/wake cycles and can help reset our circadian rhythm. Melatonin aligns us with the seasons with higher levels in long nights of autumn and winter, and lower levels in the light of spring and summer. For animals like wolves, the hormone is essential in the timing of reproduction and their growing and shedding of fur. Without melatonin, they are not equipped to survive in the wild.

DEEP SLEEP

Night is when we are closer to ourselves, closer to essential
ideas and feelings that do not register so much during daylight
hours.

CLARISSA PINKOLA ESTÉS

Look to your experience in dreams to know how you will fare
in death. Look to your experience of sleep to discover whether
or not you are truly awake.

TENZIN WANGYAL RINPOCHE

If I live to be one hundred years old, I will have slept for about thirty years
of my life, and since I want to make even those years count, I work with
my dreams. When I bring their lessons and insights into waking life, I feel
like I'm contributing to a continuum of consciousness. I don't always know
how to decode them right away, and sometimes I don't need to, but I work to
pay attention to my dreamscape.

   In last night's dream, I was in a dense, dark pine forest with red wolves,
the most endangered canid in the world. I was making paper masks for them.
I don't remember why I was making masks for them—in my dream my effort
was a human idea. The wolves and I were on one side of a fence and the human

241

world was on the other. When I went to place a paper mask on one beautiful red wolf like I was "supposed to," he started making faces at me, seeming to mock me. His face began shape-shifting, flattening, expanding, and contorting into what looked like ceremonial masks. I understood. What I was witnessing was a transmission, communication. He was showing me that they, the wolves, have more power and wisdom than I and other humans could possibly imagine. I began to make faces back and it felt liberating. The wolf was drawing out my primal power too.

Then we heard people coming and he put the stupid paper mask on. As he did, a veil seemed to drop between us and everything was "normal" again. The people who appeared were pleased with the paper mask and began to point to the red wolf and explain who he was, demeaning and patronizing this powerful being. The wolf and I seemed to shrink and tame ourselves in this ignorant human world, but as soon as they walked away, the veil lifted again and everything grew darker, more alive, more ominous, and the fence disappeared. All around me was now an endless forest. I was in the wolves' realm and as I walked through the woods, my senses were heightened. I understood through scents and subtle movement, and every sound was amplified. I heard a fawn calling. She had fallen into a forest ditch and seemed to be suffering, so a feral wolf dog killed her. I hoped it wasn't a useless kill, and that it was swift. I knew the fawn's death was part of the rules that I would have to accept in the wild world.

When fear or doubt crept into my mind during the dream, I began to straddle realms and could see into the human world, almost through a wall of mesh. An electrical power line was down and a man looked as though he was dead and his son was nearby, scared. People were mad at me about it, I don't remember why. I was blamed for the accident but it was a misunderstanding in the human world. I slipped further into the wild world where I felt I belonged, and I became less interested in what was happening in so-called reality. The presence of the red wolf seemed to be everywhere. I think he was our god. And then I woke and could tell I had been grinding my teeth, growling maybe.

AS A YOUNG TEEN, MY TEETH WERE LIKE FANGS AND I WAS SO SELF-CONSCIOUS about them that my dentist sanded them down. In fact, he suggested it since they were indeed a little weird-looking and really sharp. The rest of my teeth were beginning to wear down from me grinding them at night anyway, and for some reason, I never got a nighttime mouthguard even though it was a conversation I'd had with the dentist at every visit. Since I've been working with plants as an adult, skullcap has been a savior for my nighttime gnashing. The tincture or tea is specifically recommended for bruxism (teeth grinding or jaw clenching) and helps me relax toward more receptivity, calming without spaciness or drowsiness.

We are vulnerable when we sleep and when we are alone at night every sound can become amplified, our primal senses may be on alert; the strange banging in the radiator, a creak in the staircase, and the rattle of the wind that was a pleasant breeze during the day suddenly seems menacing. Each sound may make our nerves stand on end, trigger our fight-or-flight response, and cause tension. I woke the other night after walking around my grandmother's kitchen in a dream and it occurred to me that I might be the cause of disturbance for the people who live there now. Many of my dreams have taken place there since we sold the house, and they are so vivid that I imagine the new residents must feel me haunting in the middle of the night. Who's to say that ghosts are dead people? Whatever the cause, skullcap can calm the feeling of hypervigilance and extreme sensitivity to external influences that can become a pattern of response in our body. If left unchecked, the tension that is created can take on a life of its own.

For some, dread accompanies nighttime; when we lay down to sleep, our mind can become extremely busy. But if we can engage practices to clear excess mental and external noise during the day, our sleep can be more peaceful and even profound. It is difficult to enter visionary or meditative states when our mind is reeling or we feel tense, and as a powerful nervine with high concentrations of melatonin, skullcap can help awaken the third eye, helping us see beyond ordinary sight. The pineal gland, not the pituitary, is actually the master gland of the endocrine system and is responsible for synthesizing melatonin, a hormone released in response to darkness.[1] This organ lies deep in the center of the brain and has unique connections to light, moon cycles, "enlightenment," and our alignment with the wild. Through dreams we can reach directly into our instinct, intuition, powerful inner vision, and imaginal realms.

AT HOME, I SLEEP ON THE FLOOR WITH MY JOURNAL AND A TINCTURE OF SKULL-cap next to me. My partner and I have been sleeping on the floor for six years now and when we lay against something solid, our bodies, our muscles, and tension can fully let go. Sleeping on the floor is simple, has made camping easy, and is much better on my back. Since I've been here in the cottage in the High-lands for months now, I have also moved to the floor, and though the bed at Al-ladale is cozy and luxurious, the floor feels so much better on my body. My lower spine healed a bit strangely after the accident, overcompensating in what my acupuncturist calls a "step-down." I didn't pay the back pain much mind while I was fighting, but later I had intense spasms, so sleeping on the floor is preventive medicine for me. My acupuncturist commented recently on how much better my back has been. When I told him I'd been sleeping on the floor, he said, "Oh yeah, that's good. I sleep on a special slab of stone." Those who know, know.

I've slept with a journal by my bed to write and record my dreams when, as a teenager, I began to have to have disturbing, repetitive dreams that I wanted to understand. I learned about lucid dreaming then too: the practice of awakening in a dream to change its outcome while our body is in a highly suggestive state. With practice, I became aware that I was dreaming and real-ized I have a voice and agency, even in my dreams. I write down my dreams most mornings now too. I usually jot a list of the key elements, sometimes just a doodle that helps me remember or if it feels particularly significant, and sometimes I write them out in as much detail as I recall and type them into my computer later. I have thousands of dreams written down and it's been interesting to go back to see what my dreamscape has predicted, which ones shifted my perception of reality and have profoundly influenced my actions. Not all dreams are profound, of course, and some seem completely irrelevant, but when I make note of them anyway, I have found that some make sense days, weeks, or even years later. Dreams point us to the mythic content of our lives, and like an epic miniseries, sometimes they only add up when we string them together over time. We rarely learn or heal from something overnight, and those of us who've had repetitive dreams or nightmares know that sometimes we need to be startled awake before we pay attention to what our body and our psyche are telling us.

I had a repetitive dream during a period of transition in my early twenties. Night after night I found myself being driven by two strange men, in the back seat of a car that was moving way too fast, frighteningly out of control. We spiraled on precarious roads along the edges of mountaintops and never arrived anywhere. I was terrified, scared speechless. In waking life, things were in limbo and I didn't know where I was headed. The fear of the recurring dream forced me to dive inward in waking life and ask what the dream was showing me, while confronting the situation in my dream.

After being afraid to go to sleep for a number of nights, worried I'd be driven out of control, I went to sleep with the intention to "wake up" in my dream, confront the men, and tell them to *Let. Me. Out!* It was terrifying and I was barely able to speak, but I did it, and as I confronted the men, and what the dreams were pointing to in waking life, the dreams ceased. Similar dreams return over the years when my unconscious mind knows I am "asleep" and being led in some aspect of my life instead of being behind the wheel.

DREAM SCHOOL

There is a great deal of intelligence at play within me right now that I am completely unaware of. I don't tell my kidneys to filter my blood, actively ask my skin to regulate my body temperature, or command my heart to beat. I would have no idea how to go about it if I had to, and would be consumed (and soon dead) trying to handle all of the intricacies that happen automatically. Most of our body's functions happen involuntarily in a subconscious or unconscious state, and shifts of consciousness can impact these involuntary systems. For example, we know that chronic stress impacts heart rate, digestion, and mental health and that the practice of meditation can reverse the damaging effects of undue stress.[2] If we receive a deep insight and shift of perception during a dream, perhaps we can initiate healing in a similar way.

I've always been attracted to subversive knowledge, especially the kind that is too powerful to be written down. I've fantasized that finding this esoteric knowledge would happen in a way that would echo cinematic moments that, despite how stereotyped they seem now, called to me: training with Jedi masters like Yoda, or in faraway places like Uma Thurman's character did with her sensei in *Kill Bill*, or with Dr. Stephen Strange's teachers who merged science and mysticism behind an unassuming door in Nepal, or in a back room in Chinatown where the "real" martial arts systems are shared only after getting through fortresses of secret knocks, riddles, and passwords.

Dreams can also be doorways to deep wisdom, and we are the gatekeepers. We decide, consciously and sometimes unconsciously, who and what resides in our ethereal spaces. And while awakening the third eye in order to access visionary or dreamlike states is a goal in many spiritual traditions, most also warn not to venture beyond ordinary reality before grounding into this three-dimensional world. Fierce dwellers live at the thresholds of new realms and we must be sure we're ready for what we encounter there. We may have to face our own demons before we gain access to these deeper realms.

IN TIBETAN VAJRAYANA BUDDHISM AND BÖN TRADITION, THE INDIGENOUS animist belief system of Tibet,[3] there is a concept of terma: sacred teachings hidden by ascended masters for the benefit of the future masters. Energy doesn't go away; it simply gets transmuted so ascended masters and open, willing, and receptive students may be able to access important teachings that may no longer be in material form but wait in the ether to be transmitted. Even when the material objects are gone, as in the case of many ancient religious scrolls and texts that were burned or oral traditions that were never written down, the knowledge, wisdom, and information encoded within them is still in the ether. Whether that hidden, ancient knowledge can be accessed, translated, and applied is a different story. Ekajati, a powerful goddess in Vajrayana Buddhist cosmology and "the mother of the mothers of all the Buddhas," is a fierce guardian at the gate of these teachings, testing potential students to make sure they can be trusted with what they find. Terma may be found in physical locations such as caves, within elements such as water, in the medicine of a medicinal plant, or in dreams and visionary experiences. The students who discover terma and receive the transmission of ancient teachers are known as tertons, or "treasure finders." The teachings may emerge as an epiphany, a sudden embodied understanding that initiates awakening.

The Akashic records are also believed to be encoded in a nonphysical plane of existence—in ether, space, or the void—and accessed in deep meditation, transcendent or in-between states of consciousness, and dreams. Within Bön, Akasha is viewed as the Great Mother, a primordial space from which all ideas, forms, and beings emerge and eventually dissolve back into. This tradition of Buddhism then held the potential for practitioners to access unlimited knowledge when, through practice, they arrived at enlightenment. In Tibetan dream yoga the purpose of dreaming is to move beyond our illusions and wake up.

I'VE COME TO BELIEVE THAT HEALING CAN HAPPEN IN THE DREAM REALM whether our minds understand it or not. There will always be mystery we cannot touch. I often felt like I was getting transmissions in dream time that were stored in my unconscious and meant for me to use or understand later. I found this writing from after a dream in 2004: *I had a growth spurt last night that is beyond my understanding. Messages transmitted to me in the dream realm were as important as learning to stand and to walk. Now awake, my mind can't quite grasp what my body already knows, though I understood perfectly the language of my dream. Symbols and images and words were put together in ways that made more sense than they do in this waking world, and made this reality almost sadly simple. I know that I'll grow into the knowledge, or in the process of clearing my mind, come to see how wise I already am.*

While dreams may be relevant today in psychotherapy, especially Jungian therapy, on the whole, most of us don't develop ourselves through dreams to the degree that we could. These experiences may seem "out there"; there is no way to prove or offer evidence of a dream, which is why I think so many of us discount the dreams of others or keep our own private. But for the Anishinaabe people of northeastern North America, dreams were an important part of their holistic worldview, an aspect of personal development from childhood and a way to assert one's direction in life.[4] Dreaming was, and in many cases still is, the true way someone became a healer or herbalist—they were chosen in a dream.

In my thirties, as my life's work was becoming more clear, the line between dreams and reality became blurred. At that point, I had emptied a great deal of inner space through years of meditation, mindful movement, and creative exploration. I found myself more receptive to what the Earth needed. My dreams not only showed me what I needed to confront within myself, but also what I needed to bring to fruition and share with others. I will never forget the first time I saw energy emanating from a tree: in waking life, I was meditating with a soft gaze and saw what looked like strands of illuminated webbing between the branches, pulsing with energy. It was a beautiful, deeply emotional light show and I felt that I was being trusted with something truly sacred.

It's worth mentioning that while I work with plants like mugwort or skullcap, I haven't used psychedelics. Since I can tap into visionary states easily I have been afraid that if I experimented with psychedelics, I might not return to everyday reality. When I was young, my mom told me stories about her own frightening experiences and her friends who overdosed and died or took too much LSD and went permanently crazy. I was amply warned, and I know myself well. While entheogens like psilocybin can have incredible therapeutic value when taken mindfully, I also feel that the power of these more potent plants and fungi can obscure the magic of common ones, whose power can be just as transformative as long as we participate in the work.

When I began working with mushrooms like chaga and reishi and started finding them in the wild, I had a dream about their dimension and language. I woke up and jotted *limitless love*, which were the only words that could capture the sentiment I felt about the mushroom language. In the dream realm, there was no communication barrier between us. The connection was so sweet and I felt like I was being welcomed into the mycelial reality in my waking life that I was beginning to tap into. I began to "understand" them.

As I began to dream about communicating with nature in a more direct way, I found myself guided to integrate and embrace my path toward herbalism, and these dreams accelerated my work in relationship with nature and with plants. I grounded the teachings I was receiving into this three-dimensional reality of my waking life, where there is much work to be done.

I dreamt about plants night after night, and at the start of many dreams, I found myself in a circle with people I would receive the teaching from. The dreams had a succinct order: circle and ceremony, teaching about an aspect of nature or holistic healing and then something within my own life or body that I needed to clear. To my waking mind, the order of the dreams evolved to follow three descending layers that sent me deeply into my psyche. The most wild were times I was waiting in line for registration before I went to a class in what seemed to be a "Dream University." I told my friend Nita about this, as well as some healers I trusted, and they were unsurprised. Nita told me, "A friend of mine had a similar experience. Maybe you were in some of the same dream classes!"

When I woke up each morning I had a deep understanding that seemed to penetrate the layers of my conscious, subconscious, and unconscious mind. Sometimes I dreamt about particular plants and when I woke to look them up, the information I remembered aligned with what naturalists and researchers knew about the plant. Sometimes I woke up with the image of a plant and searched outside or online until I could find the image in waking life. My dreaming and waking lives informed each other and both became far more rich. I was learning, growing, and deepening my connection to the Earth through the day and night and achieving a continuum of consciousness.

At times, it was difficult to determine what was coming from my imagination or what seemed to be a download or vision. While I may never really know, I see visions or downloads as information that comes to me seemingly out of nowhere and offers insight that I didn't have access to before. I was looking for a teacher to guide me, but as I dreamt of the Earth night after night I realized that, duh, my teacher was here under my feet all along.

IN A RECENT DREAM, I WAS GRANTED ACCESS TO AN ANCIENT TEXT. I WAS driving down from the Highlands along the east coast of Scotland and stopped at an old library. It was dusk and the stone library, which seemed to have its own pulse, peered from below a steep hill and pulled me in. I was doing research for an upcoming book and searched through the stacks to find information about Scottish pre-Christian relationships with animals. There was little there until I found a note hidden in one of the books, *The Animal Codex*, about an ancient and yet ever-evolving text about the Gaels' relationship with animals.

It read, "Bringing back the animals indigenous to our land would bring back our heritage." The loss of the animals meant loss of our animate world.

I found a man who seemed to be waiting for me to arrive and we went into a special rare book room where we were alone. He asked me many questions and told me I could access the book only if I met certain criteria: among other things, I had to be a writer and of Scottish heritage. He laid stones on the table and left. I had to choose the right stones, and I vaguely remember a box with a piece of jewelry I had to recognize. If I passed the tests and chose to access the book, I would become affiliated with the library and have to go through some sort of ceremony to become formally associated and granted all access.

While I was wishing it was a library closer to where my ancestors lived (in my dream, the library was between the Highlands and Fife but there is still so much I don't know), I passed the tests and agreed. It was an incredible honor. I've had a few dreams about the library and book since. Perhaps *The Animal Codex* is encoded in the void. Maybe I'm contributing to a new chapter.

RITUALS

If we don't give ourselves enough space to breathe and simply be during the day, our dreams may need to filter all of our doing so we can function again when we open our eyes. I hate watching television at night (and pretty much in general) for exactly this reason. The screen creates static and I may wind up dreaming of things that are entirely irrelevant to me. Of course, sometimes we need a break from processing and so a movie can be like taking a deep breath. But constant numbing or external entertainment can add an extra layer of useless noise that muffles our minds and prevents us from healing on deeper levels.

There are also times I've made the mistake of reaching for my phone even though I know I'll regret it when I do. Emails, texts, news alerts, and social media notifications take me out of those precious liminal moments when I have access to messages from my unconscious. What a sad waste if important information gets lost in the ether as I thrust myself into the busyness of the outer world. The other night I dreamt that I fed my phone to a magical walrus. Maybe that's an option. But when I get pulled away momentarily, I can meditate, tune back into my body, and breathe, and it usually comes back to me.

Creativity loosens barriers and dissolves the doors that the mundane and rote aspects of life sometimes close in my mind. The process of releasing images from my body and moving a pen across a page opens mental barriers, allowing dams to break and dreams to flow. My latest pieces of abstract art contain images and writing about various dreams. When I look at a tiny collection of images, I can reenter those parallel worlds. A small drawing of a turtle amid a collection of other dream images acts as a key to a profound dream and waking experience. The other night I took a photo in a dream. I wanted to show people the beautiful landscape, what was possible. But then I remembered I was in a dream. But still, that image is a clear snapshot in my mind, a reality to manifest.

I recently dreamt that my partner and I were talking about the anger he was holding beneath the surface. As he spoke about it, I could see it visually and he asked me to draw his anger on his body. It was a beautiful work of art—all of his pent-up feelings became symbols on the surface to be seen.

He looked at himself in the mirror and could see all of those feelings for what they were. He could read his emotions, and I stood there with him, reading the shapes and images, understanding him better too. After a while, he washed it off. And while I was sad to see the art go, I saw a change in him. He was cleansed from the inside out. The dream felt like a real transmission, and we have become more adept at letting anger rise to the surface and then washing it away. Dreams show us how we are connected to each other, to our planet, and to our authentic selves through universal archetypes and symbols that transcend culture and time. They show us when we are stuck, warn us of danger, and affirm when we are headed in the right direction. Our dreams often hold mirrors to our lives and we are able to see more clearly where our lives are headed and can decide to change course if we don't like what we see.

FIVE YEARS AGO, I WAS INTERVIEWED FOR A PODCAST AND WAS ASKED IF I HAD to create a superhero, who would they be and what would they do? I thought about it and came up with a being that changed the world through dreams, an ally of wild animals and the Earth. She is a shape-shifter with the face of a wolf, the body of a monkey, and the wings of a bat who can slip into our subconscious as we dream. She creates such powerful, visceral dreams that when people wake, their consciousness completely shifts. CEOs of corporations wake with complete changes of heart and halt environmental destruction; abusers wake, repent, and change their ways; politicians wake and right their wrongs while setting acres and acres of land aside for the commons and the wild. The Wolfbat shifts consciousness for the benefit of all creatures, and leaves people with no one to point fingers at but themselves, and by doing so, she changes the world.

I may try to reenter the red wolf forest through meditation tonight, or in a lucid dream, or maybe I'll call upon the Wolfbat. Like them, we are also powerful shape-shifters, able to sculpt our reality.

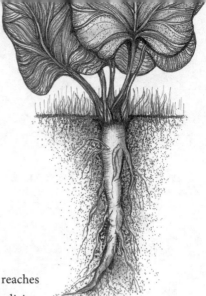

BURDOCK ROOT
Arctium lappa

Family: Asteraceae

Burdock root is a concentrated taproot that reaches deep into the soil to help us ground. With medicine that nourishes the adrenals, burdock root calms the fight-or-flight response and can ease our worries about the unknown. Burdock roots go deep into the earth to access minerals held in the subsoil, and like all taproots have a nourishing quality as they act as a storehouse for vital nutrients. A powerful yet gentle medicine, burdock acts as a blood cleanser, liver support, and prebiotic for our diverse microbiome. The tincture and tea nourish the skin, lymph, kidneys, liver, and gallbladder and strengthen immunity.

Since burdock is a biennial, the root, the most commonly used part of the plant, is generally harvested in autumn at the end of its first year of growth or in the second spring. By fall of the second year, burdock flowers become brown burrs full of seeds that attach to passing animals. The plants seed themselves at the edges of woods, roadsides, in meadows, and anywhere the Earth has been disturbed. The botanical name *Arctium* is derived from the Greek *arktos*, meaning "bear," and some speculate that the name Artemis, the goddess of wild animals who has strong association with the bear, may also derive from that root.

DEPTH

There are more life forms in a handful of forest soil than there are people on the planet.

PETER WOHLLEBEN, *THE HIDDEN LIFE OF TREES*

Our brain matter is, in fact, merely the soil that contains the neural net we use to process and store information. Plants consciously use the soil itself to house their neuronal nets. This allows the root system to continue to expand outward, adding new neural extensions for as long as the plant grows.

STEPHEN HARROD BUHNER,
PLANT INTELLIGENCE AND THE IMAGINAL REALM

It was October 4, almost dusk, when we walked into Prospect Park to harvest burdock root for our friend's birthday. Autumn is an ideal time to harvest roots since the energy of Earth is moving underground. That night, the dark sky of the new moon ensured even more potent medicine and we found the perfect collection of first-year plants in a secluded wooded area with moist, mineral-rich soil. Burdock roots are notoriously hard to unearth; the deep taproots seem to be magnetically attached to the Earth's core and I hate breaking them off, so harvesting from the wild is quite the job. I expect to dig deep and have my hands in the soil with dirt under my nails for days, but that is typically the state of my fingernails anyway.

With their claws, bears dig and eat roots, tubers, tree bark, and copious amounts of berries, catch fish, and eat honey. The majority of their diet is plant based and fall is a critical foraging time when they need to pack on as much fat as they can to see them through their long winter sleep. Burdock, with their brown fur-like burrs and oily roots, is classified as a bear medicine in both Native American tradition and in ancient Europe—indicated by the botanical name *Arctium*. When a plant is strongly associated with an animal or if the animal uses the plant as a medicine, the plant is said to have extra healing powers.

The Celts venerated the bear goddess Artio, the Celtic counterpart of Artemis whose name derived from the Gaulish word for bear, *artos*.[1] She was a protector of nature and all wild creatures, and a mother goddess with attributes of earthly fecundity. Both Artio and Artemis, like mother bears, were and are fiercely protective of the young, and especially young girls. J. Donald Hughes, author of *Ecology in Ancient Civilizations* and a scholar in early environmental history, speculates that the second element in the Greek goddess's name, -tem-, comes from *temno*, a verb meaning to divide or set aside, which is the root of the Greek word *temenos*, meaning a sanctuary. Thus the etymology of the name Artemis would be ark-temnis, "bear sanctuary" or "she who establishes (or protects) the bear sanctuary."[2]

In ancient Greece, prepubescent and adolescent Athenian girls were sent to the sanctuary of Artemis at Brauron to serve the goddess for one year, and during this time, they were known as *arktoi*, or little she-bears. Excavations of the sanctuary and its enclosures reveal that the girls slept in what look like caves while Artemis was worshipped as the Great Mother Bear.[3] The myth surrounding the dedication at Brauron is about a bear that visited the town, was fed by the people and, over time, became tame. When a village girl cruelly teased the bear, the bear killed her or, in some versions of the story, clawed her eyes out. The girl's brothers killed the bear in revenge and Artemis was so enraged that she brought a plague to the city. In order to lift the curse of illness, she demanded that young girls "act the she-bear" at her sanctuary in atonement for the bear's death.

In the sanctuary, children were given a sense of identification with the bear in enactments that were part of an initiation and underwent a period of ritual wildness. Vases recovered from the sanctuary ruins depict images of bear masks in rituals, races, and dancing to honor the goddess. One dance, called the arkteia, was made up of slow, solemn steps meant to imitate the movements of a bear and was performed to a tune from a diaulos (double flute). Little is known about each stage of the ritual, which I imagine was kept in secrecy, but from what we can glean, each gesture communicated a devotion to Artemis and all that she represents in return for her protection and guidance as they transformed from girls to women. As midwife and patron goddess of childbirth, Artemis also helped the she-bears move toward, and through, the role of potential mothers. Early on, the participants wore actual bear skins, but by the fifth century bears had become scarce so the skins were substituted with krokoton—short, saffron-yellow chiton dresses meant to symbolize the bear skins that were "shed" during the final ritual to symbolize the participant's transformation and shedding of the old self.

BURDOCK SUPPORTS MOTHERS-TO-BE BY BALANCING HORMONES AND GROUNDING us, bringing us toward the healing support of Mother Earth. Burdock supports sacred warriors and periods of intense transformation through stability by nourishment of the adrenals, the glands that regulate our body's functioning and produce hormones, including cortisol, a hormone activated when our stress levels rise. Our adrenals signal our body to enter a heightened state of emergency, alerting us to pick up our feet and run, and if they are triggered too often, we will feel less and less grounded. Cortisol secretion is cyclic, rising in the morning and slowly falling in the evening like the rhythms of a hibernating bear.

Burdock can help to decongest the liver and support overall function for improved hormonal balance, and can help this process flow. As we explored in previous chapters, the liver is our gate of protection on the inside that removes toxins and other biologically active molecules from the blood and converts them by changing their structure or inactivating them. If there are too many hormones overwhelming the liver (such as BPA, synthetic estrogen), they may be stored up, not only in the liver but in other parts of our body, affecting hormonal and reproductive health.

Herbalist Matthew Wood taught me about the Native American tradition of "spirit signatures" that categorizes herbs according to animals. Bear medicines are brown, furry, oily roots like burdock that act on the adrenal cortex to strengthen the parasympathetic nervous system. People with bear constitutions have big builds, similar to kaphas in the Ayurvedic tradition, and tend to be introspective dreamers who enjoy cozy periods of hibernation. Burdock also increases bile secretion to help us digest oily foods more easily, increases oil uptake, helps the liver process lipids, and distributes lipids to the skin, hair, tissues, adrenals, steroids, and the hormonal system. Wood explained that burdock is something of an endocrine and female remedy since steroid and sex hormones are made from oil and require oil for transmission through the body. People who need bear medicine might be thin, weak, with exhausted adrenals, like the vata dosha, and need dietary oils to rebuild their system. Oil builds the adrenals, one of the many reasons why nonfat diets are no good. Bear medicines offer reserve, power, and stamina.

SOIL AND OUR MICROBIOME

When living on St. Marks Place in Brooklyn, I religiously brought my compost to the community garden one block away from my apartment. To earn the key, I had to pay a nominal fee, spend time tending to the land and opening the sanctuary to the public during garden hours, and attend a couple of meetings a year—easy steps for private access to beautiful green space in the city. I put my name on a list for my own garden plot knowing it might be a couple of years before I could grow my own food and medicine, but after just one year, I got the anticipated email saying that I had earned my own raised bed where I could plant what I wished. I was ecstatic. I could not wait to get my hands in the soil.

I planted varieties of lettuce, kale, lemon balm, skullcap, echinacea, and what many would consider to be weeds: chickweed, motherwort, violet, stinging nettles, and even dandelion. In just a five-by-four-foot space it was amazing how much food and medicine I could grow. As spring became summer and then fall, my little plot was overflowing. In spring and summer, I harvested dandelion's bitter leaves for salads and waited to harvest the roots in autumn. The bitterness of dandelion and burdock root stimulate the release of bile from the gallbladder and the production of more in the liver, helping our body digest fats, and work as mild laxatives, toning the whole digestive system. Most of us are sorely lacking bitters in our diet as modern changes in farming include plant breeding that reduces the bitterness of plants such as broccoli, cauliflower, and cabbage. But bitterness helps plants to resist pathogens and it does the same for us.[4] Bitters have been shown to trigger a wide variety of biological processes, including regulation of blood sugar and activation of the immune system in response to infections.

I used to believe that if I had a parasitic, fungal, or bacterial infection that I needed to take an antifungal, antibacterial, antimicrobial herb like oregano, thyme, or wormwood to kill it off. Sometimes they are called for, but too many antimicrobial plants for too long can upset the balance of life within us and kill the little creatures in our bodies that are working hard on our behalf. While antibiotics have their place and have saved lives, nuking our insides too often kills beneficial organisms too. More often than not, we need to build instead of attack, and burdock is a perfect building block for our immune system. The "hygiene hypothesis," an idea proposed by Dr. David Strachan in 1989, suggests that environments with rich microbial diversity protect against allergies and autoimmune disorders. Research shows that children encountering early contact with environments that are less hygienic or overly sanitized, such as outdoor settings and farms, are less likely to develop allergies and autoimmune diseases.[5]

The soil and the human gut are similar ecosystems that follow circadian rhythms and consume, digest, and cycle nutrients for plants or our bodies to absorb. About one hundred trillion bacteria compose our microbiome, and just one gram of fertile soil contains up to one billion bacteria. The millions of species and billions of organisms in soil in the form of bacteria, algae, microscopic insects, plant roots, earthworms, beetles, ants, mites, nematodes, and fungi represent the greatest concentration of biomass on the planet. Sadly, the diversity of both our gut microbiome and the soil's has decreased dramatically in recent years because of the overuse of antibiotics, processed food, agrochemicals, pesticides, and monoculture.[6]

Even the commonplace practice of plowing soil decreases biodiversity by impeding structure, destroying the habitats of microorganisms, and reducing organic matter. Tilling or plowing also increases the potential for erosion by causing soil pores to collapse and seal over so that rain runs off instead of soaking in. In contrast, the no-till method adds organic matter in the form of garden compost from above, which helps the soil retain moisture as the compost breaks down. This not only feeds the soil but improves the structure so that the communities of plants, animals, fungi, and bacteria can flourish.

One of the constituents of taproots like burdock, dandelion, and elecampane is inulin, a prebiotic and rich food source for the diverse microbial ecology of the gut.[7] By consuming foods and herbs rich in inulin, we feed these tiny creatures inside us so that their populations remain strong and they can assist in the breakdown of our foods to provide optimal absorption. When I feed my body now, I think about the fact that I am not just feeding my cravings but all the microscopic beings that work hard to keep me healthy. And since rich, healthy soil contributes to the health of our gut microbiome, the act of merely harvesting burdock root can be medicinal too.

I HAD A DISCIPLINED PRACTICE OF HERBALISM BY THE TIME I PLANTED MY weeds, and every few months, I rotated herbal infusions of plants like nettles, burdock root, red clover, and dandelion root—all plants in the category of alteratives. Alteratives support the body's innate healing capacity and coordinate metabolism so vital organs and their related secretions are working in sync. The result, when applied over a period of time, is an improvement in the body's metabolic functions—nutrients are absorbed and energy is used more efficiently. With consistent use, the plants in this category can resolve the root cause of long-standing physical issues. I drank at least two to three cups a day for a few weeks or even a season. After months and years of consistent use, and regularly getting my hands in the earth through foraging, wildcrafting, and gardening, I began to look back and notice I hadn't been sick in some time. For most of my life, I had been reluctant to plan anything too far in advance because I knew at some point, I would be out of commission. But that wasn't happening anymore. With consistent use of alteratives and inulin-rich herbs, along with planting, harvesting, and using my own medicine, I improved my body's essential metabolic functions of digestion, absorption, and elimination and was increasing the vitality and resilience of my inner ecosystem.

SKIN DEEP

I rarely wash my hair, get it cut once or twice a year by a dear friend, don't style it, and usually brush it with my fingers. This seeming disregard is really my love for these sprouts on my head. And it helps, of course, that I like it best when it's long and a little unruly. I do have my rituals though. I just took a shower and when I turned the water off, I ceremoniously poured a warm half gallon of burdock root infusion over my hair and scalp that I intend to leave in. As I poured the amber-colored liquid onto my hair and into my skin, I felt nourished the way the root nourishes me when I drink mugfuls of rich infusion. What we see on the surface has everything to do with the health of what is inside, and one of the best plants we can turn to for hair and skin is burdock root. In herbalism, health or issues on the outside speak to problems below the surface in soil or in our organs.

Like tiny roots, millions of hair follicles can be found on our heads, most of which are constantly growing. Burdock root contains all the necessary amino acids for building the protein that creates hair, along with tannins, essential fatty acids, and vitamins that strengthen hair, promote growth, and prevent rapid shedding. Burdock root oil also helps with scalp irritation issues, dandruff, and itchy scalp and is an excellent ally for skin. A supreme blood purifier, burdock treats imbalances such as eczema, psoriasis, and acne.

Prolonged use of burdock can, over time, improve the metabolism and help restore the proper channels and functioning of elimination. If the liver, lymphatic system, and kidneys are not effectively detoxifying and excreting toxins via the kidneys, then the body will attempt to cleanse itself through our other organ of elimination: skin. Whether this elimination takes on the form of eruptions such as acne or dry inflammations like psoriasis depends on our constitution and the nature of the imbalance.

BAREFOOT

Deep roots are not only beneficial for us, but for soil evolution, groundwater and streamflow regulation, soil carbon sequestration, and moisture content in the lower troposphere. In the wild, burdock grows on injured soil, drawing nutrients from deep underground to replenish the land, offering steady healing. With all of the ecological benefits and centuries of use in traditional medicine, most people still overlook burdock as a weed. The more I learned, the more I felt it was my job to rewire that perception.

I returned to training clients as I practiced herbalism and pursued my art career in earnest. As I reentered the boxing world, I realized I still had skills, along with a better understanding of my body, mind, and spirit. I found myself entertaining the idea of fighting again. If I trained hard, I had connections to move up the ranks and fight for a championship and have something to show for all of my early training. I sought coaches who would get me into shape quickly, trained hard, and, although rusty, started sparring. Training again felt liberating and exciting as I integrated all I had learned through meditation, holistic herbalism, and my deepened connection to the Earth. Still, the early spark and seduction boxing held for me wasn't there. After a few months of intense training, I remembered the tunnel vision the sport required and realized going professional wasn't worth risking the big-picture thinking and deep interconnectedness I'd begun to cultivate. I had too much going on in my life at that point and found myself moving toward redefining the word *warrior* as one who has the courage to go within, confront the self, and heal. And above all, I wanted to fight for the Earth far more than to fight in a ring. Unless it became a platform for other things in life, success in boxing seemed pretty unimportant.

While boxing, I carried Bruce Lee's book *Tao of Jeet Kune Do* everywhere with me. But it took a long time before I embodied the principles he espoused. He wrote, "Jeet Kune Do, you see, has no definite lines or boundaries—only those you make yourself."[8] As I worked with local plant medicine, understood holistic and elemental theories of herbalism, and applied principles found in nature, I developed my own sort of style and approach without lines or boundaries. When working with clients, we integrated movement, meditation, creative meditation, and plant medicine and trained barefoot in Prospect Park.

Barefoot contact with the earth can produce nearly instant physiological changes, and we always began our sessions with rooting down, connecting to the Earth, and dropping into our bodies through grounding. Burdock root was the first plant we worked with; I brought an infusion to share and made sure clients could identify the plant as an ally for anchoring, receiving energy, and plugging into Mother Earth. The more relaxed we are, the more power we have and the more difficult we are to knock down.

Our species evolved in direct contact with the Earth's subtle electric charge, but we have lost that sustained connection because we spend our time in buildings, wearing heels or synthetic soles. Forest bathing, grounding, Earthing—all are names for "new" systems of healing, and while they are important concepts, I also find them a little ridiculous. Do we really need these new modalities and scientific studies to tell us that it is good for us to walk barefoot on the grass, spend time in a forest, or unplug from technology? The term "forest bathing" was coined in 1982 by the Japanese Ministry of Agriculture, which explained that it "refers to the process of soaking up the sights, smells and sounds of a natural setting to promote physiological and psychological health."[9] Great, but seems pretty obvious to me.

WHEN I LOOK THROUGH MY JOURNALS, I FIND WORDS LIKE *DEPTH, DIVE,* AND *deep* over and over again. I know life doesn't stop at the soles of my feet, so today I take a moment to close my eyes and tune in, feeling the pulse of life beneath me where root systems are engaged in a vast web of underground communication. I take a deep breath, exhale, and let go. I picture the depth and mystery of the fertile darkness below and ask permission to plug into her source energy, my source energy. Asking permission in my own way connects me to the living Earth with reverence and awakens my intuition as I wait for an answer. When I feel ready, I imagine roots growing down through my tailbone or the soles of my feet and into fertile ground. I take a moment to visualize my roots and notice how deep into the soil they dive and if they are deep taproots or rhizomes intertwined with the roots of trees, strands of fungi, or other plants around me.

Once I've plugged in, I draw life force energy all the way into my body with each inhale, further dislodging stagnant energy and helping me to rise tall, from the ground up, into my full height and full strength like the stalk of a second-year burdock plant. As I exhale, I compost anything I need to release. I do this as long as I need to and then thank the Earth in my own way.

Roots supply us with the energy of survival, inviting stability and balance into our bodies, our lives, and our practices. And when we ground, we calm. The more grounded we are, the more we can let go and still stand firmly in our power. I might be mobile, but I need roots nonetheless.

LINDEN TREE
Tilia spp.

Family: Malvaceae

Sitting beneath a linden tree in summer feels like a cool, nourishing embrace. Their calming presence and the moistening, honey-like infusions of their leaves and flowers can soothe frayed nerves and raw emotions, coat sore throats, ease dry coughs, and calm digestive distress. You can see linden's expression of water in the downward cascade of the branches, the soft, supple, heart-shaped leaves, and the flowing patterns of deeply furrowed tree bark.

Tilia is a genus of about thirty species of trees native through most of the temperate Northern Hemisphere. In some places they are called lime trees, and in others, *Tilia*, or linden, is called basswood.

The roots of linden dive into the earth as the branches reach toward the stars and pour down again, creating a cool, protective sanctuary. While holding, supporting, grounding us, linden can ease our pain and help us let go.

IMPERMANENCE

We cherish things . . . precisely because they cannot last; it's
their frailty that adds sweetness to their beauty.

PICO IYER

I walked out into the courtyard this morning and felt an empty space, a
void. A tree that grew by my side for years while I meditated and wrote was
suddenly gone. No one said anything, no one asked or alerted the people
who sat by the tree, the birds who made the tree a home, the squirrels who
foraged the nuts, or the mushrooms, chickweed, and violet that surrounded the
roots. The tree supported a small community. Sometimes we don't realize the
meaning and depth of connection to a person, animal, plant, or place until
they are gone.

There are times when I have felt stripped bare after a breakup with a partner, the death of a family member, the loss of an animal companion and even
creatures I have never met. I wailed at the loss of the last northern white rhinoceros in Africa, now extinct in the wild because of illegal killing and human
greed. I felt, and still feel, I had lost a piece of myself. That we all had. Sometimes I don't want to fill losses like that with joy, and instead keep their voids
as empty caverns in remembrance of what once was.

Our inner wells run deep and most of us never come close to feeling how far they might go. I believe that's because they are bottomless and that they grow deeper in relation to our experience and capacity to feel. I know those empty spaces can become sacred vessels if I allow myself to fill them with love, joy, or wonder, but when we lose any living being that we love, we may struggle to find who we are in their absence.

I grew up in New England where the culture is connected to maple trees—maple syrup, maple sugar candy, and the artistry of the autumn leaves. They give us such intense, fiery color before the trees become bare. The fall is a vulnerable time, when many of our green friends die back and the veil between worlds becomes thin. When I sit with the sensation, my skin feels thin too. My emotional nakedness and sensitivity increases.

Maybe it's being born at the end of summer or having my moon in the watery, emotional sign of Cancer, but I've always identified with the bittersweet peak of impermanence. In the Wheel of the Year—a way to mark time that is used by many herbalists and Earth-based practitioners—autumn is in the west, the direction of the setting sun. In the traditions I've studied, water, the element that moves down toward the earth like falling leaves or ripe, heavy fruit, is associated with the west. And like the nourishment and moisture created by dying leaves and overripe apples, depleted soil can also be nourished by our tears.

WHEN ZEUS TOLD HIS DAUGHTER ARTEMIS THAT SHE COULD CHOOSE HER gifts as a young girl, she chose, among other things, the wilderness and all the world's mountains. In ancient Greece, certain hills and valleys were known to be hers, along with wild forests and meadows. One of her sanctuaries was a stretch of sand dunes, while others were marshes. Whether located on a mountain, in a marshy area, or near a river, water was often a focal point in her sanctuaries. At Sparta, Epidaurus Limera, and Sicyon she was known as the Lady of the Lake.[1] Clearing obstructions or pollution from a stream was an act of devotion to Artemis. The presence of the goddess in the Greek pantheon inhibited human invasion of sacred waters and forests and helped to preserve acres and acres of wilderness along with the wildlife that lived in those sacred lands. Since her groves were numerous and often large, they protected their diverse species of flora and fauna for hundreds of years.[2]

One of the most celebrated healing wells on the Isle of Skye is Loch Sheanta well, whose guardian is a sacred trout that swims in the loch into which the spring drains.[3] People who sought healing would circle the spring three times in a clockwise direction (a common practice in Gaelic ritual) after drinking the water and make an offering of scraps of clothing, colored threads, pins, or coins. For this reason locals would never fish in the loch despite the abundance of trout. No wood would ever be cut from the area near the spring either, which means the spring can be found today in the middle of a hazel grove, and the water is still pristine. Healing wells have a long tradition in Scotland, and at one point there were over six hundred operating in every corner of the country. While the human keepers of the wells were traditionally women, the spirit guardians came in many shapes and forms.

Throughout the world, water was, and is, held sacred. And when guardian spirits or deities watch over spaces, they become literal land protectors. It doesn't matter if we think taboos or stories like the trout are made up or superstitious. Reverence for these guardians, deities, or spirits of place prevent people from taking more than they need or harming the land.

THE LINDEN THAT LINES THE SIDEWALKS OF BROOKLYN WITH DEEP, KNOWING furrows in her grayish bark has been sacred to pre-Christian cultures throughout the world.[4] Polish legends say cutting down a linden, a symbol of the goddess, will bring great misfortune. Early Germanic people believed that linden unearthed the truth to restore justice and peace, and Slavs believed that lightning never hit the holy tree, and if people or animals were ill, linden cuttings, infused with spirit, were used for healing. In Baltic mythology, Laima, the goddess of fate, lives in the linden tree where she makes her decisions as a cuckoo bird. In *The Living Goddesses*, anthropologist Marija Gimbutas writes, "The tree on which the cuckoo sits becomes sacred and imbued with the powers of the goddess." Those who still ascribe Laima's power to linden might pray and give offerings to the goddess of fate under these divine, healing trees.

INNER WELLS

I have brought all of my students to sit under linden trees, whether in Scotland, Brooklyn, or Western Massachusetts. We share an infusion of the leaves and flowers and tune in to the way the presence of the tree makes us feel. As we take the soothing infusion into our bodies, we observe the expression of the leaves, branches, flowers, and bark with all of our senses. Students study the obliquely heart-shaped leaves, the unusual leaflike bracts, and the sweet-swelling blossoms that provide ample nectar for bees.

It no longer surprises me that hundreds of students have said the same thing—they feel held and feel a sense of belonging in the presence of a linden tree. Linden soothes us when we are sick and is like a trusted caress that can ease our nerves when they are frayed. On hot summer days, the cooling, sweet-smelling embrace of a linden tree is sanctuary. We can lean on their sturdy trunks, melt into the shade, and, if needed, feel safe and sheltered enough to cry. Tears allow deep aches to move through us, washing us clean so we can see more clearly, sometimes beyond the veil. Linden eases angry and grief-stricken hearts and supports the physical heart with use for conditions such as atherosclerosis, angina, and heart palpitations, easing our nervous system and stress while softening edges inside us and between realms. To many, linden is a nurturing feminine spirit.

My student Nathalie shared with me her experience of meditating beneath a linden tree during our herbal apprenticeship: "It was the first time I felt the profound and specific healing of a plant without ingesting the medicine. When we spent time with linden during our apprenticeship, my nervous system felt plugged into the nectar quality of the medicine and I felt something enveloping me, a thick protective coating of energy. As I let go, I began to feel angry as feelings and experiences of intergenerational trauma began to arise. I wanted to step away, but linden was holding me, coaxing me to lean in. I let go of my resistance and was able to sit in the discomfort and rage that had risen to the surface and melt into sadness. After that experience and others like it, I feel strongly that linden supports intergenerational trauma and is an ally, especially to folks of color that are willing to touch into rage, especially since sentient and supportive linden allies are everywhere, even in urban areas."

WHEN FALLING IN LOVE, I HAVE ALWAYS GONE THROUGH A PERIOD OF GRIEF, even when my lovers are next to me. I worry about losing them and my love makes the fragility of life more present. Sometimes it's a poignant and dramatic inner conflict that intensifies moments and makes them sweeter, but sometimes my grief creates imagined and unnecessary pain.

I'm listening to *Fulfillingness' First Finale* by Stevie Wonder as I write this. I haven't listened to this album in its entirety since Ernesto and I broke up the first time. For two people who love each other as much as we do, it's not a surprise that we are terrible at saying goodbye. "Love is everything, but it isn't everything," Ernesto said. "Sometimes life gets in the way."

I always dreamt of Ernesto during pivotal points in his life. I knew when he was getting married, when he had his first child, when he was about to get separated. After the dream about his marriage, I couldn't stop crying for what seemed like weeks, and when I was walking around in public, I was crying inside.

A few years into his marriage he admitted he was still in love with me, but he was committed to his promise to his wife and his family. We began to talk and confide in each other and at least become friends again and that felt good. It was always understood that if his marriage didn't work out and he decided to leave, he would let go of his stubborn resolve against me and we would be together again.

When I had a vivid dream about us wandering together and crashing on couches and floors without a real place to stay, I sensed something had shifted for him. I texted him to say hi and find out what was going on. It had been a while since we communicated, and I learned that he had and his wife had separated. He was living in his recording studio, in limbo. When we saw each other, we were immediately emotionally entangled but he wasn't ready for another committed relationship. Not yet. Our earlier angst was reversed, and while I was trying to prove my undying loyalty—he wanted me there and slept next to me most nights—he now needed to be free. Still, he asked me to be patient and assured me I was "the one." So in an unsettling space of emotions, I waited, and as I waited, I began to build my life's work. He wasn't interested in coming to camp at the Wolf Conservation Center where I had begun what would become a most cherished partnership. He joked about me eating things from the ground like a wild animal, and while we laughed about it, we knew his disinterest in my work could pose a problem. My wild exploration was expanding, and it was not just what I did, but who I was. When we walked into my garden to see my medicine plants, he was worried about his sneakers getting dirty. We existed in different habitats and slowly the story of our undying love began to unravel. We started to admit that as much as we loved each other, and as much as we had grown in each other's minds, hearts, and stories, our problem might be more than bad timing. Our love was a sticky, resinous glue but our needs and our callings were pulling us in different directions.

So it was after an ambiguous second separation from Ernesto that I put my Raggedy Ann and Andy blanket and all essential belongings that didn't fit in my suitcase in storage and left for Costa Rica (it would be two and a half years before I'd go through this storage unit with Alex). I was committed to my path, to the wolves, and to the plants, and I didn't know what would happen next, but the Earth needed allies and she was calling upon me to deepen my work. I was heartbroken, exhausted from being in emotional limbo, but there was a part of me that was also relieved. I'd made it clear that I would have done anything to be with him again, and now I didn't have to. Ultimately, we knew that no matter how much we loved each other, love shouldn't keep us stuck. We could love each other and still leave.

ATKA'S GARDEN

Growing up in a family of musicians, and in the circles I've encountered, I've met many celebrities. But meeting a wolf? Well, nothing compares to that and nothing ever will. Atka, whose name means "guardian spirit" in the Inuit language, was the first wolf I met. I fell in love right away, and he always answered my howls. Raised in captivity and too accustomed to humans, Atka could not be released to the wild but instead greeted thousands of visitors to the conservation center over the years and traveled to libraries, classrooms, auditoriums, and government meetings to help change the human perception of his species.

Wolves live in large, wild enclosures on the Wolf Conservation Center's twenty-eight acres. The center's mission is "to protect and preserve wolves in North America through science-based education, advocacy, and participation in the federal recovery and release programs for two critically endangered wolf species—the Mexican gray wolf and the red wolf."[5] The center's setup isn't ideal—wolves shouldn't have to be in enclosures at all—and at first it seriously depressed me, but we've brought ourselves and our environment to a place where we have to intervene and reserve protected spaces for species to survive.

Red wolves once ranged across the southeastern United States, but years of hunting and habitat loss drove this small wolf species to the brink of extinction. There were only fourteen left in the wild by 1970. In order to save the species from extinction, the U.S. Fish and Wildlife Service captured the fourteen remaining red wolves in the wild and initiated an ambitious captive-breeding program to keep them alive. Those original wolves are the ancestors of the wolves at the Wolf Conservation Center.[6] They are the first animals to be successfully reintroduced after being declared extinct in the wild. Sadly, all but one of the wolves released by the Wolf Conservation Center into their "protected" habitat in the Albemarle Peninsula in North Carolina were killed by poachers. Once a growing population of over one hundred, the red wolves in the wild are now down to a population of about twenty-four.

When I bring groups to the Wolf Conservation Center, we greet all the wolves with a howl to let them know we're there, sharing their space. When the fifty-one wolves reply, their primal, haunting howls stir the depths of our souls and move most of us to tears. Somewhere inside, we know that these keystone predators are missing from our inner and outer landscapes.

If only they were protected by Artemis.

As a protector and defender of the wild, Artemis exacted retribution from hunters in cases of disrespect or improper injury or killing. She punished violators like the poachers with her well-aimed arrows, winds of plague, and revenge of her sacred animal allies.[7] In the story of the hunter Teuthras, a wild boar he chased sought shelter in a sanctuary of Artemis and appealed to the hunter to spare his life in the name of the goddess. When Teuthras mercilessly slaughtered the animal anyway, Artemis afflicted him with leprous scabs and drove him insane. When Orion, once Artemis's companion, boasted that he would slay all the wild beasts on Earth, Artemis called upon a scorpion to sting him to death.

The worship of Artemis in ancient Greece led to taboos around hunting and customs that affected the treatment of animals and her wild land. Sanctuaries of Artemis and other gods often consisted of tracts of forest where hunting deer and other animals was forbidden, affecting attitudes and practices relating to wildlife, forests, and the wilderness.

Despite their reputation as killers, wolves kill the weak, sick, and injured animals and support other species with their leftovers—coyotes, grizzly bears, black bears, and eagles have all been seen dining on wolf kills. Many historians believe that humans learned to hunt by watching and imitating wolves and that at some points in history, we had a mutually beneficial relationship, helping each other survive. Artemis herself is a huntress who grants success in the hunt and accepts or even demands a portion of the hunter's bag as an offering. This may seem a contradiction, but primal hunting societies see animals not as game, but as powerful, sacred beings whose spiritual protectors must be honored.

Game is defined as "an activity that one engages in for amusement or fun," and in English hunting terminology, "any wild animal hunted for sport."[8] African mammals, specifically the big five "game"—lion, leopard, rhinoceros, elephant, and Cape buffalo—are hunted as trophies, and in wildlife-killing contests in the United States, coyotes are slaughtered in vast numbers. Whoever kills the most animals wins. It is sickening, sanctioned murder. Anyone who thinks it is fun or amusing to go around killing innocent animals for a trophy or for "sport" must have a hardened heart or be in a lot of their own pain. Perhaps copious amounts of linden to soften and heal wounded places would help open them up to empathy and respect for their extended family of living creatures.

The Artemisian code of ethics demands respect for animals and plants, and permits their slaying only when it is necessary for ritual, ceremony, or for human beings to survive. The rules and rituals in ancient Greece demonstrated reverence for life and the acknowledgment of the wounds created by the absence or suffering of slain creatures. Arrian, the ancient author of a handbook on hunting, warned against incurring the wrath of the goddess and other nature deities. "So men who are interested in hunting should not neglect Artemis of the wild . . . or any other god of the mountains. If they do neglect them, needs must so that their endeavors fall short of completion. Their hounds will be injured, their horses lamed; their men come to grief."[9]

The only hero who managed to claim one of Artemis's sacred animals without being punished was Heracles, who had to perform twelve labors in penance to the gods. His third labor was the capture of the Ceryneian hind, a beautiful animal that was larger than a bull and had bronze hooves and, although female, golden antlers. Heracles pursued the deer for a year until she collapsed in exhaustion and he was able to capture her. Artemis forgave Heracles because he had not spilled a drop of her blood.[10]

ATKA WAS SEVENTEEN YEARS OLD WHEN HE PASSED AWAY ON THE AUTUMNAL equinox, old for a wolf. But it doesn't matter if someone you love dies because their time is up or if they are taken too soon. The loss still hurts. I laid goldenrod on his body during his memorial services and he was later burned with the flowers of transition. I drank sweet linden infusion to ease my raw heart. Loving can be painful. But I know that if I dwell too long on my losses, I won't be present enough to prevent new ones.

Along with my herbalism students and Wolf Conservation Center volunteers, I have since planted a medicine garden at the Wolf Conservation Center in his name. The plants grow in memory of his incredible life.

DEATH EXPOSES OUR INTERDEPENDENCE AND FORCES US TO ADJUST TO WAYS of being amid absence. Now most of us are driven to protect land not because of taboos, water guardians, or goddesses like Artemis, but because of conviction, science, love, connection, or because it is the "right" thing to do. But recalling these protectors and guardians may also be a beautiful way to honor sacredness in our world. We lose a part of ourselves with every wild space that is lost. Protecting the Earth isn't something we do as a favor for a world beyond us—we are directly served and nourished when we think of Artemis and other guardians of the wild.

The reality of impermanence can help us cherish the now before it slips away. Life asks us to awaken to the beauty of the moment, but also not to forget who and what we have lost. This can be a challenging balance to strike. But we must notice our wild, interwoven family and come to know who is here so we can work to protect the vulnerable before they become nothing but memories. I imagine that endangered or threatened species like red wolves would not want us to despair too long about their dwindling numbers, but instead to remember and feel the beauty of our interconnection. If we are moved enough by the magic and reality of our coexistence, we might be compelled into action before it's too late, becoming part of their survival.

RED TRILLIUM
Trillium erectum

Family: Melanthiaceae

Throughout most of trillium's extensive range, they are classified as an endangered or vulnerable species. Trillium is a slow-growing plant whose seeds take two years to germinate, three years to grow the first leaf, and up to fifteen years before flowering. And though the flowers are beautiful, picking them may result in the plant's early death, or if flowerless plants do survive, render them unable to flower for many years. When able to establish themselves without interruption, these sacred plants can live for up to thirty years.

Gently parting the forest floor will expose trillium's thick, gnarled rhizome, the part of the plant most commonly used as medicine. Also known as bethroot, birthroot, or wake robin, trillium exudes a faint smell of rotting flesh. As a spirit ally, this mysterious flower is known to help cleanse the root chakra of fear, open the way for a grounding connection with Mother Earth, and help us to accept death and decay as part of life.

DECAY

The boundaries which divide Life from Death are at best
shadowy and vague. Who shall say where the one ends, and
where the other begins?

EDGAR ALLAN POE, "THE PREMATURE BURIAL"

The Robert Frost Trail meanders through the woods in Amherst, Massachusetts, just feet away from my mom's house in Echo Hill where we moved when I was twelve years old. Over the years as I grew, left Amherst, and returned, I've explored the woodland path and have come to know the stretch of land well. Mugwort, wild rose, and poison ivy guard the entryway, and along the wooded path, the forest thrives through a healthy balance of life, death, and decay.

Empty, old trees provide homes for chipmunks, squirrels, owls, and foxes who use spacious hollow trunks as scaffolding for their dens. Remnants of their kills feed the soil, as fallen evergreen limbs decompose and are lined with gorgeous fans of turkey tail mushrooms, the fruiting bodies of mycelium. Nutrients would remain forever locked in the dead tissues of dead animals or plants if it weren't for essential underground creatures like fungi, bacteria, worms, and insects. More like animals than plants, mycelium digest food outside their bodies by releasing enzymes into the surrounding environment and breaking down organic matter to create valuable, fertile ground. If the only purpose of organic matter were constant growth, the earth would be entirely depleted.

I have come to harvest the mysterious saprophytic ghost pipe, *Monotropa uniflora*, an endangered plant that has popped up everywhere after constant rain. I've been reluctant to harvest this medicine since, like many species of trillium, ghost pipe is on the endangered species watch list. But lately I've felt called to explore this medicine and right now they are prolific in these woods. The strange plant, that some call the corpse plant, lacks chlorophyll and offers both a vertical and horizontal consciousness as a combination of saprotrophic fungi, like the turkey tail, that procures carbon from dead plant material, and mycorrhizas, whose vast, weblike strands sit just under the surface, sometimes covering miles as they obtain carbon from living trees whose roots move deep into the earth.

As I engage with the ghost pipe and ask permission to harvest from the land, I feel like I'm being watched. When I turn, I notice a beautiful barred owl sitting in a tree above me. Her huge eyes, fixed in place by a bony structure called a sclerotic ring, stare at me. She turns her head to follow my movement and I walk as silently as possible. But when I get too close, she dives down out and around the trees, a four-foot wingspan above me, barely making a sound.

In many cultures, owls symbolize death. In Celtic lore, the owl is a sign of the underworld and their appearance at night, when humans are lost in darkness, connect these winged creatures to the unknown. In my grandfather's native Russia, hunters carried owl claws so if they were killed, their souls would be able to climb through darkness into the heavens.[1]

Before my grandfather died, he told my mom, aunt, and me that three women were sitting on his bed. They were ancestors and "very kind," he said. I had known him through his ever-rational, scientific outlook, yet he told us he was talking to these women and could see them clearly. They were visiting to ease his mind and keep him company, and, I imagine, guide him as he released his grip on life.

LAST NIGHT I DREAMT OF MY CHILDHOOD BEDROOM ON SUMMER STREET. Though someone else lived there, my stuffed animals were still piled high upon my bed, and in the dream, I reached for my Peter Rabbit doll that I loved but was afraid to take back. *Is the doll still mine after all these years?* The dream was so vivid that I could feel the texture of the comforter on my bed, and I found a ceramic Snoopy music box that I'd been looking for in real life. I wound it and listened to the bittersweet song. And the large wooden box was there, in the middle of the room painted sky blue, with a graceful fawn that lay on the grass with butterflies dancing around her and pollinating colorful wild-flowers. My father had commissioned the box to be painted for me with my name on it: Vanessa. I hadn't thought about that box in years.

When I received the gift as a child, my mom hadn't sorted out her memories and didn't like or trust my father. She didn't have to tell me explicitly; as a porous soul, I felt it. But the box was so beautiful and I loved it. I was confused. I didn't want to love it too much because I was afraid it would mean I loved him too, and that might betray her. So I put strange things in it: the Halloween candy I didn't like but wasn't ready to throw away, old toys I didn't use but didn't want to let go of, pens and pencils that kind of worked, but not really. Even with all of the junk inside, the box continued to look beautiful on the outside, but one day when I opened the lid, I noticed a fuzz. Fungi had arrived to consume it, and it was beginning to rot. I became afraid to open it after that day so I put it in my closet out of sight where it began to stink with ambiguity.

After a while, no matter how beautiful it looked, even with the lid closed it exuded a faint smell. I vaguely remember the uncomfortable job of cleaning it out with my mom when she found it, and now I have no idea where it is, if it still exists. My father took it as an insult, but the truth is I just didn't know where to put him, or the box.

It took me years to understand that everything needs to be processed and composted; nothing real stands frozen in time. The things we throw away don't really go anywhere—they just shape-shift, but their matter, their energy is ever present in our universe. When I was young, I did notice that all the things we didn't want to deal with could be put in a deep, dark bag, out of sight. Then everything could seem neat and tidy again. I could throw things in the bin under the sink and poof! Gone. It felt good to throw things away. Since our household garbage magically disappeared when we were ready to let it go, why not our inner garbage too?

————

THE COMMON NAME FOR TRILLIUM IS WAKE ROBIN, ALLUDING TO THE DANGER of rousing the goblin Robin Goodfellow if the flower is picked, or, some say, alluding to the time the familiar birds with red chests waken.[2] In terms of the goblin, otherwise known as Puck, legend says that he might even help us to sort out our garbage and organize our homes while we sleep if he likes us. But if we're not on good terms with him, and especially if we pick a sacred plant like trillium and make him upset, he might lurk in our bedrooms at night and bring terrible dreams.

Trillium seeds have oily appendages called elaiosomes that ants, chipmunks, mice, and other woodland creatures like to dine on, inadvertently dispersing seeds. Since these animals and insects are territorial, the plant tends to appear above ground in clusters. Red trillium blooms between April and May, once red-breasted robins have begun hopping on lawns, city parks, and meadows looking for worms. Robins have incredible hearing and can locate worms underground while their keen vision shows them exactly where to strike. Because the robins' eyes are on the sides of their head, they cock their heads to look with one eye and then the other before piercing the soil. Sounds like a nightmare for worms.

Charles Darwin believed that we wouldn't exist without the humble worm. He wrote, "It may be doubted whether there are many other animals which have played so important a part in the history of the world, as have these lowly organized creatures."[3] By increasing soil fertility, recycling waste, and providing food resources for creatures like mycelium, earthworms are underground allies working hard to decompose in the darkness, feeding life above ground.

WAKE ROBIN

It might take more time to walk our food scraps to the farmers market or our community garden, drive them to the town dump, or process them in our backyards, but what was once alive deserves a proper burial. It pains me when I see people throw food in the trash that could feed the earth if it didn't end up in a landfill, creating more greenhouse gases. There's a reason this shortcut contributes to climate change; it is a clear message from our planet that living matter is meant to go back into soil to support the cycle of life. The collective benefit of nurturing the earth and properly disposing of waste outweighs any time lost in the lure of quick convenience.

Like the rotting stench of trillium, decay is essential. If we allow food, flesh, and fallen trees to compost, they can give way to incredible beauty. But if we try to "clean" or sanitize our environments by removing traces of death like leaves or rotting logs, or attempt to freeze time by injecting our living faces with botulism or embalming dead bodies (which entails being drained of blood, then injected with a poisonous cocktail of formaldehyde, methanol, and other solvents that prevent decay) so we can appear youthful or lifelike for a little longer, we withhold essential food for the soil, and all the toxic chemicals that were pumped into our bodies get leached into the land when we decompose eventually. By trying to avoid death, our world becomes lifeless.

Our garbage doesn't magically disappear, and if not properly composted, it only creates pain. Stray dogs may rummage through waste and sever their tongues on edges of carelessly discarded cans, turtles suffocate in unnecessary plastic bags that find their way into the ocean, whales die from bodies filled with discarded debris, and devoted albatross parents fly thousands of miles to forage for food floating on the surface of the sea only to come home to fill their nests with buttons, bottle tops, and other undead waste while their chicks starve to death.

If it's time we're worried about, we could enjoy more of it in autumn if we let leaves stay where they fall. Fallen leaves form a natural mulch that fertilizes the soil as they break down, and removing them by raking or using annoying, noisy gas-powered blowers not only depletes the soil but eliminates vital habitat for animals like turtles, toads, salamanders, birds, small mammals, and invertebrates that rely on leaf litter for food, shelter, and nesting material. The majority of butterflies and moths overwinter in the landscape as an egg, caterpillar, chrysalis, or adult and use leaves for winter cover.

According to the U.S. Environmental Protection Agency, leaves and other yard debris make up more than 13 percent of the nation's solid waste, and without enough oxygen to decompose, this organic matter releases the greenhouse gas methane, contributing to climate change.[4] And that figure doesn't include the carbon dioxide generated by loud leaf blowers and trucks used in leaf disposal. One of the most valuable things we can do to support pollinators and other invertebrates is to provide them with the winter cover they need in the form of fall leaves and standing dead plant material. We spend time and money and harm our environment by erasing traces of death and we forget that it is death that supports plants, that supports life.

Plant, animal, and human remains are eventually buried deep beneath Earth's surface, squished and cooked by lots of pressure and heat that turn our dead plants and animal ancestors into oil, coal, and natural gas. Plants take in CO_2, keep the carbon, and give away the oxygen; animals breathe in the oxygen and breathe out carbon dioxide. We've depended on each other for millions of years as plants and animals have lived and died. We might tell them to "rest in peace" until we interrupt their rest and use them as fossil fuels—a process of extraction that is incredibly traumatic for the body of the Earth. Our choices matter, and we often produce our own nightmares when we are seduced by promises of comfort without considering the consequences.

IF NO ONE ELSE WAS IN THE COMMUNITY GARDEN, I LIKED TO SIT, DRAW, AND meditate with the plants. One day, a flower with three petals in a triangular shape captured my attention and seemed to draw me in. Captivated, I sat on a bench near the plant, exchanged breath, and let myself gaze and enter into the center of what felt like a wise, old plant spirit. I don't remember how long I was hypnotized, but afterward I began a frenzy of writing—about my death. It was weird, nowhere near what I had been thinking about when I walked into the garden that day, but it gave me perspective. What better way to get clear about my life than to think about my inevitable death?

I wrote a stream-of-consciousness eulogy of sorts, and as I got into it, I wrote a prospective will and imagined my obituary. *How do I want to be remembered? Who matters to me, truly? If I have anything to leave, who would I leave those precious things to? What will be my legacy?* Looking at my life backward and reflecting on my eventual death helped me reclaim energy I was wasting in directions that didn't serve me. It was after this experience that I researched the mysterious plant and learned who trillium was. On a spiritual level, I have come to believe that trillium, a plant related to the two portals of birth and death, can help us accept the process of aging. There are many kinds of death. There is the inevitable letting go at the end of this incarnation, and the deaths that we experience on a daily, monthly, or yearly basis when part of who we are no longer fits.

With three large green sepals, three large green leaves, and three petals, trillium is a symbolic expression of the phases in our lives. In women, the number three marks the arrival and the death of our maiden, mother, and crone phases, and for all of us, our movement through the innocence of childhood, the responsibilities of adulthood, and the wisdom of old age. In Native American herbalism, trillium root is considered to be a sacred female herb. Also known as birthroot, trillium has been used to ease hormonal and life transitions of early menstruation and menopause by stabilizing mood and countering heavy or prolonged uterine bleeding. Extracts of the roots and poultices of the entire plant have astringent and antiseptic properties that have been used to initiate labor while keeping contractions strong and steady, and healing after-birth hemorrhage. In the wild, *Trillium erectum*, with her deep red blossom, can be found in humus-rich cool soils of the northeastern United States, southern Quebec, and Appalachian mountain states, often growing alongside hemlocks, rhododendrons, and laurels, and is considered the most promiscuous of trilliums, readily hybridizing with at least three other species where their ranges overlap.

CYCLES

For most in the Western world, there are two options when it comes to death: we are buried or burned. For some, the ritual of burying a dead body is so deeply ingrained in religious and cultural traditions that they hardly think about it, while others must choose.

If we choose to be embalmed and buried, our lifeless body might be placed in a pricey casket and then a cemetery where a sprawling, pristine lawn will consume water, chemical fertilizer, and pesticides to keep it an unnatural vibrant green. With the number of people who are going to die in the coming years, our Earth cannot handle any more of these toxic memorial parks. The amount of casket wood alone is equivalent to about four million acres of forest, and if you added up the entire square footage of all the cemeteries in the United States, it would measure about one million acres of land that could otherwise be life-giving, life-supporting forests.[5]

It seems strange that we create and even live by stories about heaven and hell yet poison the Earth on our way out, making it a more difficult place to live for those that are still around. What we destroy or create while we're here impacts everyone who is still alive and those who come after us. Even if there were a God, wouldn't he, she, or they be upset that we are destroying and poisoning the Eden that was created?

Luckily, there are other ways.

We can encase our bodies into an egg-shaped pod made of biodegradable material or a wooden urn along with a tree chosen by us before death, or our family after our death, for a living memorial. One of the companies that offers this, Capsula Mundi, writes that "cemeteries will acquire a new look and, instead of the cold grey landscape we see today, they will grow into vibrant woodlands."[6] We can seal our ashes in a concrete ball that will plunge to the bottom of the ocean to feed coral reefs (although recent studies have suggested that cremated ashes are sterile and do not supply nutrients back into the earth); there are also biodegradable casket options, including bamboo, paper, cardboard, wool, banana leaf, and willow. Or—my favorite—let fungi eat you: the Infinity Burial Suit,[7] a black ninja-like body suit worn after death, is infused with mushroom spores that consume you, leaving behind clean, pollutant-free compost. This fashionable burial suit with thread that mimics the movement of mycelium was designed by artists Jae Rhim Lee and Mike Ma. During development, Lee tested mushrooms known for cleaning up toxic environments by feeding them her own hair, skin, and nails and selectively breeding the ones that best consumed them. In her 2011 TED Talk, she said that she imagines the Infinity Burial Suit to be "a symbol of a new way of thinking about death and the relationship between my body and the environment. It's a step toward accepting the fact that someday I will die and decay. It's also a step toward taking responsibility for my own burden on the planet."[8]

IT MAY BE DISTURBING TO THINK ABOUT BEING CONSUMED BY THESE CREA-
tures, but they are the helpers of Mother Earth and I certainly want my death
to create and nurture more life. Every living being has to eat in order to live, so
it makes sense that the living Earth does too. It doesn't seem so bad to become
food for the fungi that I love, for my flesh to feed the earth and be consumed by
the wild the way it was meant to be. Becoming part of the earth—something vast
and limitless like the consciousness of mycelium, the biggest living organism
on Earth—seems incredible to me. Then who knows where our energy will go?
Maybe we'll become a linden tree or hawthorn, a field of goldenrod, a living
boundary of mugwort or a cluster of red trillium. Eventually, we all become compost and return to the womb of Mother Earth. If we think of the Earth as the
soil of our ancestors, maybe we would also think twice about her destruction.

A gorgeous barred owl perched outside my window as I was writing in
Western Massachusetts recently. I texted Carol who lives in the space next
door so she could see the owl before he or she flew away and Carol told me she
had just caught a mouse and put the mouse outside. Knowing my sensitivity,
she sent me these beautiful, moving words: "I hope you are not saddened by
the little mouse who brought the Barred Owl so close—he/she is part owl now
and can fly."

Every ending is a new beginning.

"It doesn't happen all at once," said the Skin Horse. "You become. It takes a long time. That's why it doesn't happen often to people who break easily, or have sharp edges, or who have to be carefully kept. Generally, by the time you are Real, most of your hair has been loved off, and your eyes drop out and you get loose in the joints and very shabby. But these things don't matter at all, because once you are Real you can't be ugly, except to people who don't understand."

MARGERY WILLIAMS, *THE VELVETEEN RABBIT*

PART FIVE

The Center

THERE IS A SACRED SPACE INSIDE ALL OF US THAT IS STEADY, UNWAV-ering, and at peace. While most of us have to embark on arduous, uncomfortable journeys to find this treasure, it has been patiently waiting within us all along.

SOLOMON'S SEAL

Polygonatum spp.

Family: Asparagaceae

Solomon's seal is a woodland perennial with native species in North America, Asia, and Europe whose rhizomes spread rapidly in healthy soil with space to grow. The plant is named for King Solomon, who appears as a prophet in the Talmud, the Quran, and in the Hebrew Bible as the builder of the first temple in Jerusalem. The Seal of Solomon was his signet ring engraved by God and given to him directly from heaven. This ring aided him in magical workings, allowing him to command demons, both helpful and malevolent, and to speak with animals.

According to legend, King Solomon placed his seal upon the underground stems of his namesake that resemble gnarled bones, knuckles, and vertebrae when he realized the profound ability of the plant to heal and elicit change. Solomon's seal is a sweet, cooling, moistening, and restorative medicine for the musculoskeletal system, and if we look closely and with an open mind, we may see the impression of the seal on circular scars left by the stem after the plant dies back.

In the spirit signatures of Native American tradition that categorizes herbs according to animals, Solomon's seal is a wolf medicine. Solomon's seal acts on the gallbladder, tendons, and ligaments and nurtures our joints so we can roam as far as wolves, who can travel up to thirty miles a day.

ENDURANCE

Walking . . . is how the body measures itself against the earth.

REBECCA SOLNIT

Most days I walk with Charlie, my friend's animal companion in Western Massachusetts, and the only sounds I hear are the crunch of his paws and my boots against the snow. Sometimes the white flakes are so light and airy that we barely make a sound. After a night of cold rain, we glide across a thick, frozen surface, suspended until a sudden crack drops us into a foot of cold, compacted powder. It startles us, and all of the quiet creatures that surround us—birds, squirrels—fly and skitter away. But soon all is still again. I find yesterday's tracks frozen over and carefully shuffle by rows of apple trees covered in ice and sparkling in the winter sun as though encased in pristine glass.

Walking has always been medicine for me, a slow and steady rhythm that allows my body and mind to come into sync with my surroundings. When I allow myself to be guided by instinct and have time to wander, I feel inner tugs that tell me to *leave the trail and visit the tall white pine*, or *turn left off the path*. When I listen, there is always something wonderful to discover, something I've never seen before. Sometimes, repetitive patterns appear outside of me for a period of time: a crow perched oddly everywhere I seem to go, butterflies fluttering around me in the strangest places, turtles crossing my path after dreaming about them, or continuous stands of plants like Solomon's seal. I see these patterns from nature as signs that I'm headed in the right direction.

I find Solomon's seal when I walk through shady, forested land. Their flowers dangle like white bells from their flexible green stems that arch toward the ground. I only harvest the rhizome if the plant is abundant and if I need it, since they are on the endangered species watch list. But if I carefully harvest a bit by taking just the center section and then replant both ends, the plant will continue to grow.

Solomon's seal supports and facilitates fluid motion and is helpful in releasing old patterns of tension in the body and places where we lock in memories and emotions. While muscle memory usually refers to something we do without conscious awareness, like riding a bike or walking the same path over and over again, the same could be said for the habitual stories that narrate our lives. From the unprocessed traumas to the conditioning of our culture, old memories stored, or "storied," in our bodies might lock into our minds and into our limbs instructing us how things are and how things should be, making our routines more rigid and preventing us from seeking new paths.

I was at Flower Power Herbs in the East Village of Manhattan when I saw a flyer for Spirit Signatures: Animal Totems in Herbalism, a weekend-long course by visiting teacher Matthew Wood, a celebrity in the herbalism world. I signed up immediately and that was the first time I heard about Solomon's seal. Matthew taught us that wolf medicine (the spirit signature of Solomon's seal) gives us the capacity to change profoundly: the way a wild wolf can transform into the domesticated dog, or the human can become a werewolf, or even more subtle changes like work into play and anger into laughter. Restoring fluid movement can help us be more flexible not just in our bodies but also our minds and emotional states, allowing us to travel down paths we may otherwise have feared. In the past, the rhizome was worn as an amulet to keep bad spirits at bay, attract helpful ones, and increase one's wisdom.

I loved Choose Your Own Adventure books as a child. As I read, I assumed the role of the protagonist and became a mountain climber, knight, doctor, warrior, archaeologist, or spy, and after a couple of pages, I was confronted with important decisions about my direction. My decision led to a new outcome, more options, and one of many possible endings. Turning down a dif-

ferent street, leaving five minutes early or ten minutes late, reaching out (or
not) when I was lost—all of it could change the course of my life and, in turn,
the lives of others. While the choices at the crossroads of each adventure in the
books and in my own life differed, the underlying desires and sense of purpose
were the same—to find love, fulfill my mission, stay true to my purpose, to know
myself. There were, and are, many ways to get there.

IT TOOK ME A LONG TIME TO GET MY DRIVER'S LICENSE. GROWING UP IN AMHERST,
I walked almost everywhere. People I met in town or at UMass said they often
saw me wandering and had a nickname for me: "the Girl with the Backpack."
I always felt a need to be prepared. I carried at least three books—one reference,
one novel, one poetry—a change of clothes, water, snacks, and, of course, my
sketchbook and journal. It felt like carrying a bag full of rocks. When I moved
to New York City, I did the same thing. I always needed a change of clothes
after the gym and since I might be out all day, I needed books, my journal, and
all of my creature comforts. With my heavy bag, I wandered from Brooklyn to
Manhattan and back, walking over bridges, exploring new streets, or searching for something new in familiar ones.

    In Scotland, there is a law called "the right to roam" that allows people
to camp, walk, and wander anywhere, trusting that we'll do so with respect.
There are few fences that can't be crossed and I've never encountered a NO
TRESPASSING sign. When our relationship with the land isn't explicitly man-
dated by laws and signage, we can have a less fragmented relationship. There
is less of a foreboding feeling that I may "get in trouble" or enter someone's declared territory if I veer off the path.

HUMAN ANATOMY BOOKS TELL US THAT OUR BODIES HARBOR AROUND SIX
hundred separate muscles, but it may be more accurate to imagine that our
bodies are really one muscle poured into six hundred pockets of fascial webbing. Tom Myers, author of *Anatomy Trains: Myofascial Meridians for Manual
and Movement Therapists*, writes, "The 'illusion' of separate muscles is created
by the anatomist's scalpel, dividing tissues along the planes of fascia. This

reductive process should not blind us to the reality of the unifying whole."[1] Every organ, including the brain, is encapsulated in this connective tissue that determines the shape and volume of each organ and provides a framework in which they connect, communicate, and move together. This system starts in utero as a fibrous gel that surrounds all the cells in our developing bodies, and in all mammals works like a mycelial spiderweb providing a communication network and netting that surrounds every muscle, allowing for integrated functional movement.

Like every other tissue in our bodies, our fascia is made of 70 percent water and works and feels better when lubricated.[2] Moistening herbs like Solomon's seal are so helpful. Connective tissues that are dry lack pliability, and when we restore moisture, or remember to stretch and play when we feel stuck or overly serious, we can restore fluidity to the web that holds our body together, literally. Strong emotions have physical or postural responses: we slump or protect our hearts when we are hurt, stand tall when we feel confident or proud, and let our shoulders relax and chest open when we trust our surroundings. We are constantly expanding and contracting, making mental, physical, and emotional adjustments based on the behavior of others and the state of our environment. Some circumstances stretch us further than we imagined we would go, and others create tension and cause us to shrink in self-protection. Fascia is what solidifies our unique default posture. We can choose to let go or hold on, and depending on our choice, we carry ourselves differently.

Chronic tension can cause fascial fibers to thicken in an attempt to protect the underlying muscle, just as lack of activity can cement once-supple muscle fibers into place. Over time, these adhesions can get strong enough to inhibit range of motion, making us feel trapped with few options for safe, pain-free movement. But the truth is, we are malleable. The body replaces itself with a largely new set of cells every seven to ten years, and some of our most important parts are replaced even more rapidly. Even our bones, the part of us that seems most solid, are ever changing—the cells in the skeletal system regenerate almost constantly. And every time we take a step toward healing, to some degree we shape-shift.

I began to feel myself growing lighter in Scotland, as I traveled out for longer and longer stretches of time and found acres of land where I skipped, walked, and roamed, seeing nothing but heather, gorse, and various shades of green for miles. "No one really skips unless they're happy," Alex said when I told him I skipped in the wilderness today. Can skipping make you happy then? We've been trying it and it seems to work.

As my sensory awareness and relationship with nature evolve, the distance I travel becomes much less important than intimacy with place. I became fascinated by small patches of land with sundew, yarrow, butterbur, stonecrop, gorse, wild mountain thyme, and even by the never-ending changes of a single plant. Like friends, family, partners, and lovers, the people we think we know are growing, changing, and evolving every day. The land is the same way, in that she is never the same.

WOLF MEDICINE

Over the past eight years, I've come to know the Wolf Conservation Center lands well and yet the plants there always surprise me. Last year I found more lobelia than I ever have, a plant that helps us deal with panic, anxiety, and involuntary muscle spasms and is used in ceremony to soften the edges between worlds.

I have always been in awe of wolves and worked sporadically on their behalf, but they didn't become my focus until I went to a talk by Deborah White Plume, a Lakota activist born and raised on the Pine Ridge Reservation in southwestern South Dakota. She spoke about the social and environmental issues affecting her native land and how those of us at the talk could get involved. Every single issue was something I cared deeply about, so I took notes and reflected upon the ways I'd engage. But when she began to talk about wolves, my whole body burned. She spoke about their persecution and their struggle to survive in the midst of political battle. Still endangered, they were losing their status as an endangered species, pressured by states that allowed hunting and trapping on their ever-diminishing territory. As Deborah White Plume spoke, she activated the visceral connection I have always had with these animals. It was as though she was talking about my family. Well, she was. And I knew that through her, the wolves were calling me to my work. When I was finally in the presence of wolves, something in me felt complete and at home.

WOLF PACKS ARE TIGHT-KNIT FAMILIES, EACH WITH THEIR OWN HISTORY, unique skill sets, and traditions. When humans kill one member of a pack or break them apart, the wolves are severed from family tradition and vital knowledge that would have been passed down through generations: hunting skills, raising pups, pack structure, language and communication. Skills that are critical to their survival in the wild. Killing wolves and breaking up their families takes a toll on our environment too.

When wolves were reintroduced to Yellowstone National Park in 1995 after a seventy-year absence due to hunting and persecution, they transformed the strength, resilience, and biodiversity of the land.[3] They were brought in to manage a rising elk population, which had been overgrazing much of the park, but their impact went far beyond that. The wolves dramatically changed the park's rivers and forests, providing increased habitat for other animals like eagles, beavers, and bison, which began to increase in numbers and, in some cases, return. They even improved the health and well-being of their prey, illuminating the Keewatin Inuit saying "The caribou feeds the wolf, but it is the wolf who keeps the caribou strong." But when their pack structure is dismantled by hunters or decreased habitat and they can no longer hunt as a unit and take down elk or deer, they'll go after easier prey like livestock, the source of recent and ongoing conflict in the United States and other parts of the world where wolves still roam but where domesticated spaces encroach upon the wild.

WHEN I STARTED CONDUCTING RETREATS AT THE WOLF CONSERVATION CENTER, one of the first questions people asked was "Can we pet the wolves?" And I admit, when I first saw them, I was frustrated by the enclosure. Not just for their sake, but for mine. I wanted to connect, bond, and touch. But wolves are not domesticated dogs. They might look a lot like our husky or German shepherd companions, but they aren't interested in pleasing us, nor should they be. Even though the wolves at the conservation center can't (yet) roam free, they are sovereign. No wild animal should be captive, but until we restore our relationship with the wild, we need places that keep these essential animals alive. As much as I love the Wolf Conservation Center, I wish it didn't need to exist.

I once had my own wolflike companion, a husky-Doberman rescue who was clearly descended from wolves. Gray wolves and dogs diverged from an extinct wolf species some ten to thirty-two thousand years ago. While researchers continue to debate when, where, and how dogs were first domesticated, most agree that a friendly wolf ancestor likely initiated the first contact with humans, probably through what they were taught at home—play.

I grew up with dogs as part of my family so it was only natural that I was missing my pack members when I moved to New York City. While living in the East Village and reading *The Village Voice* one day, I came across a rescue center in Staten Island, and I got that feeling in my gut. I knew I had to go. When I arrived at the shelter, a beautiful caramel-colored dog with stunning hazel eyes and boundless energy captured my attention, and we bonded immediately. The people there warned me that he was difficult, but I was undeterred; I knew I had come for him. They put him on a leash and we walked together. He pulled, was desperate to run, and had intense, spastic, pent-up energy, but that seemed only natural after being cooped up for so long. He jumped on me and communicated in all the ways he knew how, as though pleading for me to set him free. I fell in love immediately. I went through the paperwork and just days later, he arrived to live with me in the East Village. The first night I slept curled up beside him on the floor was heaven and I committed to giving him the best life I could.

I arranged my days so that we could go for long walks or runs in the morning, spend ample time at the dog run in Tompkins Square Park in the afternoon, and go for long walks again in the evening. At the time, I was mostly freelancing and training clients in the park or nearby and along the East River, and sometimes I even brought him along. I cooked his meals as I cooked mine, and when he barked and lashed out at certain tall white men with baseball hats who must have reminded him of his abusers, there was something in me that felt his reactions were justified. As I began to spend more time at the boxing gym, I began to lash out more and more on the heavy bags, then come home and cool down as we walked together for miles. For those first two years, we bonded and helped each other heal.

On days I had to work longer, I hired someone to walk him. But over time, as my clients moved away, along with my income, and I got more involved in boxing and coaching, he was stuck in the apartment alone. It made me restless; I imagined him depressed or going crazy to be free so I always rushed home, feeling guilty along the way. I took him out of the city to run wild as much as I could. We went to the beach off-season, to the forests in Western Massachusetts, but I knew it wasn't enough. He needed more. He needed freedom to roam without so many interruptions, a loving home where he wasn't cooped up and could run in the forest to his heart's content. I knew deep down that clinging to him would keep both of us stuck. He needed to live the life he deserved. Finding that home for him would be one of the hardest things I'd do, but it would have been selfish to make him stay.

I put the word out to friends and family in Western Massachusetts and was specific: he needed someone who was kind, compassionate, would treat him like family, take him hiking, running, rarely leave him alone, and give him an incredible life of love and freedom. Eventually, I found just that. After a number of long visits, one day I left my sweet canine companion to play with his new friends and soon-to-be family. It was intensely heartbreaking, but I knew it was right. I spent time with them and kept in touch, but after a while, once I knew he was happy and loved, I let go. He was thriving, and that was enough.

His picture still travels with me as I take his spirit on adventures, reminding me that loving sometimes means letting go. I will always miss him, but I know I did the right thing. And that's what I want for the wolves. I worry about the wild world—it's what keeps me up at night, motivates me, and gnaws at me more than anything else. I would rather know the wolves are safe and thriving in the wild, living the life they were born to live, than interact with them at all.

WE NEED THE SAME THINGS THAT WOLVES DO: PROTECTED PUBLIC LANDS AND uninterrupted wild places where we can roam free without the fear of destruction or being preyed upon. I think about the fact that for over 95 percent of human existence, we have been nomads, carrying and taking only what was essential and dependent on the availability of forageable fruit, nuts, roots, and greens, the movement of animals, and changes in weather. Sometimes I wonder if we're even meant to stay in one place. Certainly, we're not meant to accumulate so much unnecessary stuff that exhausts the Earth while keeping us bogged down and tethered.

TWO WOLVES GREET ME AS I WALK UP TO ALLADALE'S MAIN LODGE. THE FE-male wolf is crouched down, playful and ready to pounce. The male has his neck stretched up to the sky, howling. These lifelike sculptures represent what is to come. Every day for the past three weeks, they have been knocked down by intense, overwhelming winds that whistle through every crack in the lodge. And every day, I stand the wolves back up. I know they'll get knocked down again, but resetting them has become a daily ritual of persistence. There are days I'm tempted to pass them by, knowing that keeping them upright is a futile effort, but something compels me to walk up the hill where they reside and set them tall. I can't give up on them.

There are about twelve thousand wolves in Europe today, about twice as many as in the United States, and in the past two decades, wolf packs have returned to the Alps and begun repopulating parts of Germany, Italy, France, Austria, and Switzerland.[4] But we need to foster education alongside these repopulations efforts. European Union law allows the killing of wolves if they pose a danger to humans, and as their numbers grow, that chance for misunderstandings or misconstrued encounters also grows. In many places, wolves provoke so much unfounded fear that the line between threat and safety blur. We need to stretch our minds and revise our stories so that they reflect reality, and support wild spaces and our interdependent survival.

Heeding the call of the wolf has helped me clarify my own boundaries and step more completely into my role as a steward of the land. These words are my howls as I find my way across today's ever-evolving landscape and do my best to create new stories so that wild spaces can expand, and all creatures can roam free.

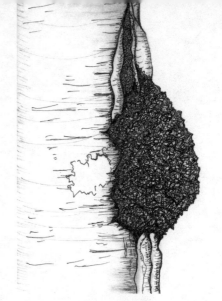

CHAGA
Inonotus obliquus

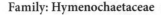

Family: Hymenochaetaceae

Chaga is not the fruiting body of a mushroom, but a medicinal mass of mycelium known as a sclerotia. Unlike most mushrooms, chaga is a polypore, a fungus with pores instead of gills, and rather than growing in soil, chaga prefers birch trees. Birch is a pioneer species that grows quickly on the devastated land, creating conditions and habitat for other woodland species to thrive. Some argue that chaga's relationship with birch is parasitic, while others say the relationship is symbiotic, and that chaga helps to heal the tree's wounds. Whatever they go through in their partnership, the combination of the two is potent, and chaga, in the most medicinal form, does not exist without their host tree. The rapid life cycle of birch pushes upward fast, causing them to fall and rot and break easily, and in collaboration with the fungi, their rotting creates more fertile ground for generations to come.

INTIMACY

Guard well your spare moments. They are like uncut diamonds.
Discard them and their value will never be known. Improve
them and they will become the brightest gems in a useful life.

RALPH WALDO EMERSON

eing with you feels like swimming in the ocean," you tell me. The ocean
is your favorite place, and swimming makes you feel free, so I know
this comparison is the highest compliment. Safe in each other's arms,
we can relax and let go. We say "I love you" to each other all the time and yet
the words' meaning never dulls.

Now, in the chaos and uncertainty of a pandemic, we're apart—me in
Scotland and you in Brooklyn. We stay connected thanks to the mycelial web
of technology, but we can't touch. It feels right for me to be here in the Highlands, but I miss you. Especially since our most tender moments have been
beyond words. I'm filled with nostalgia, but I don't want to squander my time
here pining for our home.

I feel in a strange limbo today, as though I'm going through the stages
of grief: denial, anger, bargaining, sadness, and acceptance. I'm softening
into sadness, a kind of melting, and I long for your hands that can hold so
much. When you reached for my hand as we walked down Washington Av-

enue to harvest nettles from my overgrown garden plot six years ago, I knew you were my person. You continue to reach for my hand in the darkness of our bedroom, and in our tent as we're camping under the stars. I reached for your hand last night out of habit as I was falling asleep, and nothing was there.

It's spring of 2020 and proper management of the global pandemic means many plans need to be put on hold; when someone suggests I might be stuck in the Highlands for six months, my body, always longing for the freedom of wild nature, feels relief. *I can't go back to the city, not even if I wanted to.* But my heart, confused, yearns for you even while beating faster at the thrill of the wild here. On these twenty-three thousand acres of wilderness there is no urban sprawl, no concrete, no ceaseless noise. I don't have to watch my back as I roam, and it's liberating. My nervous system relaxes and I have solitary time to crack open again—something I've been craving even though I know how uncomfortable it might be.

Once I cried, I could be more present here. After the existential sadness and the sadness of missing you abated, I'm now unraveling, letting go, and everything is more vivid. The sound of your voice on the phone touches me and I feel the embrace of all living things—the rain pouring down, the wind caressing my face, the fur-like grass, the pillowy mosses, the birch trees, the thorny gorse, the moments of sunshine. This is the wild solitude I've been longing for, and it feels like swimming in the ocean.

CHAGA DOES NOT EXIST WITHOUT A HOST TREE. AND USUALLY THAT HOST IS birch, a pioneer tree species that grows quickly on the devastated land, creating the conditions and habitat for other woodland species to thrive. Silver birch and downy birch have been here in Scotland since the end of the last Ice Age when they moved into newly exposed areas and settled with their windblown seeds. Beithe, or birch, is the first symbol of the Ogham alphabet, representing the letter *B*, and ancient birch woodlands are immortalized in many Gaelic place names such as Gleann Beithe, Allt Beithe, and Beith in Ayrshire.[1] Here in the Highlands, the birch trees with chaga are thriving.

LIKE THE CHAGA AND BIRCH, MY PARTNER AND I TAKE TURNS COMPOSTING each other's pain. On our way to the beach, he talks to me about his mother. He smiles as he tells me about his weekends growing up in Venezuela, when he sat in the sand and ate coconut sorbet served in hardened coconut shells while his mom pretended to be part of the beach club. Going to the beach, just the two of them, was their weekend ritual and their happiest time together. I look at pictures of him playing in the sand and recognize the childlike innocence he still has even as he tells me about the note his mom left when she decided that her pain was too great to go on, and decided to die.

Tears emerge from deep within his gut—a deep pain that makes him heave, almost vomit. Feeling his pain, my body reacts, hurts, something in me moves, adjusts, and I taste salt on my own lips. I imagine losing my mother, which terrifies me, and I imagine him, the little boy who loved her—and still loves her so much—losing her. I reach out to him, hold him. It is so hard to know what to do in those moments when someone we love is reeling. Even tenderness can smother sometimes. And as raw and painful as it is, I'm so glad he allows the tears to break through layers of pain, washing and healing something inside of him. Those moments of softening, feeling, and letting go have created more space inside each of us, allowing us to move closer together.

We had our first date at Fort Tilden beach, and while we were sitting on the sand, he told me that he loves to swim in the salt water because he feels free to cry there. "My tears become the ocean," he told me. Now, his beautiful mother is ever present, with him on every beach, everywhere.

WHEN TREES LOSE BRANCHES OR SUFFER DAMAGE FROM STORMS, THE CHAGA mushroom will grow over the wound to serve as a protective scar. The dark hyphal mass of chaga, the sclerotia, on the birch tree intertwines with it to form a unique fungi-and-tree interaction. The mushroom has the appearance of an irregular, cracked mass of burnt charcoal. When chaga is harvested, we find a beautiful color of rust inside. The birch tree can continue living for many years while mounds of chaga adorn her trunk, just as we can survive and even thrive while adorned with scars from old wounds.

IN 2019, AT THE END OF SUMMER, ALEX AND I WERE GOING THROUGH AN IN-tensely emotional transition. I had just returned from a month in the Scottish Highlands and did indeed now feel trapped in the city. Even though we live near Prospect Park and the botanical garden, there was nowhere I could go to be in nature and not have to watch my back, not have to deal with constant noise and steady streams of people. I wanted solitude and I was exhausted from negotiating and compromising for it.

Brooklyn has been a wonderful base, but it's been years since I called Brooklyn a home. It is a hub from which to be transient. I spend much of my time in wild spaces, and then come back to him, my friends, my community, and the culture of the city. But I am finding it harder and harder to adjust to the noise after being in nature. For a while, I enjoyed the contrast, but it increasingly affects my nerves and I find myself yearning for the wild where I can expand.

We cried a lot that fall. I was feeling done with the city. I felt trapped with nowhere to go where I wasn't surrounded by people. I needed creative space, I needed to leave. I wanted him to come with me: "Why don't we move to a rural area right outside the city?" But that's not what he wanted, and the more we talked, the more it seemed we wanted different things. We teetered on the edge of painful emotional depths, but I also thought that we might be breaking through something.

I went away for a few days and I asked him to read Skeleton Woman, an Inuit story of healing and one of my favorites in Clarissa Pinkola Estés's *Women Who Run with the Wolves*.[2] In the beginning of the story, a daughter is rejected, punished, and thrown into the ocean where eventually she disintegrates and becomes nothing but bones. When a lonely fisherman goes out to sea, farther than others dared to go, he sends his line into the depths and catches her by the ribs. He believes he's finally caught the ultimate fish, one that will feed him for days, but what is caught is not this imagined treasure. As he pulls the Skeleton Woman from the depths of the ocean, she struggles to break free but instead becomes more and more entangled in his line. Eventually, she rises to the surface and terrifies the fisherman. Heart racing, he tries to run, but she is already caught and follows right behind him. Attachment has happened.

The fisherman is exhausted from trying to escape when he finally makes it home, and as he arrives something shifts for him. He turns to look at her, *really look at her*, and as he does he is struck with compassion. He begins to untangle his net, put her bones in the right places, and dress her in furs to keep her warm. She accepts his kindness and, afraid to break the spell, does not say a word. Finally, the fisherman, in an act of trust, sleeps. And as he sleeps, a tear escapes from his eye during a dream. Skeleton Woman, so parched and so thirsty for true and deep connection, drinks his tear and in doing so, nourishes the dry, depleted spaces inside her. As a result of these new feelings, and the power of compassion, she begins to come back to life.

SALT WATER IS A MAGICAL SUBSTANCE. LIKE THE OCEAN RUNNING OVER ROCKS, our tears rounded our jagged edges so we could bump up against each other again without causing damage and find new ways to merge. The rupture of potential change brought Alex and me closer together and made us realize how deeply we love each other. Prior to that, prior to the raw honesty on both of our ends, I found it easy to imagine leaving. Now I know if I can resist the urge to run in moments like those, I might soften inside, finding new space for close connection.

I'm here again in the Scottish Highlands, repeating in some ways the trip that had left me restless last year. I'm here indefinitely due to this life-altering pandemic. Neither of us could have known this would happen, but somehow we already processed and prepared for separation. We grieved, knowing somewhere in our bones that I would, in fact, be far away for a while.

SOLITUDE

The silence here is palpable. I can hear the sounds and stirrings of my body in a way I can't usually when life is more crowded with noise and technological interference. I don't know if I can live in that amount of noise anymore. Even as I write, I feel my body sinking into Scotland amid a beautiful serene canvas from which to call forth my memories, allowing them to pour out of my body onto the page. Though the transition to being alone can be difficult, once I adjust, I cherish the solitude. Even when I'm in bliss with a beloved partner, I hunger for time alone. And even when I have it, I worry that it might be interrupted. Creativity is another form of freedom, and I need time and space to swim in the deep end.

The act of creation has always been intensely personal for me. I have always had a hard time writing, but especially drawing or painting, with others around. It's an act of pouring my insides out, a liquid flow that tends to look messy at first. My drawings always go through an ugly phase, and with my abstract work, I rarely know what I'm setting out to draw. Lines have their own life, it seems, and I try to let them move up and out of my body by starting with my nondominant hand. I feel a physical relief when I allow my left hand to create. It's as though she has been bound for most of my life because she wasn't good enough, half of me that hasn't expressed herself and is aching, yearning to be seen. The left-handed lines are shakier, like a child learning to draw, but there is also something more pure and direct about the expression. Somehow, that part of me knows how to sneak out onto paper without encountering my editing, critical mind.

I'm fortunate that I've come to enjoy my own company, and even when I didn't, I understood solitude was necessary to grow comfortable with myself before I could be completely comfortable with anyone else. In her book *All About Love: New Visions*, feminist bell hooks wrote, "Knowing how to be solitary is central to the art of loving. When we can be alone, we can be with others without using them as a means of escape."[3] There are layers of conditioning, memories, or trauma that must be peeled back in order to truly be close to someone else and let them in.

I love the mornings. I look forward to my coffee made with my chaga and oatstraw infusion. This savory blend has been part of my morning ritual for a couple of years now. Oatstraw promotes calm steadiness and flexibility, and chaga is a powerful immunomodulator. Together, they balance the bitter, caffeinated dark roast coffee. I simmer the chaga and oatstraw to get the most out of their medicine, then pour them over my grounds with a drop of coconut oil, mix, send them into my cup through a tea strainer, and savor the bitter brew.

I say "I love you" to myself every morning. I say it to my body, my mind, my loved ones, to Mother Nature. I greet my environment and often greet each direction—east, the direction of the rising sun and the element of air; south, the direction of the high noon sun and fire; west, the direction of the setting sun and water; and north, the direction of midnight and Earth. I greet the sky above and ground below and orient myself in the center of it all. This practice helps me to know where I am in relation to the natural world. Then I rub places in my body that are tense, roll out my joints, move stagnant energy, greet my body, check in, breathe, and reflect on my nighttime dreams.

The morning is when my thoughts are most clear. When I wake, I allow inspiration to come through me, from the ground up, into my fingers and out. I download ideas that seem to come from the ether, from the plants, from the spirits, and upload information from the soil or caverns of memory. When I wake up early, at 5 or 6 a.m., I am energized. I feel the cortisol coursing through me, the waves of energy. I like to write and meditate before the outside world invades my inner world; it has always been the time I write best. I try to take advantage of the sweet spot between dreaming and fully waking, downloading what comes to me first thing in the morning. When the rest of the world wakes up and the invisible buzz is around me, I feel a faint distraction even if I don't have to do anything.

I LOVE THE MORNINGS WITH HIM TOO. HE GREETS ME WITH "HELLO, SUNSHINE" or "Buenos días, mi cariño" every day. Somehow he is in a good mood every morning, which bewilders me, but I'm so grateful for it. But then there is also always a moment of tension: *Is he going to turn the radio on?* We want to stay in bed and cuddle, but we know whoever gets downstairs first will define the morning environment. I've explained my need for quiet, we've gone through uncomfortable negotiations, and now he often wears headphones—but he doesn't like them. He likes to enter the day knowing what's going on in the outside world, while I need to attune to my inside world first. It's a tricky balance we strike. I struggled to maintain my morning practices when I first moved in with him. We've come to better compromises lately, but here in the Highlands, I can drop in more deeply, knowing I don't have to negotiate sacred space.

A BIRD, AN ADORABLE BLUE TIT, FLEW INTO MY ROOM THE OTHER DAY. HE OR she had seemed to want to come in for days and had been pecking at the window. Whether their visitation was some sort of sign or simply their own curiosity, I don't know. But that day, they flew through the window I had opened just enough to get fresh air, barely enough for the little body to enter the room. When I walked to my desk after making my morning infusion, the little bird was sitting on the edge of the chair. They didn't seem fazed or afraid. While I wanted to soak in the interaction, I can't stand birds being stuck in the house and flapping against the walls. But since the bird didn't seem anxious, I was able to be present for that small moment he or she perched on my chair, blessing my writing desk. This little creature seemed to know exactly what they were doing. Then I opened all the windows, and a few minutes later, they perched on a windowsill, flew through one I had opened wide, and took off into the sky.

THERE IS A PART OF ME THAT ALWAYS FEELS ON EDGE ABOUT MY TIME AND space being encroached upon. Even in a remote cabin in the Scottish Highlands, alone in the hills of Western Massachusetts, or in the jungle of Costa Rica where it would take some serious effort to come and find me, I want to know I will have uninterrupted time. I feel desperate for it. I have no kids, I have a partner who supports my need for solitude, and still I have wasted time worrying about being interrupted. Maybe it's all the women who came before me who felt that way. Maybe it's something I'm working out for the women in my family who didn't get their time. I worry if my solitude is broken that I won't write as well or that I'll enter a space that isn't quite as deep and have to start all over again. Like a bird thrashing against the walls, I want freedom.

I don't want children. I have never had much of a craving for kids. In the midst of a passionate love affair I've had romantic notions of creating a child with my partner. I've wanted them to want that with me, and I wondered what our children would look like or be like. But the truth is, parenthood is not my calling. I have come to believe that I am healing for the generations before me and any trauma that has been passed down stops with me. There are other ways to give birth.

While women living alone have been stigmatized, pitied as spinsters, or feared as witches of the wood, they are free. I suppose swimming or flying on the symbolic broomsticks with entheogens made women feel like they were suspended without strings, but groundedness is limitless too. Roots can grow endlessly as long as they aren't constrained by concrete, and sometimes break through even if they are.

CHAGA MUST "FEEL" WHEN THE BIRCH IS INJURED. THESE TWO SPECIES ARE intimately connected, sensing one another's needs under the soil just like I intuit the feelings of those I love and move to support them when they need to lean on me. Chaga is a mound of protection, a scab around an area of woundedness. But protectiveness itself can become parasitic or smothering, so it's no wonder people debate whether chaga is good or bad for the birch. We all need a healthy balance of intimacy and solitude in order to thrive. At its core, independence is an illusion. Even where we're alone, we are tethered to others.

I'VE BEEN CONNECTING WITH FRIENDS ONLINE IN WAYS THAT REMIND ME OF curling up on my couch and talking on my landline for hours before the days of cell phones. Before the pandemic, it seemed there was hardly time to text back with such an oversaturation of messages, alerts, social media, doing. So many interruptions. Now all that has slowed and it has become clear who I want to talk to.

I've been getting lots of messages like: "You must miss him. It must feel lonely there. It must be hard" and "Don't worry, you're not alone."

I don't feel lonely or alone. I try to explain, but they are caught up in their own imagining. I appreciate the empathy, and though I can easily describe and explain how I feel, my truth doesn't seem to sink in. But I listen to my friends anyway and don't feel like arguing. Of course there are moments when I miss those I love, but mostly, I am enjoying my solitude. Those who know me well know I have been craving time like this for so long.

I CAN BE AWKWARD IN GROUPS, UNLESS THE GROUPS ARE CURATED BY ME. Alex and I often argue about my lack of desire to go to parties. I rarely enjoy parties, but he thrives on social gatherings while I usually come home feeling drained. One-on-one get-togethers and small curated groups work well for me, but there always needs to be a level of depth or I just disappear. I'm an introvert by nature, and I wish I'd understood what that meant when I was younger because I always worried that my silence was interpreted as stupidity.

I always remind people who come to any retreat I host, whether two days or two weeks, that "this is your time for you." I remind them to listen to what they need and if something is happening but they'd rather be alone, to take that time for themselves. Together, we hold a safe space for authenticity, where we can be real without judgment. We can be alone, together.

SYMBIOSIS

The mycelium under our feet are sensitive to changes in their environment, and as a sentient network, form a sort of forest consciousness. As we walk into old-growth forests, or any area of woodland that is intact, the mycelia sense our movements and tell the rest of the community. I imagine they also sense our intent.

In the best circumstances both the fungus and their host benefit from the relationship—the fungi act as fascia, connecting and supporting the host's root tissues, improving their moisture and nutrient absorption capabilities, and in exchange, the host plant provides the fungi with carbohydrates produced through photosynthesis. The fungi also provide greater connectivity with the larger forest web, which in turn helps the forest function as one unified ecosystem. Mushrooms also help by breaking down organic matter as they draw food and nutrients from decaying plants, dead animal bodies, and trees. Thus making the nutrients available to the forest community.

All fungi begin with a spore that germinates and grows strands called the mycelium. The fruiting body of a mushroom is like the familiar portobello mushroom, and the mycelium is the vast feeding body that we might not recognize as well. But in the case of chaga, the perennial growth on tree trunks is a mass of mycelium, not the fruiting bodies usually thought of as mushrooms. So in a sense, wild chaga could be seen as a mass of the land's consciousness. They are a slow-growing species, taking three to five years to fully form, and because of that, when I gather chaga for medicine, I leave plenty on the tree and take only as much as I need.

WHEN I HARVESTED TODAY, I ASKED PERMISSION FROM THE CHAGA, THE BIRCH, and the surrounding forest and let them know that I'd come to gather medicine for Lincoln, Innes MacNeill's Labrador retriever, who has cancer. He has a large tumor on his torso that looks itself like chaga protruding from the trunk of a birch tree. I sensed a yes, permission and openness from the tree that I doubted for a moment when I began to harvest the chaga since the mass was so difficult to remove from the birch. I rarely use tools to harvest; I prefer my hands whenever possible, but for this I had to rely on a tool. I borrowed Innes's knife and released just a bit from a healthy part of the forest populated by birch trees and left most intact. It was a good agreement, and I am so grateful for the gift. In my small muslin bag, the chaga looks and feels like a pouch of gold.

In his 1968 semi-autobiographical novel *Cancer Ward*, Russian author Aleksandr Solzhenitsyn wrote about the powers of chaga, especially when it came to treating and even preventing cancer.[4] The novel follows the work of Sergei N. Maslennikov, a Russian doctor who noted that he didn't have any cancer patients among the peasants he treated who saved money on buying tea by harvesting and brewing chaga. He felt they had unknowingly (or maybe knowingly) been preventing and treating cancer for centuries. In order to test his theory, he began treating willing cancer patients with varied extractions made from chaga. His notebooks record the results of ideal methods of medicinal extraction and dosage and of his treatment of cancer with chaga, with many patients making full recoveries. It's perhaps not a surprise then that chaga has been an approved anticancer drug in Russia since 1955.

While chaga can grow on grains, it is the combination of chaga and birch—the predigested betulinic acid derivatives and melano-glucan complexes—that make chaga a potent healer. The name *chaga* is the Russian word for mushroom in the language of indigenous people living west of the Ural Mountains. Deemed "the Mushroom of Immortality" by Siberian Russian shamans,[5] this wild healer is a powerful adaptogen that helps bring the body into balance through beneficial effects on the nervous system. The immunomodulating properties of chaga can strengthen the immune system by regulating the production of cytokines and supporting the immune system with better cell communication. Autoimmune issues are a result of our body overcompensating—our system is trying too hard and overcorrecting. The mycelial mass is also a strong source of vitamin D, which is helpful for the long, dark winters here in Scotland and the other cold climates where chaga lives.

The birch tree has also been an ally to people in the cold north for thousands of years, and has been used for everything from adhesives to baskets, boats, vinegar, spirits, and medicine. The ceremony of the maypole on Beltane is symbolic of renewed life and sexual union. The pole, usually made from birch, is a phallic symbol. The discus at the top from which ribbons are tied represents the feminine, and the wearing of ribbons represents the union of the male and the female and fertility. In some parts of the British Isles, it was the custom to erect a maypole outside every house, or for young men to assemble one outside the home of their beloved. It was also common practice to bring a new pole into the village every year, representing the nature spirit who would bless the celebrations and bring fertility to land.

In early spring before the birch leaves unfurl, the abundant sap can be used for irrigation therapy to flush and reinvigorate the body after winter. The flow from the birch is best on sunny days following a heavy frost, and as long as the tap is plugged after using and a tree isn't tapped too frequently, this harvesting won't harm the tree. The healing liquid reduces fluid retention and swelling, clears up many skin problems, and makes a clear and refreshing drink that can also be preserved as a wine, beer, or spirit.

Birch leaves can also be made into tea or dried and infused into oil to ease arthritis. In each form, birch is tonic, helping our kidneys and urinary system wash away what our body doesn't want or need while easing inflammation. The bark was generally seen as a famine food when other forms of starch were unavailable or in short supply. The inner bark, called the cambium layer, can be cooked or dried and ground into a powder, then used with cereals for making bread. But it is very important not to strip the bark all the way around the tree—a wound called girdling. This causes the tree to bleed to death. In cold forests, and where the wounds are more localized, chaga might rise up from the earth to build a strong scab.

LONGING

Chords connect us at the heart and I feel him pull. But in those moments, I wonder if it is love I feel or attachment. Sometimes he thinks I'm too sensitive, and sometimes I think he's too desensitized. There are moments when we are both distracted, unaware we are treading on tender spaces, and we wound each other without meaning to. But as long as we have the words to describe our feelings and don't allow scabs and scars to build barriers between us, our wounds can be repaired.

Like chaga and birch, each of us contains the stories and memories of those we love. Some stories and experiences are harder to digest and compost, and sometimes they are one-sided, making a relationship parasitic instead of healing. If we can learn to digest our own pain instead of putting it onto others, or if we can process our pain together, our relationships can be strengthened by symbiosis. Sometimes, one of us will lean in and let go while the other stands strong. Then we exchange roles.

Like most animals, I adore coziness and sometimes wonder why I am so compelled to head out into the wild when I am so warm and snug and in love. Why leave the nest? Even though we want each other to stay in those moments, our relationship would lose its wings if we gave in to codependence instead of cultivating interdependence. We've done enough work on ourselves to feel that a relationship should make us feel free and not burdened. The tenderness of growth hurts and I wonder if plants have growing pains, if buds grieve the loss of their tight, close, cozy quarters before they open to the eyes of the world and become flowers.

Closeness to a person or place can mean depth or limitation, and sometimes it's difficult to see each other in close proximity. There are times when we have to zoom out and get some distance to realize how beautiful those closest to us are, and how much they mean to us. While we may never marry, our bond is sealed in moments of pure sweetness, wild laughter, ocean waves, and bittersweet tears. Together, we may continue to negotiate sound versus silence, city versus wild nature, parties versus quiet evenings at home. And we still choose each other every day. My freedom came when I didn't need partners to need me anymore, but to choose me.

We can never really know what will befall a partnership or even how we will change, and I'm grateful that we give each other the freedom to go off in our own directions supported by an almost invisible net of intimacy. Our love keeps us connected even when we're far apart.

"MAYBE YOU NEED TO ACCEPT THAT THERE WILL ALWAYS BE A PART OF YOU that is longing," a friend said to me recently. The words rang true. There will always be a contradictory pull between my need for solitude and partnership, between my community in the city and the healing expanse of the wild. When I'm alone, I may cherish the space but also long for his touch. But there is a beautiful tension in longing. Things always taste better when I'm hungry, water is pure bliss when I'm thirsty. When I take a bath, the moment my body enters the hot water is the best part. The parts of me that are submerged can forget how good they feel, and if I stay too long, I turn into a soggy prune. If I let go and dive into the embrace of it all, I can ride the waves of intimacy and solitude, and in those moments, it feels like swimming in the ocean.

RED CLOVER
Trifolium pratense

Family: Fabaceae

Red clover appears to be one flower, but when we look closely, we find that the flower head is actually a collection of up to one hundred tiny purple-pink flowers whose petals look like wings. Often found growing in sunny fields with three-parted white chevron-embossed leaflets, this plant in the legume family invites other creatures to thrive. Clover works hard to improve soil health, attract pollinators and beneficial insects, and promote healthy meadows, lawns, woodland edges, and gardens. The magnanimous plant converts nitrogen in the atmosphere into forms that plants can more easily absorb through their root systems, resulting in more diverse soil life and higher capacity to hold nutrients. For our inner ecosystems, red clover is just as generous as a highly nutritive plant with significant amounts of calcium, magnesium, chromium, niacin, phosphorus, potassium, thiamine, and vitamin C. The medicine acts as an antispasmodic, expectorant, and alterative, helping our bodies remove metabolic waste and experience more vitality. Native to Europe, Western Asia, and northwest Africa, red clover has naturalized in North America and throughout the world, nurturing communities of plants, insects, animals, and people wherever they grow.

COEXISTENCE

To be healed we must come with all the other creatures to the feast of Creation.

WENDELL BERRY

I stepped outside of the small crofting cottage in the Scottish Highlands to walk along the narrow road edged with rowan trees, rose bushes, rolling hills, and wandering sheep. It was almost 10 p.m. but still bright when I saw a creature across the tiny street who was moving quickly, low to the ground. He or she was coming closer and closer to me, disappearing and reappearing under small green hills, weaving toward me in waves among a flock of indifferent sheep. It was summer solstice, the longest day of the year, and I had just finished facilitating my online herbal apprenticeship where my students and I shared a solstice ritual, set personal intentions, and spoke about plants like St. John's wort that peak in late June, harnessing the energy of the sun.

When I saw the flash of her lush fiery tail I knew she was a red fox—a vixen, I imagined. When she felt me staring at her, she edged closer, curious. Then she stopped, sat, and stared at me too. In that moment, the gorgeous animal and I were taking each other in, locked together as one. We stared without moving for what seemed like ten minutes, maybe more. While I was mesmerized, I also needed to move my body after sitting for hours so I started to walk, wondering what she would do.

As I walked, she did too, and we moved parallel to each other. Then I stopped, and she stopped and sat again, and we stared. Then we walked some more. This pattern repeated and I was hypnotized as time slipped away in our creaturely communication. It was the most incredible solstice gift. When I turned and walked back to the cottage, the fox followed, parallel for a while until she gradually walked diagonally up the hill, farther away from me. That's when I thought, *I should take a picture!* But no, it seemed like an experience that was not meant to be captured. I hesitated. In that brief moment when I looked down at my phone, the spell was broken, and when I looked up again she was gone.

I basked in the solstice interaction though I was disappointed I'd stepped outside of our trance with the thought of severing that sacred moment with a screen. But I sensed I would see her again, next time with no phone in my pocket. I looked through the window all of the next day and finally saw her trotting across the hill in the evening. I walked outside and again she stopped when she noticed me and we stared at each other. She sat a little farther up on the hill this time, on top of a small mound. So graceful. We gazed at each other in stillness, but when I began to walk, instead of following me, she spun in a circle on top of the mound and vanished. I waited for a while, thinking she might reappear, but she was nowhere in sight.

Her spiral turn seemed playful, almost to beckon me, so I decided to hike up the mountain and, without disturbing her or any other creature, visit the mound and follow in her direction. As I did, I came upon a space with magical energy where many of the plants I had been writing about and looking for grew—eyebright, yarrow, self-heal, nettles, and red clover. I had been seeking eyebright, intending to write about the plant, and though usually prominent in the Highlands, this wild patch was the first I saw in bloom. I sat with tiny flowers the next day, and that chapter moved through me in one sitting. Red clover was prominent here too, rising from the ground with slender, flexible, and hairy stems and three-sectioned ovate leaves, each imprinted with a light-green V. The deep pinkish-purple blossoms were visited by fuzzy bumblebees. I recently read that red foxes like the taste of red clover flowers too. I gathered a few plants to munch on and to dry as keepsakes to take home, leaving plenty for the fox and the bees.

AS I RODE DOWN ATLANTIC AVENUE FROM JFK AIRPORT TO BROOKLYN AFTER my unexpectedly long stay in Scotland, mugwort and goldenrod were among the first friends to greet me. Mugwort was the plant I allied with for a year during my herbal apprenticeship, and after that, red clover. While I always worked with many plants, allying meant that I would spend time with my chosen plants everywhere I could, listen to their messages, observe their behavior closely, engage with their medicine in ways that felt right, and be a devoted and trusted friend and ambassador. When I sat alongside red clover in rural fields or city parks, the message I continued to receive was *We are all in this together.* Red clover is self-seeding, but the seed alone can do nothing without the presence of soil microbes, the sun, water, and other plants and creatures that help facilitate growth.

I saw my partner for the first time in six months and returned to shelves full of beloved plants and herbal tinctures, vinegars, oils, and the memories they carry. I decanted Japanese knotweed root tincture, one that I'd been craving, and placed the liquid in a small dropper bottle on my desk. I unpacked a small circular box made of birch bark, a recent gift from my father to celebrate our reunion. He wanted to get me something special, something with a wolf on it, but we found this sweet treasure with a fox carved on the lid instead and now it seems no coincidence. I carried the small treasure to Scotland and brought it back to Brooklyn full of dried eyebright and red clover I gathered from the fox hill, St. John's wort that grew outside my cottage, and a tiny ancestral stone from Argyll. The box joins a circle of dried mugwort from the Wolf Conservation Center, chaga from Alladale Wilderness Reserve, red clover from Western Massachusetts, and goldenrod from Fort Tilden beach. A fox figurine and a photo of a fox pup also watch me at my desk and have become my writing companions. Whenever I gaze at the plants or the picture, I go back to the hypnotic moment when the solstice fox and I were woven together, in sync. I wonder if she carries something of me too.

TWO WEEKS AGO, ALEX AND I STOPPED TO FILL UP THE GAS IN HIS SCOOTER after coming back from the beach where we saw three dolphins playing just fifty feet away. It was late September so Fort Tilden was nearly empty except for a few volunteers picking up trash, some people fishing, and others, like us, simply savoring the environment. Just a thirty-minute ride from our Brooklyn apartment, at Fort Tilden goldenrod is beginning to bloom along the dunes while gorgeous monarch butterflies drink in their nectar, and there is a protected plover nesting site nearby. Lately, we've seen dolphins on every visit.

The first time we spotted them, a dolphin leapt out of the water while a pod of twenty or more fins followed. It was so exciting and I came home wanting to know all about them. I learned that every dolphin develops a unique whistle pattern called a signature whistle and that they remember the whistles of companions for up to twenty years. Their social memory is the longest ever recorded in the animal kingdom and is essential as they swim in and out of different pods over a lifetime. One type of pod, called a nursery, is made up of mothers and their calves. These caregiving pods might also include elderly dolphins and "dolphin daycare" called allomothering that may even include female dolphins of different species. Bottlenose dolphins often come to the aid of injured dolphins, using their signature whistle to call for help when needed, providing support for the weakened mammal by bringing them to the surface to breathe.

As Alex filled the small tank, I looked up and noticed a huge, majestic red-tailed hawk perched atop one of the buildings. Then an iridescent pigeon walked by. Some people call pigeons "rats with wings," but I think they're beautiful. Domesticated about ten thousand years ago, pigeons are the feral descendants of the rock dove and were once worshipped as companions of fertility goddesses and celebrated as messengers. They carried vital messages for us over centuries, and homing pigeons like the famous Cher Ami have been awarded for saving thousands of lives during wartime. Now these intelligent birds, who mate for life and once symbolized love, carry on with little recognition or respect, and at worst are reviled. Still, they persevere gracefully.

While Alex and I were at the beach, a pair of pigeons sat on the sand gazing at the ocean just like us. It was so touching. We're lucky that these creatures and many others—like seagulls, squirrels, robins, racoons, chipmunks, starlings, blue jays, chickadees, crows, and the peregrine falcons that live high above Prospect Park—have adapted and are tenacious enough to live with us in urban areas.

In New York City, people live on top of each other like bees in a honeycomb yet rarely know their neighbors and often come and go without saying a word. Up until the time of COVID, we squeezed into subways and acquired the art of pressing against strangers as close as we would to a lover and yet look through them and see no one. We are surrounded by a growing population of people, but it is increasingly easy to feel isolated. Material progress and the desire to come out on top take over a sense of interconnection in many places where we live in our own boxes, houses, or castles, guarding possessions with locks, fences, or security cameras as we plan to acquire more. It's a strange and lonely way to live. Impersonal, "time-saving" acts designed for our convenience, like picking up vegetables at the grocery store or even by the click of a button with no idea who grew or harvested them, creates even more distance and, ironically, more dependence. Computers and industrialized machines that do things our hands and hearts used to do sever people from each other and from land and make people who have been essential feel unnecessary.

I'll admit, even as someone who enjoys solitude, I liked being in the creative energy of New York City and still being able to weave through streets anonymously. But I know that my solitude was made possible by a web of loved ones who hold and support me near and far. In *Ishmael*, Daniel Quinn writes about the community of gorillas in Africa. He believes that if they could speak on our terms, they would say that their "family is like a hand, of which they are the fingers. They are fully aware of being a family but are very little aware of being individuals. . . . In the zoo there were other gorillas—but there was no family. Five severed fingers do not make a hand."[1]

I was worried that the pandemic would separate our communities even further, but what I found in my Brooklyn neighborhood after being away for six months was a feeling of solidarity. There was no rush to and from subways— people were coming up with creative, communal solutions to education and childcare, there were more banners, murals, and peaceful protests for Black

Lives Matter. Instead of being cloistered in separate apartments, nearby streets became playgrounds. Vanderbilt Avenue, the street I walk most frequently from my community garden to Prospect Park, was closed to cars on weekends so people could gather safely outdoors at restaurants while bands played and people danced in the streets. Even with people six feet apart, and wearing masks when necessary, the neighborhood felt more alive and connected. In my building, people were in less of a rush and seemed to crave connection in a way they hadn't before. While sitting outside and writing in the communal courtyard, I got to know neighbors I'd passed by before with little more than a hello. I talked to them about turning what had been a lovely ornamental garden and public space into more of a functional and educational space that would be easy to take care of while benefiting essential pollinators. There was an opening for that conversation that wasn't there before.

I had the opportunity to share that there is no such thing as a weed. They listened as I explained the ways in which plants like dandelion, clover, plantain, and chickweed provide nutrients for grasses, food for urban birds, and important groundcover. I proposed planting lots of clover, explaining that the generous plant helps heal soil and creates potential for more life without the need for chemical fertilizers. Butterflies and other beneficial insects like ladybugs and lacewings enjoy the nectar and then feed on surrounding aphids, whiteflies, cabbage worms, and other creatures that can be harmful to neighboring plants. A network of creatures gather to create balance in gardens when we allow the red clover to thrive.

I suggested native perennials like goldenrod and aster around the perimeter to provide food for butterflies and bees that are struggling. In the large center container where beautiful but dying birch trees stand, we could plant a medicinal garden and herb spiral that the building's residents could use, and we could fill existing empty boxes and pots throughout the garden with mints and easily grown aromatic plants such as lemon balm, peppermint, rosemary, and lavender that attract beneficial pollinators while helping to keep bugs like mosquitoes away. They listened, and the vision grew roots, and after talking to the co-op board, I'm happy to say that this will become a reality. Everyone is excited about the prospect of a healing garden that they can interact with, not just look at. The plants are already working their magic.

There is more awareness about our interconnection, and a desire for a space that we nurture and that nurtures us in return. In times of strife, when our everyday routines are interrupted and we are forced to go inward, we often come together and remember what matters most.

HARMONY

A retreat—time and space to pull back, tune in, reflect, and reemerge with a new perspective—is much different from an escape. In the retreats I curate, I do my best to share practices and experiences that can be integrated into our everyday lives. Most people arrive as a group of strangers, but over the course of days or weeks, with intentional space to unplug and be seen and heard for who we are, we become family.

After everyone settles in, we gather in a circle to introduce ourselves and share what led us to be there. Often, it is our wounds that draw us together, and through telling our stories and listening to one another, we find aspects of ourselves in others, and of others in ourselves. Together, we create space for thoughtful revisions so we can rewrite the tales that are harmful to ourselves and others, and are untrue. As author, mythologist, and storyteller Martin Shaw writes, "Bad storytellers make spells. Great storytellers break them."[2]

Deep roots like those of dandelion and burdock help us ground on day one, and we often share red clover on the second day, which I devote to water, flow, and cleansing. The nourishing infusion is a floral, harmonizing medicine that benefits the whole body, helping all our systems work together optimally. With an affinity for the water element, red clover moves congested, swollen, stagnant spaces, and with deep nourishment, benefits our lymphatic system, digestion, reproductive system, musculoskeletal system, nervous system, and skin. Red clover offers an easily digestible, complete protein that provides our bodies with the material to create neurotransmitters such as serotonin and dopamine, helping to steady our moods. Regular use helps balance hormones and is recommended for all phases of a woman's life, creating a more fluid, rhythmic, and less painful moon cycle and then easing the transition into menopause. When I drink the infusion for months at a time, I feel more harmony throughout my body. Where there was rigidity or lack of rhythm, I reestablish flow.

When I share the infusion brewed from freshly dried flowers, or point out the beautiful but overlooked pink-purple blossoms during nature walks, they often spark remembrance. I hear nostalgic stories as people realize these flowers have always grown alongside them as they played in fields, parks, or meadows as children, or even ate the honey-like blossoms. The taste and scent of red clover always bring me back to experiences of deep connection.

When we come away from our retreats, plants have joined us as healers that join us when we return home. Jahan, like many others, told me she became "totally sidetracked walking down Brooklyn streets, entranced by plants that have always been there" though she had never noticed them before. Many have told me that they engage with sidewalks, lawns, meadows, weeds, and their extended wild communities in a completely different way. Holistic healing—becoming whole—includes the recognition that the human psyche, spirit, body, and soul is an expression of nature.

While we might perceive ourselves as being separate individuals, we are truly a collection of creatures from the past and present. In his book *The Self Delusion*, ecologist Tom Oliver explains that "The molecules in your body have been recycled through the dinosaurs that walked the earth millions of years ago. All the organisms that have ever existed on the earth since the origin of life, approximately 3 to 4 billion years ago, are made of these same molecules, recycled in a never-ending cosmic dance. And each molecule has followed a different path through time before ending up together in your body at this moment."[3] We *are* nature and we can decide right now to break free from the spell of separation, remembering that we are just one miraculous member of a furred, feathered, and flowering family. When we lose essential species like wolves or bumblebees, or cut down sentient old-growth forests, we lose integral aspects of ourselves.

Like mycelium, the connective tissue that brings forest communities together, our capacity to see a fox, insect, or our human neighbor across inevitable differences to what unites us can help us build a stronger, healthier, and more biodiverse world. But we must not forget that our own ongoing healing is a prerequisite for healing one another. When we love ourselves, we're less likely to pollute our inner waterways, to harm or abuse our bodies. And when we love the land and understand that our actions impact our multispecies communities, we think not only of ourselves, but the health and resilience of the whole.

A healthy forest works for the benefit of all species within it, and it can be the same way for us. Relationships offer a web of connection, a web to catch us and hold us even in periods of solitude. When we come together with intent, we have the power to initiate healing for generations and, like red clover, create and nurture habitat for our wondrous wild family.

PINE
Pinus spp.

Family: Pinaceae

With a spiraling growth of branches, needles, and cone scales, pine offers year-round medicine that can clear our lungs, strengthen our immunity, and cleanse our environment. Pine trees are emblematic of the forest and invite us into the present moment through our exchange of breath. These trees are thought to have evolved from now-extinct ancient evergreens about 95 million years ago. They were on this planet long before we were and there is much we can learn by spending time with these wise elders that can live for thousands of years. Estimated to be 5,067 years old, a Great Basin bristlecone pine in California's White Mountains is the oldest living tree on Earth.

A home for animals like the owl, which can navigate darkness, and the eagle, which nests upon the highest branches, pine can help us move through shadows and look out upon all of our wild possibilities. In the Celtic "tree alphabet" known as Ogham, alim is pine or conifer and is associated with contemplation, finding one's purpose, and finding home. To Haudenosaunee First Nations, white pine is the Great Tree of Peace.

EVER-PRESENT PEACE

Nothing stands up more free from blame in this world as a pine tree.

HENRY DAVID THOREAU

Pines always seem to be with me in every step of the creative process. As I began organizing the material for this book, I found myself sorting through memories of the redwoods in California. Then, in the cold New England winter, I walked through pine forests whose branches bowed heavy with snow toward the earth and found I was able to dive deeply into myself, where I found the words I needed waiting. My perspective expanded among the tall, majestic Scots pines of the Scottish Highlands. And now I look out upon the white pines in Western Massachusetts once again, circling back to the place where my relationship to the wild world began.

Pine trees have been a steady presence in all of the places I've called home. As a child, I climbed the tall white pine that stood peaceful watch over our house on Summer Street. Scots pine, among the oldest living trees in the Scottish Highlands, surrounded me at Alladale Wilderness Reserve and the small cottage I rented nearby. A white pine stands tall, a steady presence, in my Brooklyn community garden, providing shelter and the welcome sight of green throughout winter when most of the garden is brown and bare.

While deciduous trees shed their leaves every fall and go through intense visible changes, evergreens like pine stay steady as their efficient shapes and thin needles transform the energy of the sun year round. For cultures all over the world, pines symbolize the power of life—of surviving and thriving through the changing seasons. And though we age and shape-shift, and our emotions ebb and flow, there is a similar unwavering steadiness within all of us that we often leave untapped. I tend to find that stillness through movement. When I move my body through writing, drawing, walking, or martial arts, I circulate scattered energy and find peace. My body no longer craves the intensity of boxing so I have shifted to the subtle movement of archery.

Archery asks for focused intent and reminds me to breathe into that space of stillness. Artemis, the moon goddess, Mother Bear, and protector of wild creatures carries her silver bow and uses her arrows with discernment. When I began practicing four years ago, I was happy to stand tall, stretch my shoulders back, look far, and open my heart and engage my instinct as I pulled the taut string of my longbow. After the first few sessions, I found myself standing and walking taller. And like Artemis, the Mother Bear, I've learned to breathe into my calm center and guard the boundaries of my sacred space.

ONE OF MY FIRST ASSIGNMENTS AS AN HERBAL APPRENTICE WAS TO FIND A guardian tree. I understood a guardian tree to be an elder, one who would watch out for me, a special relationship I would build upon. I knew I would need to visit the tree regularly to cultivate a connection, so it seemed like a good idea to find a tree close to my apartment in Brooklyn. I wandered around Prospect Park looking for my tree. But this act of looking and analyzing put too much in my head, and took me out of my feeling body. So instead of seeking, I opened myself to recognize the feeling of being pulled. I stopped intellectualizing and categorizing and simply walked, inviting trees to call to me. I was drawn to many, but none of them seemed like "the one." I finally lay under a horse chestnut and felt a sense of ease. Was this my tree? Maybe. I decided to come back to spend time with the tree again and see.

A day or two later, after working in the community garden, I had the impulse to walk out using a different, more narrow path. And that's when a tree I had walked by for years grabbed me. As I squeezed past, trying to maneuver around the trunk, the branches caught my coat, the needles scratched my face and stopped me. Clearly I needed an obvious signal, but it was more than that; I realized this had been my guardian tree for years. *Why hadn't I noticed?* The evergreen stood by every season as I walked in and out of the garden to compost, plant seeds, harvest, or simply relax, sit with the green allies, and learn.

That day, I felt tremendous gratitude. I sat and meditated under the tree and dropped into a centered, peaceful state almost immediately. I continued to sit with the tree year after year and still do, sometimes bringing gifts of water, meaningful herbs, and thanks for the steady presence. When I visit, I feel the guardian tree is also grateful to be noticed and to have a steady, watchful, and loving friend in me too.

AGAINST FORGETTING, A FINE-ART PIECE BY ARTIST NINA MONTENEGRO, IS A wax rubbing of a tree stump adjacent to an inked human fingerprint. Presented side by side, they are almost identical. The artwork showing our kinship with nature went viral in 2019, proving that we yearn to remember that *we are nature*. The artist in her statement shares that she encountered the enormous stump, likely a Douglas fir, and took a rubbing with wax crayon. She writes, "I had always marveled at the similarity between the rings of a tree and the rings of our human fingerprints, but I was shocked to see the rings actually align when I took an inked fingerprint and enlarged it to the scale of the tree rings. What resulted was a harmonious depiction of humanity's kinship (and belonging) with nature."[1] I believe this relationship is one that we yearn for; we are dogged by an emptiness and searching that can only be filled by coming home to the reality of our interconnection with nature. The plants and trees around us now, that have always been there supporting us, are a perfect place to begin. As herbalist David Hoffman writes, "Through respiration, our oneness with trees becomes a manifest act."[2] Whether we are aware of it or not, we are always in communion with the Earth.

BY KEEPING THEIR LEAVES THROUGH THE WINTER, PINE FORESTS ARE AN OASIS for wildlife, providing food and shelter for animals that face increased scarcity in cold, harsh weather. Chipmunks and squirrels eat the seeds of pine cones, while deer and bears snack on tree bark. Owls can be heard in the cold winter air hooting from their roosts in old trees. Pine warblers spend most of their time in pine trees, red-tailed hawks nest in pines close to edges and openings in the canopy, and bald eagles may use dead pine trees as lookouts for clear, unobstructed vantage points. For woodpeckers, squirrels, and bats, a hollowed trunk is a protective cavern. Longleaf pine forests in the southeastern United States are home to hundreds of different plants and animals, including over thirty endangered and threatened species that rely on longleaf pine for habitat, such as gopher tortoises and red-cockaded woodpeckers. Some researchers estimate that the longleaf pine ecosystem is one of the most diverse outside of the tropics.

The tallest tree in the Northeast, white pine, is found in woodlands, forest edges, yards, parks, and old meadows along the Eastern Seaboard and is known as the Great Tree of Peace by the Haudenosaunee Confederacy. According to Native American history, the Mohawk, Oneida, Onondaga, Cayuga, and Seneca tribes who live in present-day New York and Pennsylvania were often at odds with each other.[3] They experienced chaos and ongoing conflict until the Great Peacemaker Dekanawidah brought the tribes together to form a political and cultural union known as the Iroquois Confederacy. As a symbol of peace, they planted a white pine to proclaim the Great Binding Law and buried their arrows beneath the roots of the tree, pointing in the four directions. The slender needles of white pine that grow in bundles of five came to symbolize these Five Nations joined together as one.

The majestic tree thrived and covered most of northeastern North America until the extensive logging of the 1700s and 1800s.[4] Now, sadly, only about 1 percent of the original trees and old-growth pine forests remain.

When a pine tree is cut or wounded, a sticky, golden-colored resin oozes out to seal over the wounds and prevent organisms from entering tender places. Resin is a vital aspect of the tree's immune system. While the sap is highly antiseptic and has a number of treatments for us, I don't like to harvest it, knowing that the function of the resin is to heal the trees themselves. After millions of years, if the resin finds its way between layers of sediment, the sticky, healing substance becomes amber: hardened, stable resin from the wounds of ancient trees.

I usually collect branches and needles from the forest floor after strong winds or a storm. A tincture or fresh tea from young green pine needles is extremely high in vitamin C, perfect for fighting the common cold or to boost our immune system in winter. The needles and twigs can be used for a revitalizing, clearing steam for congestion or a warming circulatory-stimulant bath for a winter chill or general aches and pains. The new spring shoots covered in brown or whitish bud scales point upward and are sometimes called candles. The pine essence, the vibrational medicine collected from the candles, was derived by Dr. Edward Bach—the physician and homeopath known for developing the Bach flower remedies—from Scots pine (*Pinus sylvestris*) to help release feelings of guilt, self-blame, and self-condemnation. With a range that stretches from western Scotland to eastern Siberia, the Scots pine is the most widely distributed conifer in the world. In the Scottish Highlands, the tree, now the national tree of Scotland, was used to mark burial places of warriors, heroes, and chieftains.

Every species of *Pinus* contains edible seeds that we call pine nuts. Harvested from cones, they can be used as a wildcrafted ingredient in pesto, but the seeds of most species are small and take time and patience to shell. Red squirrels love them and are skilled at shelling, and as they feast on them, they help spread the seeds. Their nickname, "pine squirrels," reflects their strong symbiotic relationship and devotion to these evergreens.

Pines are mostly monoecious, meaning the male and female cones are produced by single trees at the same time. The familiar woody, egg-shaped cones are the females that produce seeds, and the male cones, whose elongated, scaly structures grow in clusters and are substantially smaller, produce yellow pollen that has recently been touted as an adaptogenic superfood. In most species, both seeds and pollen collaborate with wind, and studies have shown that pollen can travel hundreds of miles to find receptive females and produce viable seeds. In the case of species like white pine, second-year cones open up in dry weather so gusts of wind can catch and carry them. Pines with large seeds rely more on animal dispersal by birds and furry creatures like the red squirrel. Wet weather just washes seeds away, so these intelligent trees close their cones to protect the seeds when it's humid or about to rain. This is why hanging a pine cone from a string outside is a traditional method of predicting dry or wet weather for people of temperate climates.

In environments where fires are frequent, some pine species have evolved thick, hard, serotinous cones that are glued shut with a strong resin. They hang on a pine tree for years, long after the enclosed seeds mature. Only when a fire sweeps through and melts the resin do these heat-dependent cones open up, releasing seeds in huge numbers that are then distributed by wind and wildlife to repopulate desolate ground. While these seeds have adapted to fire to break their dormancy, unnaturally severe fires are destroying forests, even those where controlled fire existed historically.

Deforestation displaces wildlife species that depend on them, bringing them closer to one another and to humans. Scientists have been warning for years that this increases human exposure to new infectious diseases and makes us more vulnerable to pandemics.[5] Thinking about it in this way, it makes sense that Artemis was not only the protector of the wild, but also the goddess of the plague, infecting those who abused the land she held sacred. Deforestation also contributes greatly to climate change since forests are some of the most vital resources for carbon sequestration and cooling the atmosphere. When we cut down the intelligent, sentient old-growth forests that support so much life, we lose irreplaceable sacred spaces, ancient species, and vital aspects of ourselves.

Many of us just need to look down and see the beautiful brown wavy lines and other patterns on our golden wood floors to connect with pine trees. White pine is one of the trees most commonly cut to become our floors and each beautiful marking speaks to a moment in their lives. Even after they are gone, trees are still solid ground that supports us.

LOOKING AHEAD

While we have all experienced dramatic, upending changes in our lives, most change happens gradually. We age every day and hardly notice unless we measure our inches and centimeters of growth as we move through adolescence, or obsess about the gradual lines and wrinkles that set in from our worries and our smiles. In the same way, outside of us, our neighborhoods may be as beautiful as ever with subtle shifts over time—a small clearing for a new shopping center, a few less bees and butterflies, a few more houses on our street—but all in all, little may appear different. Without visible, noticeable change, it is easy to keep doing what makes us comfortable, consequences seemingly far away. For others, contending with floods or fires that are destroying homes and the sanctuary of ancient pine groves, the reality of ecological change is impossible to ignore.

But even if we don't experience changes in our immediate environment, when we tune into the news, we see and hear about ecological imbalance and suffering happening at a pace that can be hard for our emotional bodies to keep up with. The speed with which information is coming our way is overwhelming, and we cannot administer triage to the entire globe alone, especially when we need healing too. But if we turn down the volume of the outside world long enough to breathe and remember our innate connection to the Earth under our feet, our personal and collective wounds become easier to mend. When there is so much to distract and alarm us, it takes an assertion of our boundaries and engaging practices that remind us we belong here. And when we're ready, we can begin tuning our antennas to the stories of regeneration and find that the movement to rewild is also growing. There are increasing opportunities to halt or even reverse abusive ecological trends, and our own healing is an essential part of it.

MOST OF US HAVE TO GO THROUGH ARDUOUS, UNCOMFORTABLE JOURNEYS AND peel back layers of conditioning to come home to who we are. My suggestion that we rewild the self may mean returning the body to a fully functioning, thriving ecosystem that we nurture and support instead of criticize and attack. Being healthy doesn't necessarily mean an absence of symptoms (not right away, at least), but coming to different levels of consciousness as we unearth the root causes of those symptoms. Healing might be revealing, a peeling back, a spiraling into our center, toward our tenderness as we reveal more and more of our inner wild even to ourselves.

To come to our true and unwavering core, we must let go of the stories that are harmful, untrue, that shame our bodies and shame our outer world. It's time to do away with the collective conditioning that separates us from each other, from nature, and convinces us that human comfort and material growth is more important than the well-being of our community of trees, wolves, bears, bees, fungi, water, forests, or air. What we do to the environment, we also do to ourselves.

Nature is always taking care of us through the creation of clean air, food, and every other aspect of life that we need in order to thrive, and we have knowledge and opportunity to return her ceaseless generosity. While some environmentalists believe the Earth would be better off without us, I believe that underneath all of the displaced pain, suffering, greed, and illusion of separation, we are an integral part of the living Earth. We can leave land, waterways, and every wild place around us more beautiful, more diverse, and more alive than we found them. There are countless ways to be involved in regeneration, and I believe that deepening intimacy to the living land is a vital place to begin.

In some places, miles of landscapes are being awakened and reconnected through reviving of mycelial networks, the creation of wildlife corridors, and reforestation. Elsewhere, towns, cities, communities, and individuals are working to create permaculture farms and habitat for pollinators, and to reduce consumption. Mitigating climate change is much more than reducing our carbon footprint, it's about remembering that every species has a role in maintaining the overall health of Mother Earth. Like the physiology of our bodies when in balance, when healthy, Mother Earth can also regenerate and heal herself. We can think of the Earth as a body, like we think of our body as an ecosystem. And like our inner ecosystem, we have to feed the land with the microbes, plants, insects, fungi, and predators that she relies on to thrive.

Successful rewilding projects have transformed areas like Yellowstone National Park with the presence and ecological impact of wolves.[6] And since many of our public policies rely on numbers to quantify "value," the presence of wolves has dramatically increased revenue as well. Wolves are coming back in Northwestern Europe too, in particular western Germany, the Netherlands, and, hopefully one day soon, Scotland. American Prairie Reserve, whose mission is to create the largest nature reserve in the United States, currently spans

419,000 acres on Montana's northern plains and is growing as it buys more private land and returns it to the commons. With a holistic model, the reserve collaborates with indigenous people of the area, ranchers, and neighbors to cocreate solutions that address their respective concerns while restoring the wild. Fence removal is among their ongoing efforts to increase connectivity and ease the movement of animals like the pronghorn. In some areas indigenous people are reclaiming their land, and in others the land herself is given rights. In January 2019, the High Court of Bangladesh recognized the river Turag as a living entity with legal rights and held that the same would apply to all rivers in Bangladesh. In areas where farmland is given space and support needed to heal after decades of excessive use, dry, lifeless land is becoming vibrant once again.

The vision that unites all of these efforts is one of interconnection and regeneration. Rewilding projects throughout the world are growing. When we channel the energy of Artemis to guard and protect wildlife, wildlife returns.

WHEN WILDLIFE RETURNS, MY INTUITION IS AFFIRMED: THE MORE I LEARN AND understand the networks of relationship and the evolution of our species, the more I know that separation is an illusion, and that the earth, the fungi, and the plants that were here long before us provided the basis for our survival.

I've embraced my sensitivity as my superpower, and that act of reclamation has allowed me to be a bridge between worlds and remind people that we all have access to the healing power of nature and can awaken to our interconnection. We can decide right now to engage our senses, throw away stories of separation, and lift the veil between ourselves and the natural world. Eugen Herrigel writes in *Zen in the Art of Archery*, "Unless we enter into mystic experiences by direct participation we remain outside, turn and twist as we may."[7] As we embrace all that is wild within us and outside of us, we might even fall in love, and as our love grows, expands, and spirals outward, it can be contagious.

GREEN LEAVES PEERING THROUGH GRAY STONE WALLS AND PAVED CITY STREETS and crawling up the sides of concrete buildings assure me of nature's resilience and remind me of my own. Plants are ready to reclaim any space we cease to tame. I know land that I love and take care of will love and take care of me in return as we watch each other grow. When I see mugwort, yew, wild rose, goldenrod, burdock, Solomon's seal, red clover, or pine on the city streets, in abandoned lots, forests, and fields, or on beaches, I feel a sense of gratitude and an ever-evolving connection. Like a weed, I've learned to thrive in the city, in the country, in the jungle, and especially along dense, wild forests of pine. As a child of the Earth, I am always home.

PART SIX

Practices and Medicine-Making Guide

THE HOLISTIC
MODEL OF HEALING

In a holistic view of health, we look at the whole picture of ourselves in relationship to our environment. If we ignore the basics of good sleep, nourishing food, hydration, way of life, or tending to our emotional landscapes, plants can only do so much. Treating symptoms without changing unhealthy habits is not a holistic approach to healing. Awareness is the first step. When we notice the way we relate to the world around us and become aware of our inner dialogue and the stories we have inherited from our families and culture at large, we empower ourselves with self-knowledge. We can look at where there is excess and where there is deficiency in each area of our lives and begin to create balance. It is from this space of self-awareness that the plants can be true allies and collaborators in healing. I like to use these four categories as a basis for exploration:

The Inner Landscape: These are things that no one else can see or ever truly know. This includes your emotional body, soul self, belief systems, and personal stories. Exploring this terrain begins with creating space so that you can listen to your physical and emotional body without judgment. To do so, create time to check in with yourself regularly. Start with a few minutes a day (or more if you already have a practice) to sit in silence to become aware of your bodily sensations. Notice and simply be with whatever comes up, whatever is there. Then, take out your journal and write from the part of you that is uncomfortable or yearning for attention. Write *as* the body, the eight-year-old-self. Let go of the words you're ashamed to say. This is for you only. As you become more self-aware, begin to explore: *What unexpressed thoughts are repeating in my mind? What actions or inactions rise from those thoughts? What do I sense emotionally, in the waters in my body? Are there deep pools of grief that have become stagnant? Raging fires of anger I've been suppressing?* Your body will be grateful for your attention. This exploration may be uncomfortable, but if you stay with it and continue to listen, discomfort will become an ally too. Begin at a pace that feels right for you. This is a continuous, lifelong practice of loving and listening.

Way of Life: Notice how you spend your time. Does your action support or diminish your well-being? Do you walk in the park regularly or stare at a computer screen? Do you get adequate sleep? Do you move your body? Meditate? Are you eating nourishing foods? Where do your products come from? Do your actions align with your ethics? When you become aware of imbalance, make two adjustments this week. Eliminate one action or habit that doesn't serve holistic health, and add one, like regular walks in nature, that does. Commit to this each day. Habits take time to build. When these two actions have shifted, do it again.

Outer Environment: Notice your outer environment and the way your surroundings impact your well-being. Who surrounds you? Do you have a loving relationship with Mother Earth? Are you aware of the plants and trees nearby? How do you feel in your home? Is it time to let go of clutter or rearrange things so the space is more supportive? What similarities do you see in your outer environment, the Earth as a whole, and within your own body? When you become aware of people or places that deplete you, begin to set boundaries and make adjustments. If there are relationships you'd like to deepen, find ways to strengthen those bonds.

Heredity: What physical proclivities, belief systems, and possible trauma have you inherited? What is yours and what isn't? Begin to untangle the web. What is your personal or cultural origin story? How has that story influenced you and your relationship with yourself, with others, and the living Earth? Allow yourself to be objective. Notice the feelings that come up. Write or draw them out and, maybe, write new narratives of your own.

Additional questions to explore: What is your definition of healing? How have you approached healing throughout your life? Does that differ from your vision of a healing practice moving forward? If so, how? What questions would you ask yourself to explore the root causes of a health challenge or symptom you're experiencing? After some reflection or meditation, write out your answers or unravel your ideas through stream-of-consciousness writing until you find clarity.

BECOMING INTIMATE
WITH LAND

I recommend using the same holistic model to explore your relationship with land. Most of us are not taught how to care for our bodies or our environment—leaving these sacred spaces to the so-called experts—but we now know how vital it is to be an empowered and aware participant in healing. We contribute to life or degradation every day, with every choice we make, and our choices affect everyone. So, with a holistic perspective, explore the land around you and look at your environment in relationship to *you*. Is your environment thriving or struggling? Is your relationship healthy? Do you view land as scenery or a living sanctuary? Go through the same four categories from the perspective of your local land and your furred, feathered, scaled, and green neighbors. Make adjustments as you uncover your blind spots and areas where you can learn, nurture holistic health, and deepen intimacy.

ENGAGE YOUR SENSES

Touch the sandpaper-like texture of a goldenrod leaf, the softness of a mullein leaf, or the velvety skin of a wild rose blossom. (But keep a respectful distance from poison ivy—she needs her space!)

Taste the sweetness of a red clover flower, a linden blossom, a pine needle, an apple, the bitterness of a mugwort leaf, or the tartness of a hawthorn berry.

Listen to the way a breeze whispers through leaves and forests. Attune to the buzz of bees, the vibration of hummingbird wings, the rhythmic release of ocean waves.

Smell aromatic plants like lemon balm: How does the scent make you feel? Walk through a pine forest and notice the changes in your breath and body.

See the plants around you as though for the first time. Which ones call to you? You may want to refer to chapter 4 about eyebright for guidance around ways to observe plants using the doctrine of signatures. Drawing is a great practice to engage; as you follow the lines, shapes, and subtleties of plants you're drawn to, you will notice more and become intimate with your surroundings.

WHAT TO EXPLORE WHEN WORKING WITH A PLANT

This is a list I give my students as they explore and develop relationships with plants in the wild. It is something they always come back around to when working with a new plant or rediscovering the ones they think they know.

- Doctrine of signatures: What does the plant communicate through their shapes, textures, colors, scent, and choice of habitat?
- If you are able to taste and experience the medicine, or be in the presence of the plant, note how the energetics of the herb make you feel. What comes up for you? Everything is valid. You are uncovering and discovering.
- Explore the "personality" of the plant: Who are they? Use your imagination and get creative, basing your conclusion on how, where, and when they grow. For example, dandelion is not a people pleaser, and is fiery, gutsy, confident, relentless.
- What is the predominant elemental makeup: earth, water, fire, air, or ether?

- Is the plant warming or cooling, stimulating or sedating, drying or moistening?
- What is the taste? Bitter, sweet, pungent, sour, or salty? Each taste communicates unique medicine. Many plants have a combination.
- Clinical use: What health challenges is this plant commonly used for? What other challenges could you see this plant being supportive of (mind, physical body, emotional body, soul, spirit)? Which body systems does this plant support and align with?
- Ritual or ceremonial use: If none exist that you can find, create one (or more).
- Folklore/mythology: Find folklore and stories across cultures (or create some!).
- Ecological role and interspecies relationships: Who are the plant's pollinators? Does the plant play a remediating role for the Earth? Do they have symbiotic relationships with certain fungi?
- Where does the plant grow? What is their species status or environmental challenges? Are there ways you can help?
- How would you go about planting this species in a garden or reintroducing the plant (if native to your ecosystem) to the wild? What conditions does this plant need to thrive?

Rekindling Wonder

Write and reflect upon your childhood connection to nature. Draw or create a collage or diorama of your real or imagined mystical forest. Put it somewhere where you can see it. You may want to use it as a tool for meditation practice, adding elements as you reconnect with the magic of your imagination and the natural world.

Dreaming and Deepening

Keep a dream journal. Develop a dreaming practice in collaboration with mugwort, skullcap, mullein, linden, or any other plant that calls to you. Ask a question when you go to sleep and journal when you wake.

New Moon Bathing Ritual

Use mugwort or any other abundant dried herb to burn to purify your space.

Prepare to take an intentional bath in the dark. Soaking in stillness and darkness is a ritual that brings clarity, blocks out incessant noise, and allows innate wisdom to arise. Make an herbal infusion to soak in for a ritual bath, and also to drink. Any herb that is calling you can be used, but especially those in your immediate environment or that you already have a relationship with; skullcap, linden, or lemon balm are some of my favorites for deep relaxation. As you fill the tub with water, reflect on aspects of the water element, set intentions, and listen.

Ask yourself:

What do I want to release on the new moon?

What is ready to be illuminated?

What am I ready to release to step more fully into my power?

What am I ready to bring to light?

What actions am I going to take moving forward?

In spring, summer, or early fall, dandelion flowers can float on the water for fiery confidence, and as the days get darker, goldenrod can be an ally for illumination.

For those of you without a bathtub, you can make your herbal brew and use large cups to cleanse your body and bring clarity. Use four cups and pour them over yourself after a shower: one pour for the body, one for the mind, one for the spirit, one for the soul. Allow what no longer serves you to be washed away.

Take time afterward to journal in stream of consciousness. Allow your whole self, from the ground up, to speak.

Symbolically bury or burn what you're ready to release to make space for new growth.

Finally, symbolically (or literally) plant seeds of intent: How do you want to grow? How will you nurture and cultivate your intentions so they thrive?

Channeling Artemis

Some of the ecological problems we face might seem insurmountable, but think of the power of a tiny seed to multiply and create new life. At first, seeds are under the surface, invisible, but once their roots or rhizomes take hold, they can be unstoppable. If we each do our little bit and come together with intention, we create momentum. We can get creative and think holistically, locally, and find what unites us in relationship to our immediate ecosystems.

How can you build community and work together with those around you? Even if we live in harmony with nature, if our neighbor is spraying pesticides or our housemate is using copious amounts of toxic "cleansing" aerosols, it will affect our surrounding land and lungs too. The air—whose wind carries pollen, seeds, voices, ideas, communication, and pollution—doesn't discriminate or know boundaries.

Here are a few ideas, and I encourage you to think outside the box and create your own.

Learn about the amazing creatures that share your ecosystem: Who are they? What are their struggles, their needs? Learn how to be a loving community member and share that love with your neighbors. Here are some simple ways to do that:

- Allow wild leaves to fall, just be, or if you must, gently rake them. Remember that butterflies and moths overwinter in autumn leaves, and queen bumblebees use them as added warmth for hibernation during winter.
- Plant perennials and native wildflowers that have long seasons of bloom to attract and offer food to pollinators like hummingbirds, butterflies, and bumblebees.

- Take on a cause: start a movement to ban gas-powered leaf blowers or carcinogenic pesticides. Start a community permaculture garden or farm.
- Develop a composting practice if you don't have one already; find a community garden or farm with a compost bin if you can't create your own.
- Become a citizen scientist to help your local ecosystems.
- Learn how to use the principles of ecological farming and think relationally with all that you do.
- Get involved with a land trust and learn how to preserve and protect your local land.

Savoring Sweetness

Write a list of all the things that bring you joy and make you feel alive. Bring something tangible from that list into your life each day.

Hike among evergreens, meditate amid their medicine, and harvest fresh pine needles for a cleansing tea, ritual bath, and household cleaner. Clear and cleanse your space for your homecoming.

And finally, through all of your practices and the messy, sometimes euphoric process of healing, allow yourself to let go of resistance and truly fall in love with your beautiful animal body and the magnificent body of Earth. Assure them both that you are here, that you are ready and willing to unlearn, remember, and fall into deep and everlasting love.

MEDICINE MAKING AND WILDCRAFTING

Herbal Infusions

Herbal infusions provide the body with easy-to-assimilate nutrition. They differ from tea because the plant material is steeped for a longer period of time, which allows for all the medicinal constituents, including vitamins and minerals, to be liberated from the herb. Regular drinking of infusions over time provides deep nutrition for the body. Infusions are typically made with dried herbs.

DRYING HERBS

The easiest way to dry herbs is to gather a bunch and hang them upside down in a dark dry area with plenty of air circulation. This doesn't work with all plants, of course, since many are too small and delicate. If that's the case, I like to lay them out on a screen to dry.

TO PREPARE YOUR INFUSION

Place your dried herbs into a glass mason jar (the amount varies with the herb and your intention) while you bring water to a near boil. I like to use the half-gallon mason jar so I have infusion to last me at least a couple of days. Pour the boiling water into the jar with your herb, mix with a wooden spoon or chopstick, and screw the lid on tight. After about twenty minutes to eight hours, depending on the herb, strain or squeeze the extra goodness out of the wet herbs with a strainer or cheesecloth and drink the liquid cold, hot, or at room temperature.

Note: Mucilaginous herbs like linden and marshmallow root may release more of their gooey healing with cold infusions.

STEEPING TIME AND QUALITIES

Flowers: Since flowers are the most delicate part of the plant, their steeping time is much shorter. I typically infuse flowers and leaves at the same time but if I infuse flowers alone, the steeping time is usually no more than twenty minutes.

Roots: Roots are the densest part of plants such as burdock, dandelion, and Solomon's seal. The medicinal aspects of most roots are often found in their alkaloid content, which dissolves slowly into water. Steeping amount and time: roughly 1 ounce of dried herb to a pint of water, steeped (ideally) for four to eight hours.

Barks: This refers to the inner bark (cambium layer), which lies just underneath the outer layer we see. The nourishment and life force of the tree moves through this layer, making it a valuable source of medicine. Remember not to take bark from the trunk of a tree. I use freshly fallen branches or the outer branches on the tree if there are none on the ground. Steeping amount and time: 1 ounce to a pint of water, steeped for about four to eight hours.

Leaves: Long steeping extracts all the healing benefits of chlorophyll, along with minerals and vitamins. Some leaves are tougher than others. Those with more delicate structures release medicine more quickly, so use your judgment. Steeping amount and time: 1 ounce of dried herb to a quart of water, steeped from four to eight hours.

Seeds and Berries: Dried berries such as hawthorn are best simmered and then steeped for up to four hours to release their healing properties, but the amount of time varies depending on the density of the seed or berry. Steeping amount and time: 1 ounce of dried herb to a quart of water; steeped from thirty minutes to about four hours, depending on the plant.

Decoction: In these concentrated remedies, water is brought to a boil, then chaga, dense roots, bark, seeds, or berries are simmered in the water for fifteen minutes to an hour or more. The amount of herb and length of simmering time for decoctions depends on the fungus or plant. The traditional method used for making a simple herbal decoction is to simmer the herbs until the liquid is reduced by half.

Tincture: The best tinctures are made from fresh plant material. Tear or chop the plant material to extract as much medicine as possible (except flowers and delicate plants). Fill a glass jar two thirds to three quarters of the way to the top with the plant material. You want to make sure the plant material is completely covered by the liquid. Then fill the jar to the top with 80–100 proof vodka, vinegar (ideally raw organic apple cider vinegar), or the spirit of your choice. Cap the jar tightly. Label the jar with the name of the plant, the part of the plant used, the type of spirit used, and the date. Top up the liquid level the next day. Let it sit for six weeks or more so that you have a potent medicine. Decant the tincture and it is ready to use.

Using apple cider vinegar: Apple cider vinegar has long been used as a solvent in medicine making. While the vinegar extractions don't break down plant constituents as effectively as alcohol, they do extract sugars, tannins, glycosides, bitter compounds, alkaloids, vitamins, and minerals. They are excellent for mineral-rich herbs like nettles. Make sure that you use parchment or wax paper between the jar and a metal lid, otherwise the vinegar will eat away at the metal.

Decanting tincture: Pour off the alcohol, put it into a tinted glass bottle, and cap tightly. To extract all the medicine from the wet plant material, put small handfuls of it in a cotton cloth and wring into the bottle. Label the bottle of decanted tincture with the same information you put on the original tincture. When you're ready to use it, put some of the decanted tincture in a tinted glass bottle with a dropper top. Use only glass droppers, as residues from plastic droppers interfere with the medicinal actions of the herbs.

Oxymels: The ancient Greek word *oxymeli* translates to "acid and honey," and the simplest definition of an oxymel is an herbal extraction of vinegar and raw honey. When combined with herbs that carry complementary actions, oxymels offer potent and tasty support for well-being. Like herbal vinegars, oxymels should be stored in glass jars with a non-metal lid, or place a piece of parchment or wax paper between the jar and a metal lid.

Cold method: Fill a small jar about half to three fourths full of herbs. Pour honey over them, then vinegar. Use about one third of the jar filled with honey to two thirds of the rest vinegar, or half of the jar honey and half vinegar. The amount is flexible. Both honey and vinegar act as preservatives, so you're not going to ruin the mixture by altering the ratios. Stir together, seal with a lid, then shake every day until blended. Let it sit for four weeks or more.

Hot method: Simmer herbs and vinegar together for ten to twenty minutes, then stir in honey while the vinegar is still warm. Place in a glass jar, seal with a lid, and let it sit for four weeks (or less if you want to use it sooner).

Poultices: These are moistened herbs applied externally and used to treat swelling, pain, and congestion. There are a few methods. Do what resonates with you. If using fresh herbs, you can simply macerate the herbs to a gooey mass, or if using dried herbs, moisten enough to release the healing qualities, then spread either the fresh or dry herbal paste over a piece of clean cloth large enough to cover the affected area. Gauze, muslin, or other light cotton fabrics work well. Place the poultice over clean skin, and then cover with a hot cloth. Another method is to use a fresh leaf such as comfrey, heat it in a very small amount of water to activate the medicinal qualities, and place it on the affected area. Since comfrey leaves may be a bit irritating to the skin for some, you may want to use a thin cloth.

Herbal Oils: Place dried herbs in a completely dry glass jar. It's important to break up the herb first as it exposes more of the plant to the oil, making for a better infusion. Flowers can be put in whole. If using dried herbs, it's helpful to warm the oil (any oil can be used but it is important to know the smoke point temperature) a bit first. Fill the jar to the brim with oil, as an air gap will promote oxidation and spoilage. Stir the contents (wooden chopsticks are good) until all bubbles have dispersed, then cap. Infuse on a bright sunny windowsill or in a nice warm spot near your heater. Shake and swirl as much as possible as it's steeping, particularly during the first couple of weeks, then leave to infuse for another four to six weeks.

Burn Bundles: You can dry and prepare herbs to burn for cleansing space, personal rituals, deepening meditation, smoke blends, or any other reason. Mugwort, mullein, and skullcap are among my favorite to use. I hang mugwort bundles upside down to dry and do the same with bundles of skullcap and large individual mullein leaves.

Herbal/Ritual Baths

STEAMING

Respiratory system: Pour boiling water over a mixture of aromatic herbs such as lemon balm and thyme, or simmer plants with a high essential oil content like pine (make sure your pot is covered) until they exude steam. Place pot or bowl on a table that is at a height easy for you to lean over. Then drape a towel over your head to capture the steam and inhale the soothing, uplifting, and decongestant medicine.

Yoni, or vaginal, steaming is an ancient practice consisting of sitting over a steaming pot of water to soften and open vaginal tissues, increase circulation, thin mucus, and cleanse the reproductive system. Plants traditionally used include mugwort and rose.

CLEANING SUPPLIES

Nontoxic homemade cleaning products can save us money, improve our health, and protect our environment. White vinegar or vodka are good options as bases for cleaner that can degrease, deodorize, and disinfect. Vodka has solvent qualities that clean mirrors and glass without streaking. Aromatic and antimicrobial plants like lemon balm, pine, thyme, and oregano can be steeped in cheap vodka, vinegar, or oil and used. Lemon juice kills mildew and mold and shines hard surfaces, olive oil works as a cleanser and polisher, and baking soda has proven virus-killing abilities to clean, deodorize, brighten, and cut through grime.

MINDFUL
WILDCRAFTING

I mportant things to consider when wildcrafting:

Make sure the plant you're harvesting is who you think they are! It's helpful to learn and work with a few plants, or even one plant at a time, to build relationships. Be mindful, and don't harvest so many plants that you threaten the continuation of that particular population. Avoid gathering near roads, power lines, or areas that may have been exposed to fertilizers, chemicals, pesticides, or other forms of chemical pollution.

Gather your herbs with respect and gratitude to the plants and to the environments they grow in. Survey the environment to make sure there's enough so they will continue to grow and feed the wild creatures that depend on them. In your own way, ask permission from the plant and land before harvesting. I like to acknowledge the indigenous people whose land I am on, the animals that live or have lived on the land, and the many species of flora and fungi that surround me. I leave a token of gratitude—sometimes herbs, often a piece of my hair plucked from my head, or simply a genuine thank-you—when I feel permission has been granted and I know I am not harming the ecosystem. It is a beautiful practice to bring or give some sort of offering that is meaningful for you. Mindful interactions initiate a relationship of reverence and open the door to deeper levels of intimacy with Mother Earth.

HERBAL SOURCES
AND INFORMATION

M ost of the herbalism information I draw from I've pulled from the
extensive notes I've taken while studying with teachers in person,
working with plants in the wild and in healing rituals, and teaching students while learning from their experiences. I have also buried my head
in books, of course. Here is a short list of resources that were influential on my
path, many of which I continue to turn to.

BOOKS

Sastun: My Apprenticeship with a Maya Healer, by Rosita Arvigo

Healing Threads: Traditional Medicine of the Highlands and Islands,
by Mary Beith

*The Gift of Healing Herbs: Plant Medicines and Home Remedies for a
Vibrantly Healthy Life*, by Robin Rose Bennett

*Plant Intelligence and the Imaginal Realm: Beyond the Doors of Perception
Into the Dreaming of Earth*, by Stephen Harrod Buhner

Eastern/Central Guide to Medicinal Plants and Herbs, by Stephen Foster
and James A. Duke

*Women Who Run with the Wolves: Myths and Stories of the Wild Woman
Archetype*, by Clarissa Pinkola Estés

One-Straw Revolution: An Introduction to Natural Farming,
by Masanobu Fukuoka

The Web That Has No Weaver: Understanding Chinese Medicine,
by Ted J. Kaptchuk

Plant Spirit Healing: A Guide to Working with Plant Consciousness,
by Pam Montgomery

Zen Mind, Beginner's Mind, by Shunryū Suzuki

Mycelium Running: How Mushrooms Can Help Save the World,
by Paul Stamets

Seven Arrows, by Hyemeyohsts Storm

Shambhala: The Sacred Path of the Warrior, by Chögyam Trungpa

The Book of Herbal Wisdom: Using Plants as Medicines, by Matthew Wood

ACKNOWLEDGMENTS

First, to the women who made this book possible: my wonderful agent, Terra Challberg, and brilliant editor Laura Tisdel. Thank you both for your friendship, and for believing in this book from the beginning. Terra, I love having you in my corner! Thank you for your support and guidance and helping to make this book a reality. Laura, your editorial and creative counsel have been invaluable. Thank you for helping me grow as a writer and being a steady presence through the many, many distractions of this difficult year.

To the lands where this book came alive: the jungles of Puerto Viejo de Limon, the urban wilds of Brooklyn, the redwoods of California, the forests of western Massachusetts, and the expanse of the Scottish Highlands. Thank you, Rachel Thomas, Maycol and Hidden Garden, Wellstone Center in the Redwoods, Gayle Kabaker, Peter Kitchell, Sonya Kitchell and Charlie, and my writing retreat companions in Fort William. Thank you, Pieter-Paul for inviting me to stay at Alladale Wilderness Reserve in early March 2020. I couldn't have picked a better place to get "stuck" during lockdown. To Natasha and Remi for welcoming me in the midst of chaos, to Paul Lister for your generosity, to Innes Macneill for all the work you do on behalf of the land, and to Derek and Kate Matheson, and Amat Estate to the remote, peaceful cottages toward to end of my stay in the Highlands, and to Carol Duke and the sanctuary of Flower Hill Farm Retreat where I finished this book.

To dear friends: Àdhamh O'Broin, Gaelic language adviser, co-teacher, and coconspirator, you have been such a huge part of this journey. Thank you for proofreading my Gaelic, helping me recover my roots, and being a constant source of inspiration. Nicola Orr for your nourishment, curiosity, laughter, and being an early reader; Heidi Smith for your comradery, writing commiseration, and plant sisterhood; Encar Villa for the amazing work you do on behalf of our beloved nonhuman animals; Ancel Mitchell for your stories and teachings; and Natalia Schwein Scott for your ongoing collaboration and being a kindred spirit. To Mallory Lance, Jenn Ruff, Matt Hall, Boyuan Gao, Jahan Matin, Queen Herawin, and Kimberly Terrence. To Tonya Callahan for being there when times were tough, Angela Cartsos for all the ridiculousness, to Morisha the maiden for the telepathic conversations, Amber King for your mystical guidance, Saga Blane for holding down the Sacred Warrior fort while I was unplugged, to Maria Katherine and Sia Mensah for all that you share during our gatherings. To Sacred Warrior teachers: Jessica Strom, Nathalie Fischer-Rodriguez, and Andrea Stopa, it has been wonderful to grow with you and I'm excited about the journey ahead. And thank you Andrea for all your admin support! Joan and Joan, thank you for helping me voice my truths and unravel my memories. To all the students who have attended Sacred Warrior retreats and workshops, inspiring me to keep going and validating my vision. To everyone who attended Herbal School at Love Is Juniper and to Deborah Claire Bagg and Shenav for creating the sanctuary. To Susan Pincus, staff, and students at Sawmill Herb Farm. To Ernesto for being a great love and helping me heal, brokenheartedness and all. To all my partners who have helped me grow. Horatio Clare, thank you for being a wonderful mentor and early champion of this book. And to dear friends that won't fit on this page: you know who you are.

Deep thanks to my boxing community and the coaches that took me seriously. To Eli Wolff and all my colleagues in the sports and social justice arena. To the amazing team at the Wolf Conservation Center: Regan, Summer, Maggie, Spencer, Rebecca, and the wolves: Zephyr, Alawa, Nikai, and ones who may someday be free. To Mavis, Izabella, Atka, Ebony, Daphne, Toby, Kobe, and my many other canine friends. To Susan Leopold and United Plant Savers, and all my friends in rewilding, conservation, ecology, environmental justice, social justice, and regenerative agriculture.

To my herbalism and ecology teachers in both flesh and book form: Robin Rose Bennett, Matthew Wood, Rachel Thomas, Mary Mullen, Eva Sengfelder,

ACKNOWLEDGMENTS

Rosita Arvigo, Stephen Harrod Buhner, Rosemary Gladstar, David Hoffman, Paul Stamets, Robin Wall Kimmerer, Clarissa Pinkola Estes, Robin Wall Kimmerer, Suzanne Simard . . . and so many more.

To the team at Viking and Penguin Random House: Victoria Savanh, Jennifer Tait, Nayon Cho, Shelby Meizlik, Britta Galanis, Bridget Gillerna, and Hal Fessenden and his rights team.

To my mom for being by my side, loving and supporting me even when my choices scared you. My beloved siblings: Alecia and Alex and Mitch for filling our home with music. To Van, I'm grateful for our relationship even though it has been rocky at times. And to my ancestors on all sides. Thank you for bringing me here.

Finally, to my loving partner for being so patient through this long process. Thank you for standing by me even when we were thousands of miles apart. I am ever grateful for our friendship, adventures, and sweet love.

Plants, fungi, and wondrous wild world, I adore you. I hope our collaboration will inspire others to fall more deeply in love with you too. And to the trees who have become the printed book readers will hold in their hands. As I write this, I am taking a moment to pause, close my eyes, and imagine who you are; who you were. May these words protect more wild spaces and bring your families justice.

NOTES

MUGWORT: THE INNER WILD

1. Clarissa Pinkola Estés, *Women Who Run with the Wolves: Myths and Stories of the Wild Woman Archetype* (New York: Ballantine, 1992).
2. Peter A. Levine and Ann Frederick, *Waking the Tiger: Healing Trauma* (Berkeley, CA: North Atlantic, 1997).
3. Siri Carpenter, "That Gut Feeling," *Monitor on Psychology* 43, no. 8 (September 2012): 50, www.apa.org/monitor/2012/09/gut-feeling.
4. Jean Shinoda Bolen, *Artemis: The Indomitable Spirit in Everywoman* (San Francisco: Conari, 2014).
5. C. G. Jung, *The Earth Has a Soul: The Nature Writings of C. G. Jung*, ed. Meredith Sabini (Berkeley, CA: North Atlantic, 2002).

YEW: BELONGING

1. Erna Gunther, *Ethnobotany of Western Washington: The Knowledge and Use of Indigenous Plants by Native Americans* (Seattle: University of Washington Press, 1973), 16.
2. Joyce Irene Whalley, *Pliny the Elder: Historia Naturalis* (London: Victoria and Albert Museum, 1982).
3. James Hunter, *Last of the Free: A Millennial History of the Highlands and Islands of Scotland* (Edinburgh: Mainstream, 1999).
4. John O'Donohue, *Anam Cara: A Book of Celtic Wisdom* (New York: Cliff Street, 1997).
5. Peter Wohlleben, *The Hidden Life of Trees: What They Feel, How They Communicate: Discoveries from a Secret World* (Carlton, Victoria, Australia: Black Inc., 2016).
6. Nancy J. Turner and Richard J. Hebda, "Contemporary Use of Bark for Medicine by Two Salishan Native Elders of Southeast Vancouver Island, Canada," *Journal of Ethnopharmacology* 29, no. 1 (April 1990): 59–72, https://doi.org/10.1016/0378-8741(90)90098-E.

7. Richard Louv, Last Child in the Woods: Saving Our Children from Nature-Deficit Disorder (Chapel Hill, NC: Algonquin, 2006).

8. Robin Wall Kimmerer, *Braiding Sweetgrass: Indigenous Wisdom, Scientific Knowledge, and the Teachings of Plants* (Minneapolis: Milkweed, 2013).

APPLE TREE: ORIGIN STORIES

1. Sorita d'Este and David Rankine, *Visions of the Cailleach: Exploring the Myths, Folklore and Legends of the Pre-Eminent Celtic Hag Goddess* (London: Avalonia, 2009).

2. Scott Leonard and Michael McClure, *Myth and Knowing: An Introduction to World Mythology* (New York: McGraw-Hill, 2004).

3. Robin Wall Kimmerer, *Braiding Sweetgrass: Indigenous Wisdom, Scientific Knowledge, and the Teachings of Plants* (Minneapolis: Milkweed, 2013).

4. David P. O'Brien et al., "The Delivery of Water during Terrestrial Planet Formation," *Space Science Reviews* 214, no. 47 (February 2018), https://doi.org/10.1007/s11214-018-0475-8.

5. Simson Najovits, *Egypt, Trunk of the Tree: A Modern Survey of an Ancient Land*, vol. 2 (New York: Algora, 2004).

6. Norbulinkga Institute, https://norbulingka.org.

7. Alexander Carmichael, trans., *Carmina Gadelica: Hymns and Incantations with Illustrative Notes on Words, Rites, and Customs, Dying and Obsolete* (Edinburgh: T. and A. Constable, 1900).

8. Merlin Stone, *When God Was a Woman* (New York: Harvest/Harcourt Brace, 1976).

9. James Bonwick, *Irish Druids and Old Irish Religions* (London: Griffith, Farran & Co, 1894).

10. Iain W. G. Forbes, *The Last of the Druids: The Mystery of the Pictish Symbol Stones* (Gloucestershire, UK: Amberley, 2012).

11. Judith Shaw, "Corra, Celtic Serpent Goddess," Feminism and Religion, August 23, 2017, https://feminismandreligion.com/2017/08/23/corra-celtic-serpent-goddess-by-judith-shaw/.

12. Thomas S. Bremer, *Formed from This Soil: An Introduction to the Diverse History of Religion in America* (Chichester, UK: Wiley, 2015).

13. Bron Taylor, *Dark Green Religion: Nature Spirituality and the Planetary Future* (Berkeley: University of California Press, 2009).

14. Chögyam Trungpa, John Baker, and Marvin Casper, *Cutting Through Spiritual Materialism* (Boston: Shambhala, 1987).

EYEBRIGHT: PERCEPTION

1. Tess Darwin, The Scots Herbal: *The Plant Lore of Scotland* (Edinburgh: Birlinn, 2008).

2. David Abram, *Becoming Animal: An Earthly Cosmology* (New York: Vintage, 2011).

3. Joby Warrick, "Pesticides and Cut Flowers," *National Wildlife*, June 2000, www .nwf.org/Magazines/National-Wildlife/2000/Pesticides-and-Cut-Flowers; John McQuaid, "The Secrets Behind Your Flowers," *Smithsonian*, February 2011, www .smithsonianmag.com/travel/the-secrets-behind-your-flowers-53128/.
4. Matthew Wood, *Vitalism: The History of Herbalism, Homeopathy, and Flower Essences* (Berkeley, CA: North Atlantic Books, 2000).
5. Jacob Boehme, *The Signature of All Things* (Cambridge, UK: Lutterworth Press, 2014).

ELECAMPANE: HEALING PATHS

1. Barbara Ehnrenriech and Deidre English, *Witches, Midwives and Nurses: A History of Women Healers* (New York: Feminist Press at the City University of New York, 2010).
2. Ian Dawson, *Medicine in the Middle Ages* (New York: Enchanted Lion Books, 2005).
3. Leigh Whaley, *Women and the Practice of Medical Care in Early Modern Europe, 1400–1800* (Basingstoke, UK: Palgrave Macmillan, 2011); Ehnrenriech and English, *Witches, Midwives and Nurses.*
4. Gearóid Ó. Crualaoich, "Reading the Bean Feasa," *Folklore* 116, no. 1 (2005): 37–50, https://doi.org/10.1080/0015587052000337707.
5. Silvia Federici, *Caliban and the Witch: Women, the Body and Primitive Accumulation* (Brooklyn: Autonomedia, 2004).
6. Leslie P. King, "The Ongoing 30-Year Lyme Disease War: Case Study of a Failure to Communicate," *Yale Climate Connections*, November 25, 2008, https://yale climateconnections.org/2008/11/30-year-lyme-disease-war/.
7. Matthew Wood, *The Book of Herbal Wisdom: Using Plants as Medicines* (Berkeley, CA: North Atlantic Books, 2017).
8. Matthew Wood, *Vitalism: The History of Herbalism, Homeopathy, and Flower Essences* (Berkeley, CA: North Atlantic Books, 2000).

PUMPKIN: SHAPE-SHIFTING

1. Gabriela Castellanos-Morales et al., "Tracing Back the Origin of Pumpkins (*Cucurbita pepo* ssp. *pepo* L.) in Mexico," *Proceedings of the Royal Society of Biological Sciences* 286, no. 1908 (August 2019), https://doi.org/10.1098/rspb .2019.1440.
2. Jane Mt.Pleasant, "Food Yields and Nutrient Analyses of the Three Sisters: A Haudenosaunee Cropping System," *Ethnobiology Letters* 7, no. 1 (August 2016): 87–98, https://doi.org/10.14237/ebl.7.1.2016.721.
3. Bahare Salehi et al., "*Cucurbits* Plants: A Key Emphasis to Its Pharmacological Potential," *Molecules* 24, no. 10 (May 2019): 1854, https://doi.org/10.3390/molecules 24101854.
4. Maciej Grzybek et al. "Evaluation of Anthelmintic Activity and Composition of Pumpkin (*Cucurbita pepo* L.) Seed Extracts—In Vitro and In Vivo Studies,"

International Journal of Molecular Sciences 17, no. 9 (September 2016): 1456, https://doi.org/10.3390/ijms17091456.

5. Karen Hursch Grober, "Pumpkins and Mexico," *Conecciones*, October 2020, https://issuu.com/lakechapalasociety/docs/conecciones_magazine_october_2020.

6. Robert Kirk, *The Secret Commonwealth of Elves, Fauns and Faeries* (London: D. Nutt, 1893), 5.

7. F. Marian McNeill, *The Silver Bough: Scottish Folklore and Folk-Belief*, vol. 1 (Edinburgh: Canongate, 1989).

8. *Encyclopaedia Britannica Online*, Academic ed., s.v. "Leshy," accessed March 31, 2021.

9. Michael Strmiska, "Ásatrú in Iceland: The Rebirth of Nordic Paganism?" *Nova Religio: The Journal of Alternative and Emergent Religions* 4, no. 1 (October 2000): 106–32, https://doi.org/10.1525/nr.2000.4.1.106.

10. "In Iceland, Elves Aren't Just Santa's Little Helpers," PBS, December 22, 2013, https://www.pbs.org/newshour/nation/in-iceland-elves-arent-just-santas-little-helpers.

11. "Alastair McIntosh: An Ecology of the Imagination, Advaya Talks," Advaya, March 25, 2018, https://youtu.be/ju0l5jJfB_E.

12. Patrick LaViolette and Alastair Mcintosh, "Fairy Hills: Merging Heritage and Conservation," *ECOS* 18, no. 3/4, 1997: 2–8, www.researchgate.net/publication/267153358_Fairy_Hills_Merging_Heritage_and_Conservation.

MULLEIN: COMFORTERS

1. Ted J. Kaptchuk, *The Web That Has No Weaver: Understanding Chinese Medicine* (New York: Contemporary, 2000).

2. Wajeeha Malik, "Inky's Daring Escape Shows How Smart Octopuses Are," *National Geographic*, April 14, 2016, www.nationalgeographic.com/animals/article/160414-inky-octopus-escapes-intelligence.

3. Krishnmurti Foundation Trust, "Krishnamurti on Mental Health," https://kfoundation.org/mental-health/.

4. Iain Gately, *Tobacco: A Cultural History of How an Exotic Plant Seduced Civilization* (New York: Grove, 2001).

5. Tengwen Long, et al., "Cannabis in Eurasia: Origin of Human Use and Bronze Age Trans-continental Connections," *Vegetation History and Archaeobotany* 26, no. 2 (March 2017): 245–58, https://doi.org/10.1007/s00334-016-0579-6.

6. Peter Singer, *Animal Liberation* (London: Bodley Head, 2015); Peter A. Schouls, *Descartes and the Enlightenment* (Ottawa: McGill-Queen's University Press, 1989).

7. Rick Gladstone, "Dogs in Heaven? Pope Francis Leaves Pearly Gates Open," *The New York Times*, December 11, 2014, www.nytimes.com/2014/12/12/world/europe/dogs-in-heaven-pope-leaves-pearly-gate-open-.html.

8. Carl Safina, *Beyond Words: What Animals Think and Feel* (New York: Henry Holt, 2015).

9. Yas Necati, "The Tories Have Voted That Animals Can't Feel Pain as Part of the EU Bill, Marking the Beginning of Our Anti-science Brexit," *The Independent* (London), November 20, 2017, www.independent.co.uk/voices/brexit-government -vote-animal-sentience-can-t-feel-pain-eu-withdrawal-bill-anti-science-tory-mps -a8065161.html.
10. Margery Williams, *The Velveteen Rabbit* (London: Egmont, 2004).

WILD ROSE: BOUNDARIES

1. Louis Durand, *The Book of Roses* (United Kingdom: John Lane, 1911).

MILK THISTLE: METAMORPHOSIS

1. Peter A. Levine and Ann Frederick, *Waking the Tiger: Healing Trauma* (Berkeley, CA: North Atlantic, 1997).
2. Ben Johnson, "The Thistle—National Emblem of Scotland," Historic UK, www .historic-uk.com/HistoryUK/HistoryofScotland/The-Thistle-National-Emblem -of-Scotland/.
3. Naomi Wolf, *The Beauty Myth* (London: Vintage Classics, 2015).

POISON IVY: NO TRESPASSING

1. "More Pernicious Poison Ivy," *Duke Magazine*, September–October 2006, https:// alumni.duke.edu/magazine/articles/more-pernicious-poison-ivy.
2. *Merriam-Webster*, s.v. "agriculture," accessed April 19, 2021, www.merriam-webster .com/dictionary/agriculture.
3. Masanobu Fukuoka, *The One-Straw Revolution: An Introduction to Natural Farming* (Emmaus, PA: Rodale Press, 1978).
4. Albert Howard, *The Soil and Health: A Study of Organic Agriculture* (Ukraine: University Press of Kentucky, 2010).
5. Rinku Singh and G. S. Singh, "Traditional Agriculture: A Climate-Smart Approach for Sustainable Food Production," *Energy, Ecology and Environment* 2 (2017): 296–316, https://doi.org/10.1007/s40974-017-0074-7.
6. *Encyclopaedia Britannica Online*, s.v. "ladybug," accessed May 3, 2020, www .britannica.com/animal/ladybug.
7. Daphne Miller, "The Surprising Healing Qualities . . . of Dirt," *Yes!*, December 7, 2013, www.yesmagazine.org/issue/food-health/2013/12/07/how-dirt-heals-us.
8. David A. Relman and Marc Lipsitch, "Microbiome as a Tool and a Target in the Effort to Address Antimicrobial Resistance," *Proceedings of the National Academy of Sciences* 115, no. 51 (December 2018): 12902–10, https://doi.org/10.1073/pnas .1717163115.
9. Andrew Marshall, "From Vietnam's Forced-Labor Camps: 'Blood Cashews,'" *Time*, September 6, 2011, http://content.time.com/time/world/article/0,8599,2092004,00 .html.

10. Stephen Harrod Buhner, *Plant Intelligence and the Imaginal Realm: Beyond the Doors of Perception into the Dreaming of Earth* (Rochester, VT: Bear, 2014).

11. Greg Rucka, *Detective Comics: Batman: A Walk in the Park #751* (New York: DC Comics, 2000).

12. Carey Gillam, "NYC Leaders Join Calls for Ban on Monsanto Herbicide," *Environmental Health News*, April 19, 2019, www.ehn.org/monsantos-herbicide-defense-falling-on-deaf-ears-as-nyc-leaders-join-calls-for-ban-2634974362.html.

13. Patricia Cohen, "Roundup Maker to Pay $10 Billion to Settle Cancer Suits," *The New York Times*, June 24, 2020, www.nytimes.com/2020/06/24/business/roundup-settlement-lawsuits.html.

14. Mark Hersey, "Hints and Suggestions to Farmers: George Washington Carver and Rural Conservation in the South," *Environmental History* 11, no. 2 (2006).

15. Carey Gillam, *Whitewash: The Story of a Weed Killer, Cancer, and the Corruption of Science* (Washington, DC: Island, 2017).

16. *The Environmental Impacts of Glyphosate* (Brussels: Friends of the Earth Europe, June 2013).

HAWTHORN: LOVER AND A FIGHTER

1. Brian O'Sullivan, *Irish Imbas Celtic Mythology Collection* (New Zealand: Smashwords, 2016).

2. "Minstrelsy of the Scottish Border," Walter Scott Digital Archive, Edinburgh University Library, www.walterscott.lib.ed.ac.uk/works/poetry/minstrelsy.html.

3. David Winston, *Adaptogens: Herbs for Strength, Stamina, and Stress Relief* (Rochester, VT: Inner Traditions/Bear, 2019).

DANDELION: GUT INSTINCT

1. William Sharp, *The Writings of "Fiona Macleod" [pseud.]* (New York: Duffield, 1910); Patricia Monaghan, *The Encyclopedia of Celtic Mythology and Folklore* (New York: Facts On File, 2014).

2. Sensei/Renshi Nathan Chlumsky, *Inside Kungfu: Chinese Martial Arts Encyclopedia* (N.p.: Lulu.com, 2015).

3. Fleur Macdonald, "The Legend of Benin's Fearless Female Warriors," BBC, August 27, 2018, www.bbc.com/travel/story/20180826-the-legend-of-benins-fearless-female-warriors.

4. Peter Aleshire, *Warrior Woman: The Story of Lozen, Apache Warrior and Shaman* (New York: St. Martin's, 2015).

5. Juilene Osborne-McKnight, *Bright Sword of Ireland* (New York: Tom Doherty Associates, 2005).

6. Peter A. Levine and Ann Frederick, *Waking the Tiger: Healing Trauma* (Berkeley, CA: North Atlantic, 1997).

7. Farjad Afzal and Sidra Manzoor, "Prolong Wearing of High Heeled Shoes Can Cause Low Back Pain," *Journal of Novel Physiotherapies* 7 (July 2017): 356; Edeny

Baaklini et al., "High-Heeled Walking Decreases Lumbar Lordosis," *Gait and Posture* 55 (June 2017): 12–14, https://doi.org/10.1016/j.gaitpost.2017.03.035.

8. Vasant Lad, *Ayurveda: The Science of Self-Healing: A Practical Guide* (Twin Lakes, WI: Lotus Press, 1984).

9. Linda Rector Page, *Healthy Healing: A Guide to Self-Healing for Everyone* (N.p.: Healthy Healing Publications, 1998).

10. Ted J. Kaptchuk, *The Web That Has No Weaver: Understanding Chinese Medicine* (New York: Contemporary, 2000).

11. Joyce Carol Oates, *On Boxing* (New York: HarperCollins, 2009).

NUTMEG: CONSUMPTION

1. Giles Milton, *Nathaniel's Nutmeg, or, The True and Incredible Adventures of the Spice Trader Who Changed the Course of History* (New York: Farrar, Straus and Giroux, 2014).

2. Ralph Waldo Emerson, *Emerson. Essays & Lectures*, ed. Joel Porte (New York: Literary Classics of the United States, 1983).

3. Chögyam Trungpa, *Cutting Through Spiritual Materialism* (London: Shambhala, 2002).

4. "Legal and Regulatory FAQs," American Herbalists Guild, www.americanherbalistsguild.com/legal-and-regulatory-faqs.

5. Milton, *Nathaniel's Nutmeg.*

ST. JOHN'S WORT: NO PAIN, NO GAIN

1. John Gerard, *The Herball, or Generall historie of plantes* (London: John Norton, 1597).

2. James Townsend Mackay, *Flora Hibernica, Comprising the Flowering Plants, Ferns, Characeæ, Musci, Hepaticæ,Lichenes and Algæ of Ireland, Arranged According to the Natural System, with a Synopsis of the Genera According to the Linnæan System* (Dublin: William Curry, 1836).

3. A. R. Vickery, "Traditional Uses and Folklore of Hypericum in the British Isles," *Economic Botany* 35, no. 3 (1981): 289–95; Tess Darwin, "St John's Wort," in *The Scots Herbal. The Plant Lore of Scotland* (Edinburgh: Mercat Press, 1996), 95–97.

4. Tess Darwin, *The Scots Herbal: The Plant Lore of Scotland* (Edinburgh: Birlinn, 2008).

5. Darwin, "St John's Wort," 95–97.

6. Ruth Trickey, *Women, Hormones and the Menstrual Cycle: Herbal and Medical Solutions from Adolescence to Menopause* (Sydney: Allen and Unwin,1998), 360.

GOLDENROD: ILLUMINATION

1. Plato, *Phaedrus*, trans. R. Hackworth (Cambridge, UK: Cambridge University Press, 1972).

2. C. L. Marlatt, *The periodical cicada: an account of Cicada Septendecim, its natural enemies and the means of preventing its injury, together with a summary of the distribution of the different broods* (Washington, DC: U.S. Department of Agriculture, Division of Entomology, 1898).

3. Joseph Demakis, *The Ultimate Book of Quotations.* Lulu.com (n.d.).

4. Mary Oliver, *Devotions: The Selected Poems of Mary Oliver* (New York: Penguin, 2020).

JAPANESE KNOTWEED: VOLCANIC SOIL

1. Kenneth R. Lang, "Sun: Tutorial: Energizing Space," NASA's Cosmos, Tufts University, https://ase.tufts.edu/cosmos/view_chapter.asp?id=29&page=1.

2. "Japanese Knotweed: What Is It and Why Are People Panicking?" *The Week*, July 4, 2016, www.theweek.co.uk/74144/japanese-knotweed-what-is-it-and-why-are-people-panicking.

3. John Bailey, "History of Japanese Knotweed in Europe," Department of Genetics and Genome Biology, University of Leicester, www2.le.ac.uk/departments/genetics/people/bailey/res/hist.

4. House of Commons Science and Technology Committee, *Japanese Knotweed and the Built Environment*, Seventeenth Report of Session 2017–19, May 8, 2019, United Kingdom Parliament, https://publications.parliament.uk/pa/cm201719/cmselect/cmsctech/1702/1702.pdf.

5. Dominique Vervandier-Fasseur and Norbert Latruffe, "The Potential Use of Resveratrol for Cancer Prevention," *Molecules* 24, no. 24 (December 2019): 4506, https://doi.org/10.3390/molecules24244506; Lindsay Carter, John A. D'Orazio, and Kevin J. Pearson, "Resveratrol and Cancer: Focus on *In Vivo* Evidence," *Endocrine-Related Cancer* 21, no. 3 (June 2014): R209–R225, https://doi.org/10.1530/ERC-13-0171.

6. Allen G. Debus, "Paracelsus and the Medical Revolution of the Renaissance: A 500th Anniversary Celebration," in "Paracelsus, Five Hundred Years: Three American Exhibits," History of Medicine, U.S. National Library of Medicine, National Institute of Health, https://www.nlm.nih.gov/exhibition/paracelsus/index.html.

7. Katja Triplett, "Potency by Name? 'Medicine Buddha Plant' and Other Herbs in the Japanese Scroll of Equine Medicine (Ba'i sōshi emaki, 1267)," *Himalaya* 39, no. 1 (July 2019): 189–207, https://digitalcommons.macalester.edu/himalaya/vol39/iss1/12/.

8. Alice E. Kane and David A. Sinclair, "Sirtuins and NAD+ in the Development and Treatment of Metabolic and Cardiovascular Diseases," *Circulation Research* 123, no. 7 (September 2018): 868–85, https://doi.org/10.1161/CIRCRESAHA.118.312498; M. Andrea Markus and Brian J Morris, "Resveratrol in Prevention and Treatment of Common Clinical Conditions of Aging," *Clinical Interventions in Aging* 3, no. 2 (June 2008): 331–39, https://pubmed.ncbi.nlm.nih.gov/18686754/.

9. W. Burgdorfer et al., "Lyme Disease—a Tick-Borne Spirochetosis?," *Science* 216, no. 4552 (June 1982): 1317–19, https://doi.org/10.1126/science.7043737.

10. "Episode #22: Healing Lyme with Stephen Harrod Buhner," *Better Health Guy Blogcasts*, April 18, 2017, https://youtu.be/oIRzVI5vdb8.

SKULLCAP: DEEP SLEEP

1. Anna Aulinas, "Physiology of the Pineal Gland and Melatonin," updated December 10, 2019, in *Endotext*, ed. K. R. Feingold, et al. (South Dartmouth, MA: MDText, 2000–), www.ncbi.nlm.nih.gov/books/NBK550972/.

2. Sahib S. Khalsa, David Rudrauf, Richard J. Davidson, and Daniel Tranel, "The Effect of Meditation on Regulation of Internal Body States," *Frontiers in Psychology* 6 (July 2015): 924, https://doi.org/10.3389/fpsyg.2015.00924.

3. Zeff Bjerken, "Cracking the Mirror: A Critical Genealogy of Scholarship on Tibetan Bon Ana the 'Canonical' Status of the Crystal Mirror of Doctrinal Systems," *The Tibet Journal* 23, no. 4 (1998): 92–107, http://www.jstor.org/stable/43301676.

4. Theresa S. Smith, *The Island of the Anishnaabeg: Thunderers and Water Monsters in the Traditional Ojibwe Life-World* (Lincoln: University of Nebraska Press, 2012).

BURDOCK ROOT: DEPTH

1. "Celtic Religion: An Overview," Encyclopedia of Religion, Encyclopedia.com, www.encyclopedia.com/environment/encyclopedias-almanacs-transcripts-and-maps/celtic-religion-overview.

2. J. Donald Hughes, "Artemis: Goddess of Conservation," *Forest and Conservation History* 34, no. 4 (October1990): 191–97, https://doi.org/10.2307/3983705.

3. Paula Perlman, "Acting the She-Bear for Artemis," *Arethusa* 22, no. 2 (1989): 111–33, http://www.jstor.org/stable/26308518.

4. Adam Drewnowski and Carmen Gomez-Carneros, "Bitter Taste, Phytonutrients, and the Consumer: A Review," *American Journal of Clinical Nutrition* 72, no. 6 (December 2000): 1424–35, https://doi.org/10.1093/ajcn/72.6.1424.

5. Ilkka Hanski et al., "Environmental Biodiversity, Human Microbiota, and Allergy Are Interrelated," *Proceedings of the National Academy of Sciences* 109, no. 29 (March 2012): 8334–39, https://doi.org/10.1073/pnas.1205624109.

6. Anthony Samsel and Stephanie Seneff, "Glyphosate, Pathways to Modern Diseases II: Celiac Sprue and Gluten Intolerance," *Interdisciplinary Toxicology* 6, no. 4 (2014): 159–84, https://doi.org/10.2478/intox-2013-0026.

7. Thaísa M. A. Moro and Maria T. P. S. Clerici, "Burdock (*Arctium lappa* L) Roots as a Source of Inulin-Type Fructans and Other Bioactive Compounds: Current Knowledge and Future Perspectives for Food and Non-food Applications," *Food Research International* 141 (March 2021): 109889, https://doi.org/10.1016/j.foodres.2020.109889.

8. Bruce Lee, *Tao of Jeet Kune Do* (Burbank, CA: Ohara, 1975).
9. Allie Wisniewski, "Shirin-Yoku: Why Forest Bathing Became a Global Health Phenomenon" *American Forests* (June 2017).

LINDEN TREE: IMPERMANENCE

1. Olga Zolotnikova, "Becoming Classical Artemis: A Glimpse at the Evolution of the Goddess as Traced in Ancient Arcadia," *Journal of Arts and Humanities* 6, no. 5 (May 2017): 8–20, https://doi.org/10.18533/journal.v6i4.1157.
2. Susan Guettel Cole, *Landscapes, Gender, and Ritual Space: The Ancient Greek Experience* (Berkeley: University of California Press, 2004), 178–225.
3. "7 'Magic' Wells of Scotland," *The Scotsman*, May 23, 2017, www.scotsman.com /whats-on/arts-and-entertainment/7-magic-wells-scotland-855602.
4. Alina-Maria Ţenche-Constantinescu, Claudia Varan, Fl. Borlea, E. Madoşa, and G. Szekely, "The Symbolism of the Linden Tree," *Journal of Horticulture, Forestry and Biotechnology* 19, no. 2 (2015): 237–242, https://journal-hfb.usab-tm.ro /rom아ña/2015/Lucrari%20PDF/Lucrari%20PDF%2019(2)/41Tenche%20Alina %202.pdf.
5. "Misson," Wolf Conservation Center, https://nywolf.org/about-the-wcc/mission/.
6. "Red Wolf," Wolf Conservation Center, https://nywolf.org/learn/red-wolf/.
7. Ruth M. Léger, *Artemis and Her Cult* (Oxford, UK: Archaeopress, 2017).
8. Edward Newenham Hoare, *English Roots: And the Derivation of Words from the Ancient Anglo-Saxon: Two Lectures* (Dublin: Hodges and Smith, 1856).
9. Xenophon and Arrian, *Xenophon and Arrian, On Hunting with Hounds*, ed. and trans. A. A. Phillips and M. M. Willcock (Warminster, UK: Aris and Phillips, 1999).
10. Frank Brommer, *Heracles: The Twelve Labors of the Hero in Ancient Art and Literature* (New Rochelle, NY: A. D. Caratzas, 1986).

RED TRILLIUM: DECAY

1. A. A. Znamenski, *Shamanism in Siberia: Russian Records of Indigenous Spirituality* (Heidelberg: Springer, 2013).
2. John Burroughs, *Wake-Robin* (New York: Houghton, Mifflin, 1885); Geoffrey Grigson, *The Englishman's Flora* (London: Phoenix, 1958).
3. Charles Darwin, *The Formation of Vegetable Mould, through the Action of Worms, with Observations on Their Habits* (New York: D. Appleton, 1896).
4. Joe Lamp'l, *The Green Gardener's Guide: Simple, Significant Actions to Protect and Preserve Our Planet* (Beverly, MA: Cool Springs Press, 2008).
5. Erin Blakemore, "Could the Funeral of the Future Help Heal the Environment?," *Smithsonian*, February 2, 2016, www.smithsonianmag.com/science-nature/could -funeral-future-help-heal-environment-180957953/; Green Burial Council, www .greenburialcouncil.org/.
6. Capsula Mundi, www.capsulamundi.it/en.
7. Coeio, https://coeio.com/.

8. Jae Rhim Lee, "My Mushroom Burial Suit," TEDGlobal 2011, July 2011, www.ted
.com/talks/jae_rhim_lee_my_mushroom_burial_suit?language=en.

SOLOMON'S SEAL: ENDURANCE

1. Thomas W. Myers, *Anatomy Trains Posters: Myofascial Meridians for Manual and Movement Therapists* (United Kingdom: Elsevier Science Health Science Division, 2009).
2. "Unwinding the Mystery of Fascia," Phys-Ed Health and Performance, www
.phys-ednm.com/fascia/.
3. Douglas W. Smith, Daniel R. Stahler, and Daniel R. MacNulty, eds., *Yellowstone Wolves: Science and Discovery in the World's First National Park* (Chicago: University of Chicago Press, 2020).
4. Cain Burdeau, "Europe's Wolves Are Back, Igniting Old Fears and New Tensions," Courthouse News Service, February 14, 2019, www.courthousenews.com
/europes-wolves-are-back-igniting-old-fears-and-new-tensions/.

CHAGA: INTIMACY

1. George McLennan, *A Gaelic Alphabet: A Guide to the Pronunciation of Gaelic Letters and Words* (Glasgow: New Argyll, 2018).
2. Clarissa Pinkola Estés, *Women Who Run with the Wolves: Myths and Stories of the Wild Woman Archetype* (New York: Ballantine, 1992).
3. bell hooks, *All About Love: New Visions* (New York: William Morrow, 2018).
4. Aleksandr Solzhenitsyn, *Cancer Ward*, trans. Nicholas Bethell and David Burg (New York: Farrar, Straus and Giroux, 1991).
5. Greg A. Marley, *Chanterelle Dreams, Amanita Nightmares: The Love, Lore, and Mystique of Mushrooms* (White River Junction, VT: Chelsea Green, 2010).

RED CLOVER: COEXISTENCE

1. Daniel Quinn, *Ishmael: A Novel* (London: Random House, 2009).
2. Martin Shaw, *Courting the Wild Twin* (White River Junction, VT: Chelsea Green, 2020).
3. Tom Oliver, *The Self Delusion: The Surprising Science of Our Connection to Each Other and the Natural World* (London: Weidenfeld and Nicolson, 2020).

PINE: EVER-PRESENT PEACE

1. Nina Montenegro on *Against Forgetting*, The Far Woods, www.thefarwoods.com
/2018/8/7/bw07ebtdk1sjgy0plw6tz7p3unnnk0.
2. David Hoffmann, *The Complete Illustrated Holistic Herbal: A Safe and Practical Guide to Making and Using Herbal Remedies* (London: Element, 1996).
3. Paul A. W. Wallace, *The White Roots of Peace* (Philadelphia: University of Pennsylvania Press, 1946).

4. Philip Marshall, "The Problem of Eastern White Pine (Pinus strobus L.) in Southern New England: Ecophysiology, Site Restriction, and Historical Land-Use Change," *Journal of Sustainable Forestry* 28, no. 1–2 (2009): 108–31, https://doi.org/10.1080/10549810802626423.

5. Anamaria Silic, "Scientists Say Climate Change Will Continue to Drive Disease Outbreaks," *Discover*, February 25, 2021, www.discovermagazine.com/health/scientists-say-climate-change-will-continue-to-drive-disease-outbreaks; Institute of Medicine and National Research Council, *Sustaining Global Surveillance and Response to Emerging Zoonotic Diseases* (Washington, DC: The National Academies Press, 2009), https://doi.org/10.17226/12625.

6. Douglas W. Smith, Daniel R. Stahler, and Daniel R. MacNulty, eds., *Yellowstone Wolves: Science and Discovery in the World's First National Park* (Chicago: University of Chicago Press, 2020).

7. Eugen Herrigel, *Zen in the Art of Archery* (New York: Vantage, 1971).